VOLUME 617

MAY 2008

W9-ANI-655

THE ANNALS

of The American Academy of Political
and Social Science

PHYLLIS KANISS, *Executive Editor*

The Politics of History in Comparative Perspective

Special Editor of this Volume

MARTIN O. HEISLER
University of Maryland

⑨SAGE

The American Academy of Political and Social Science

3814 Walnut Street, Fels Institute of Government, University of Pennsylvania,
Philadelphia, PA 19104-6197; (215) 746-6500; (215) 573-3003 (fax); www.aapss.org

Origin and Purpose. The Academy was organized December 14, 1889, to promote the progress of political and social science, especially through publications and meetings. The Academy does not take sides in controverted questions, but seeks to gather and present reliable information to assist the public in forming an intelligent and accurate judgment.

Meetings. The Academy occasionally holds a meeting in the spring extending over two days.

Publications. THE ANNALS of The American Academy of Political and Social Science is the bimonthly publication of the Academy. Each issue contains articles on some prominent social or political problem, written at the invitation of the editors. Also, monographs are published from time to time, numbers of which are distributed to pertinent professional organizations. These volumes constitute important reference works on the topics with which they deal, and they are extensively cited by authorities throughout the United States and abroad. The papers presented at the meetings of the Academy are included in THE ANNALS.

Membership. Each member of the Academy receives THE ANNALS and may attend the meetings of the Academy. Membership is open only to individuals. Annual dues: $94.00 for the regular paperbound edition (clothbound, $134.00). Members may also purchase single issues of THE ANNALS for $18.00 each (clothbound, $27.00). Student memberships are available for $52.00.

Subscriptions. THE ANNALS of The American Academy of Political and Social Science (ISSN 0002-7162) (J295) is published six times annually—in January, March, May, July, September, and November—by Sage Publications, 2455 Teller Road, Thousand Oaks, CA 91320. Telephone: (800) 818-SAGE (7243) and (805) 499-0721; Fax/Order line: (805) 375-1700; e-mail: journals@sagepub.com. Copyright © 2008 by The American Academy of Political and Social Science. Institutions may subscribe to THE ANNALS at the annual rate: $661.00 (clothbound, $747.00). Single issues of THE ANNALS may be obtained by individuals who are not members of the Academy for $34.00 each (clothbound, $47.00). Single issues of THE ANNALS have proven to be excellent supplementary texts for classroom use. Direct inquiries regarding adoptions to THE ANNALS c/o Sage Publications (address below). Periodicals postage paid at Thousand Oaks, California, and at additional mailing offices. POSTMASTER: Send address changes to The Annals of The American Academy of Political and Social Science, c/o Sage Publications, 2455 Teller Road, Thousand Oaks, CA 91320.

All correspondence concerning membership in the Academy, dues renewals, inquiries about membership status, and/or purchase of single issues of THE ANNALS should be sent to THE ANNALS c/o Sage Publications, 2455 Teller Road, Thousand Oaks, CA 91320.Telephone: (800) 818-SAGE (7243) and (805) 499-0721; Fax/Order line: (805) 375-1700; e-mail: journals@sagepub.com. *Please note that orders under $30 must be prepaid.* Sage affiliates in London and India will assist institutional subscribers abroad with regard to orders, claims, and inquiries for both subscriptions and single issues.

Printed on acid-free paper

THE ANNALS

Editorial Office: 3814 Walnut Street, Fels Institute for Government, University of Pennsylvania, Philadelphia, PA 19104-6197.
For information about membership* (individuals only) and subscriptions (institutions), address:
Sage Publications
2455 Teller Road
Thousand Oaks, CA 91320

For Sage Publications: Dan Wollrich (Production) and Sandra Hopps (Marketing)

From India and South Asia, write to:
SAGE PUBLICATIONS INDIA Pvt Ltd
B-42 Panchsheel Enclave, P.O. Box 4109
New Delhi 110 017
INDIA

From Europe, the Middle East, and Africa, write to:
SAGE PUBLICATIONS LTD
1 Oliver's Yard, 55 City Road
London EC1Y 1SP
UNITED KINGDOM

*Please note that members of the Academy receive THE ANNALS with their membership.
International Standard Serial Number ISSN 0002-7162
International Standard Book Number ISBN 978-1-4129-6879-9 (Vol. 617, 2008) paper
International Standard Book Number ISBN 978-1-4129-6880-5 (Vol. 617, 2008) cloth
Manufactured in the United States of America. First printing, May 2008.

The articles appearing in *The Annals* are abstracted or indexed in Academic Abstracts, Academic Search, America: History and Life, Asia Pacific Database, Book Review Index,CABAbstracts Database, Central Asia: Abstracts &Index, Communication Abstracts, Corporate ResourceNET, Criminal Justice Abstracts, Current Citations Express, Current Contents: Social & Behavioral Sciences, Documentation in Public Administration, e-JEL, EconLit, Expanded Academic Index, Guide to Social Science & Religion in Periodical Literature, Health Business FullTEXT, HealthSTAR FullTEXT, Historical Abstracts, International Bibliography of the Social Sciences, International Political Science Abstracts, ISI Basic Social Sciences Index, Journal of Economic Literature on CD, LEXIS-NEXIS, MasterFILE FullTEXT, Middle East: Abstracts&Index, North Africa: Abstracts&Index, PAIS International, Periodical Abstracts, Political Science Abstracts, Psychological Abstracts, PsycINFO, Sage Public Administration Abstracts, Scopus, Social Science Source, Social Sciences Citation Index, Social Sciences Index Full Text, Social Services Abstracts, SocialWork Abstracts, Sociological Abstracts, Southeast Asia: Abstracts& Index, Standard Periodical Directory (SPD), TOPICsearch, Wilson OmniFileV, and Wilson Social Sciences Index/Abstracts, and are available on microfilm from ProQuest, Ann Arbor, Michigan.

Information about membership rates, institutional subscriptions, and back issue prices may be found on the facing page.

Advertising. Current rates and specifications may be obtained by writing to The Annals Advertising and Promotion Manager at the Thousand Oaks office (address above).

Claims. Claims for undelivered copies must be made no later than six months following month of publication. The publisher will supply missing copies when losses have been sustained in transit and when the reserve stock will permit.

Change of Address. Six weeks' advance notice must be given when notifying of change of address to ensure proper identification. Please specify name of journal.

THE ANNALS

OF THE AMERICAN ACADEMY OF POLITICAL AND SOCIAL SCIENCE

Volume 617   May 2008

IN THIS ISSUE:

The Politics of History in Comparative Perspective

Special Editor: MARTIN O. HEISLER

Quick Read Synopsis

FORTHCOMING

Terrorism: What the Next President Will Face
Special Editor: RICHARD CLARKE

Cultural Sociology and Its Diversity
Special Editors: AMY BINDER, MARY BLAIR-LOY, JOHN EVANS,
KWAI NG, and MICHAEL SCHUDSON

Historical Remembrance in the Twenty-First Century

By
JAY WINTER

The role of remembrance in public life has expanded radically over the past century. In part this is due to the democratization of warfare. Before 1914, the vast majority of those who served, were injured, or died in war were volunteers or mercenaries. After 1914, conscript armies fought wars and left bereaved parents, widows, and orphans behind in numbers that were never before registered. Inevitably, this meant that the history of warfare and family history came to be bound together. War memorials proliferated in villages and towns throughout Europe and beyond, largely to preserve the names of the fallen. The overwhelming majority of these sites list names alphabetically and not by rank. Maya Lin's Vietnam Veterans' Memorial in Washington, D. C., consciously designed to follow the First World War model, does it another way, by recording the names of the dead by the date they died. The result is the same: the sixty thousand American dead of the Vietnam War are symbolically interred in the Mall in Washington, and every name counts; every name is equal to every other name.

Naming is the way democracies have honored war dead since 1914. Australian memorials since the First World War have named those who served as well as those who died. But since enlistment was voluntary in the Great War, this kind of naming was intended to shame those passersby who had not enlisted (Inglis 1998).

After the Second World War, the business of naming the victims of war became much more difficult. In part this was a problem of scale. In

Jay Winter, Charles J. Stille Professor of History, joined the Yale faculty in 2001. From 1979 to 2001, he was reader in modern history and fellow of Pembroke College, Cambridge University. He holds PhD and DLitt degrees from Cambridge. He is a historian of the First World War and is the author of Sites of Memory, Sites of Mourning: The Great War in European Cultural History (Cambridge University Press, 1995).

DOI: 10.1177/0002716207312761

ANNALS, *AAPSS*, 617, May 2008

St. Petersburg, the war cemetery honoring victims of the city's one-thousand-day siege is arrayed in 186 giant mass graves. Names vanished, but the city survived. In Hiroshima, both names and the city were obliterated. In Paris, an infant deported from the Drancy transit camp to Auschwitz was not named but was listed as the child with an earring.[1] Efforts to retrieve the names of Holocaust victims are ongoing. Thanks to the effort of Serge Klarsfeld, Parisian schools have plaques with the names of schoolchildren from the district who were deported and murdered during the Nazi occupation.

Here is the nub of the matter: when the number of civilian victims approximately equaled or exceeded the number of soldiers who died in war, previous commemorative forms, rooted in older traditions of military honor, had to be changed. It is much more difficult to design a monument to the unknown civilian than to the unknown soldier. Soldiers are said to die for a reason: love of country or fellow soldiers or simply for doing their duty. But what meaning can we ascribe to the deportation and murder of a French infant known only by her earring? Commemorating that single death (among millions) cannot be done in any conventional (or perhaps any unconventional) manner. Where there is no meaning, there is no commemoration.

There is also no history. Here is one of the key reasons for the renegotiation of the space occupied by history and memory over the past sixty years: both the act of producing history and the act of remembrance are gestures toward finding meaning in the past. The patterns we choose to give shape to traces of the past fade away or fall apart when we claim that major events, or deaths, or lives have no meaning. To be sure, this sense of disorientation is selective. Winning the war against Hitler and the Japanese had meaning. Breaking through the encircling German forces surrounding Leningrad had meaning. But within these larger events, there were massive, terrifying phenomena—the names of Hiroshima and Auschwitz among them—which in their unadorned nihilism threaten the notion that narratives of the past had "meaning" in any conventional sense of the term.

The efflorescence of historical writing about wars and the victims of war is one facet of this insistent reaffirmation of geometry, of logic, and of causality in an increasingly violent world. In the 1940s and 1950s, what Charles Maier (2000) termed "the age of territoriality" was still intact, and indeed fortified by the war, and this urgent effort to reconfirm the "meaning" of history took place in separately configured national cultural spaces. There were overlaps to be sure. The French (alongside the Belgians and the Dutch) had the myth of the Resistance to write into their history, thereby occluding the complex phenomenon of collaboration and the role of local officials in the deportation of Jews to their deaths (Lagrou 2000). The Germans could put the "catastrophe" in parentheses and align their history with that of the West just as they aligned their foreign policy with their cold war allies. The strength of Marxism in British, French, and Italian historiography mirrored the heroic image of the Red Army and the communist resistance as essential agents of victory in the Second World War.

These efforts to restore "meaning" to European history came apart by the 1970s. National boundaries were by then encapsulated in a thriving European community, with its own judiciary, the decisions of which over time came to be written into the legal framework of each constituent member of the European Union. After 1968 and the Soviet invasion of Czechoslovakia, much of the political and intellectual capital accumulated by communist parties and their followers became debased. Marxism as a theory of society—how power operates—and as a theory of history—how societies change—began to fall apart. Capitalism was in trouble, too. In 1973, the cheap energy strategy of the Western powers came unhinged after the Arab-Israeli war, creating real strains in the middle-of-the-road parties that had governed since the 1950s. Massive inflation produced industrial unrest, which in turn fueled a political backlash of which Margaret Thatcher's conservatism was the most salient product. With the superpowers' global strategy of mutually assured destruction, the heart of Europe was the bull's eye to which thousands of missiles pointed. The cost of this staggering arms race ultimately bankrupted the Soviet Union, though a good case can be made that its governing structures had already begun to collapse in 1986. What greater evidence is there of both criminal negligence and evil than the Chernobyl catastrophe, when officials in the Ukraine publicly denied the emergency while sending their families away from contaminated areas? In a tragic version of an old song of Tom Lehrer's, "Pollution," millions were left to drink the milk and water and breathe the air. We still do not know the full genetic price paid for Chernobyl or the criminal manner in which it was handled.

The efflorescence of historical writing about wars and the victims of war is one facet of this insistent reaffirmation of geometry, of logic, and of causality in an increasingly violent world.

In the 1970s, a new factor altered the way history and memory have been configured. Although video cassette technology had been developed in the 1950s and 1960s, it became part of household furniture in many countries by the 1970s. The Philips Company marketed its VCR in 1970; Betamax appeared in 1975; and by 1980, video cassette players were within the reach of millions of families. This technology revolutionized the preservation of the voices of historical actors, from the most modest to the most prominent. The archive on which history rested suddenly expanded radically. Twenty years later, the World Wide Web expanded that visual archive of the past even more radically. In those two decades, the materials from which historians construct their narratives became more digital than documentary. At the same time, the word "documentary" took on a new meaning, referring to a whole branch of nonfiction television history.

This revolution in the role of visual evidence in historical writing accounts in large part for the ways in which history and memory have intersected in the past generation. The problems remained the same: how to construct narratives in an age of globalized violence. But the means and resources available to do so changed, and did so in a way that brought to the fore the single human voice.

That voice could be anyone's, and as such, the individual's power of recollection provided evidence of a variety and durability historians had never before had at their disposal. What did these voices offer? Was it memory, in the sense of the individual retrieval of personally encountered events? Or was it history, in the sense of narratives backed up by the authority of direct experience? The answer was both, and in every new interview of the victims of war or revolution or repression, from Vietnam to Chile to Palestine, the space between history and memory was reconfigured. That space is what I term "historical remembrance."[2]

"Historical remembrance" describes a host of ways in which we try to give meaning to our violent past. Its practices overlap with liturgical remembrance, in that sacred matters and issues are touched on time and again. It shares many characteristics with family remembrance, the calendar of our domestic lives. But historical remembrance has one particular feature the other two do not always have. Acts of remembrance are informed by what professional historians and public historians write and broadcast. And the writing of history is informed by the "memory boom" of the past forty years. Anyone with eyes to see knows that there has been an efflorescence of memory artifacts about history in film, sculpture, museums, exhibitions, plays, novels, and cartoon strips, as well as on thousands of Internet sites. There are judicial records now available online and in video cassette format that provide easily accessible evidence drawn from war crimes trials and post–civil war tribunals of many kinds. We historians are being carried along on a fast-moving stream of memory studies, which we did not create and do not control.

Whenever we collectively mark a date in the calendar of when important events occurred, we engage in historical remembrance. Our meditations at a war memorial or a village square form one part of this activity. When we come together in public to exchange our reflections on the past stimulated by a film or a play or a novel or a visit to a museum, we enter this area between history and memory. I have had the privilege of helping to create a museum of the First World War at Péronne, on the river Somme in northern France. We call the museum L'Historial de la Grande Guerre. The term *Historial* is a neologism, drawing from the intersection of a memorial to the soldiers who died and the history of the Battle of the Somme, which was fought there ninety years ago.

The *Historial* has flourished because families and school parties have adopted it. Surrounded by hundreds of French, British, and German war cemeteries, the museum shows the way practices of historical remembrance overlap with family narratives and sacred stories.

This kind of public history is still not welcomed by many within the historical profession. There are multiple reasons for this hostility. In part, the financing of museums, exhibitions, and television documentaries puts pressure on historians to present the past in ways pleasing to patrons. Political pressures appear when national museums touch on sensitive subjects open to criticism by participants in historical events or by politicians with an axe to grind. When American air force veterans saw the outline of an exhibition on the dropping of the atomic bomb on Hiroshima, they demanded and were assured changes in the historians' narrative would be made (Bird and Lifschultz 1998; Boyer 1996). The treatment of Aborigines in the Australian National Museum in Canberra was similarly rewritten when nonhistorians protested its initial interpretation.[3] Canadian historians backtracked when their account of the strategic bombing campaign in the Second World War came under harsh scrutiny by some veterans' groups (Oliver 2007). George Orwell wrote that history is a discipline that stops people (usually but not only those in power) from lying about the past. If independence of interpretation can be so easily compromised, some argue, then history is reduced to propaganda.

Or it is reduced to memory (Nora 2000). This notion that survivors' memories matter more than historians' judgments is deeply problematic. It reflects the proprietary nature of the past, the sense that some people "own" it. Forty years ago, I appeared at a conference at the Royal Military Academy at Sandhurst to open part of a library in honor of Harold Macmillan, who attended. Another First World War soldier (and novelist), Charles Carrington, took me aside and suggested I choose another subject. Better not write about the First World War, he said, because only *we* know. Those who had been there *were* history; their memories were oracular; and we historians dealt with them critically at our peril. Holocaust survivors have said the same thing. Here configuring history as touching on the sacred destroys the enterprise altogether. It is evident why some historians prefer to stay inside the academy. If the mission of turning myths about the past into documented narrative is limited in this way, then history vanishes entirely.

Witnesses provide challenges for historians in other ways, too. There is a strong body of literature that questions the truth value of eyewitness testimony. Especially under pressures of combat or domestic violence, the accuracy of statements made by those who were there is suspect (Dulong 1998). There are the risks of the normal "sins" of memory—misattribution, suggestibility, and bias (Schacter 2002). And then there is time itself, which erodes and rearranges the collage of fragments that we call memory. When survivors remember, they provide evidence about the present as much as the past; they present *their* truth, not *the* truth. Here is an observation most historians take for granted, but when they enter the public domain, other rules may apply. Some truths are "better" than others; some serve political purposes. Here again, the academy is a safer place to operate. Those who retreat in this manner reinforce the notion that history is inside and memory outside of what professionals do.

The insider/outsider divide helps us understand the history/memory divide in Europe in other ways. In France, those who teach history at the level of *lycée* or university are *fonctionnaires*, paid employees of the state, who pass examinations to get their jobs. They are the carriers of history, bringing it to the young as a key element in the education of citizens. Commemoration is what others do; history is purer than that. It is objective, cold, and rational; whereas memory is subjective, warm, and emotional (Maier 1993, 2001). The historical discipline is precisely that; it has rules as to how to pose a problem, how to answer it, and how and where to make that answer public. History is a way of thinking; memory is a way of feeling. All this is true, but not entirely so. The reasons historians choose a subject are frequently personal and subjective. The art of writing is, in the hands of masters like Antoine Prost and Pierre Nora, filled with passion and literary echoes. We weave into our narratives the conversations we have had in our lives. This is the key to the linguistic turn, which is simply the commonsense view that there are no facts outside the language in which they are expressed. Positivism is dead, buried long ago, but its traces can be seen every time a French historian denies that history and memory overlap in the language historians use. My sense is that the social position of historians within a state system lies behind the strict distinction they erect between history and memory. When historians work in the private sector, as in large parts of the American university system, they have less need to insist on the pristine purity of history, as opposed to memory, which is what amateurs (or the rest of us) have.

This notion that survivors' memories matter more than historians' judgments is deeply problematic. It reflects the proprietary nature of the past, the sense that some people "own" it.

There is a danger in the nationalization of history in this manner. When historians are *fonctionnaires*, they risk being told by other public employees—elected ones—how to do their job. In July 2005, French politicians passed a resolution stating that teachers at state schools must emphasize the positive role France played in its dealings with its overseas holdings, especially in North Africa. This differs from legislative statements, largely rhetorical, denominating the murder of Armenians in Turkey in 1915 as genocide. Such statements are acts of solidarity, not pedagogy. Still, on occasion, when Holocaust deniers receive higher degrees in French universities, public authorities take action.

Here we come to the heart of the problem. Since the 1970s, what Annette Wieviorka (1998) has termed "the age of the witness" has affected the way history is taught and written. Witnesses are everywhere. They testify in courts. They speak in national commissions. They agitate, and when they are able to get an audience, they can help protect endangered populations. Rigoberta Menchu Tum won the Nobel Peace Prize for speaking out on behalf of Guatemalan Indians. They tell us what human rights are by describing the inhuman treatment they have endured and have seen. They are living documents, people who carry in their memories the tragic history of their people.

What happens when they get it wrong? Rigoberta Menchu (1999) told stories of atrocities that, when investigated, turned out to be generic rather than factual. Her brother was not burned alive in the town square, as she wrote, but other people were in other towns and at other times. Does this matter? Historians have to say yes, but when they do, they are subject to severe criticism, this time from the "witnesses" themselves or their supporters.

What is the way out of this adversarial universe? Surely the time has come to recognize that there is a field of force between history and memory, a site of interaction, overlap, contestation, and dissonance. Calling this field "historical remembrance" is simply one way of recognizing the obvious. But sometimes stating the obvious can serve a very useful purpose. In Guatemala, the Catholic Church has set up a "historical memory" project. The balance is right; memory is essential to history, especially the history of the violation of human rights, so rarely documented by the perpetrators. But history is essential to memory too, in that the testimony of witnesses needs to be treated with critical respect, precisely as we treat all other traces of the past.

I have spent much of my life studying the First World War, a conflict that produced an avalanche of war memoirs. In a sense, the memory boom of the twentieth century came out of the Great War and prepared the ground for the emergence of other voices, other commemorative acts, following later wars and atrocities. The soldiers who wrote of the Great War told stories that came out of their lives. They wrote with the authority of direct experience. But no one in the large and still growing historical profession specializing in this field believes that their memoirs tell the unvarnished truth. Many of the authors themselves state this precisely. Robert Graves said that only those who lied about the war actually told the truth. Memory plays tricks on us, and those tricks are very revealing. In a period when a new human rights regime is emerging in Europe and (in a checkered way) in other parts of the world, and when witnesses are coming forward in increasing numbers, the best service historians can offer is to go beyond conceptual apartheid and explore the creative space between history and memory. Writing the history of the contemporary world is an act of historical remembrance, one kind of signifying practice among many others. The sooner we realize this simple truth, the better.

Notes

1. I am grateful to Caroline Piketty of the Archives Nationales in Paris for this information.
2. For a fuller account of my interpretation, see Winter (2006).
3. For one view, see Windschuttle (2001).

References

Bird, Kai, and Lawrence Lifschultz, eds. 1998. *Hiroshima's shadow: Writings on the denial of history and the Smithsonian controversy*. Stony Creek, CT: Bird Pamphleteers Press.

Boyer, Paul. 1996. Whose history is it anyway? Memory, politics, and historical scholarship. In *History wars: The Enola Gay and other battles for the American past*, ed. Edward Linenthal and Tom Engelhardt. New York: Metropolitan.

Dulong, Renaud. 1998. *Le témoin oculaire. Les conditions sociales de l'attestation personnelle*. Paris: Edtions de l'EHESS.

Inglis, Ken. 1998. *Sacred places. War memorials in the Australian landscape*. Melbourne, Australia: Melbourne University Press.

Lagrou, Pieter. 2000. *The legacy of Nazi occupation: Patriotic memory and national recovery in Western Europe, 1945-65*. Cambridge: Cambridge University Press.

Maier, Charles S. 1993. A surfeit of memory? Reflections on history, melancholy and denial. *History & Memory* 5 (2): 136-51.

———. 2000. Consigning the twentieth century to history. *American Historical Review* 105: 807-31.

———. 2001. Hot memory . . . cold memory: On the political half-life of fascist and communist memory. Paper delivered to the conference on "The Memory of the Century," Institut für die Wissenschaften vom Menschen, Vienna, Austria, March 9-11.

Menchu, Rigoberta. 1999. If truth be told: A forum on David Stoll's "Rigoberta Menchu and the story of all poor Guatemalans." *Latin American Perspectives* 26 (6): 38-46.

Nora, Pierre. 2000. The era of commemoration. In *Realms of memory*, vol. 3, *Symbols*, ed. Pierre Nora, trans. A. Goldhammer. New York: Columbia University Press.

Oliver, Dean F. 2007. War and controversy. *Ottawa Citizen*, March 22.

Schacter, Daniel L. 2002. *The seven sins of memory (how the mind forgets and remembers)*. New York: Houghton Mifflin.

Wieviorka, Annette. 1998. *L'ère du témoin*. Paris: Plon.

Windschuttle, Keith. 2001. How not to run a museum. *Quadrant* 45 (9): 11-19.

Winter, Jay. 2006. *Remembering war: The Great War between history and memory in the twentieth century*. New Haven, CT: Yale University Press.

The Political Currency of the Past: History, Memory, and Identity

By
MARTIN O. HEISLER

During the year between the conception of this volume of *The Annals* in the autumn of 2006 and the submission of the completed volume, a writer/editor was assassinated; a distinguished scholar was hounded into exile; a prime minister's resignation was hastened; members of a parliament tried to impeach their president; parliamentarians in several countries accused colleagues of treason; the government of a member-state created a diplomatic crisis at a crucial summit of the European Union; a government finally dismissed an indictment against one of its most distinguished citizens— a current Nobel laureate—following widespread international protests; and the same government recalled its ambassador to a major ally, to show displeasure with a committee vote in the latter's parliament. Several of the contributors to this volume have received specific, credible threats to their safety, related to work on the subjects of their articles; and another was shouted down at an academic forum by presumably highly educated and sophisticated attendees.

These are illustrations of myriad similar events in ostensibly democratic or democratizing countries. They stem from disagreements about the past—specifically, disagreements about portrayals of historical acts committed by, or in the name of, collectivities in which the disputes occur. Such incidents are even more common and much more likely to involve repression and violence in the less tolerant parts of the world.

Martin O. Heisler, professor emeritus of government and politics at the University of Maryland, has worked in the fields of comparative politics and international relations, focusing on ethnicity and ethnic relations, transnational migration, security, and policy studies. He was special editor and contributing author of three previous volumes of The Annals. *His most recent publication, "Academic Freedom and the Freedom of Academics," appeared in the November 2007 issue of* International Studies Perspectives.

DOI: 10.1177/0002716208315024

The collective self-concepts of clans, tribes, religious groups, nations, and perhaps (overlooking the nebulousness of the term for the moment) civilizations are intimately and intricately connected with the stories they have embraced regarding the path they have traveled to the present.[1] Challenges to the accuracy, or some of the particulars, of a widely and deeply held version of our past disturbs the sense of who we are and what we stand for. As Nietzsche put it, in his well-known Aphorism 68, "'I did this,' my memory tells me, 'I cannot have done this,' says my pride and remains inexorable. In the end—memory yields" (Nietzsche 1989).

> *As Nietzsche put it, in his well-known Aphorism 68, "'I did this,' my memory tells me, 'I cannot have done this,' says my pride and remains inexorable. In the end—memory yields."*

On balance, our picture of our past is—must be—positive, though perhaps not invariably so in every detail. Acknowledging mistakes in our past is imperative if we are to maintain a positive self-image. In practice, however, as the case of Turkey developed by Fatma Müge Göçek shows, neither acknowledging nor reconciling the past with the self-image we would like to sustain is easy, much less routine. If such acts—even if they occurred decades, sometimes centuries, ago—violated our *current* sense of who we are, it is necessary to account for them and to deal with them in some fashion, but doing so is likely to prove problematic (Walzer 1994, 42ff., but cf. Smith 2003, 160-61).

The articles in this volume focus on the political dynamics of confronting the publication—in the generic sense of making publicly known—of unsavory findings about collective pasts. The issues are related to concerns about identity or self-concept, recognition, remembrance, respect, and intellectual and normative integrity, mostly at the level of entire societies or nations, but sometimes that of smaller groups and even individuals. The tensions between differing conceptions of related histories or accounts of events most often reflect the incompatibility of the simultaneously held self-concepts of two or more collectivities in the same narrative space.

Our goal here is to explicate and analyze very diverse manifestations of such politics. While some of the authors have sought to glean more general, occasionally explicitly comparative, insights from their research, we have not tried to provide sweeping theoretical propositions about the politics of history or memory.

The foreword, the first few articles, and the concluding essay do consider relationships between such elements of discourse on our subject as history, memory,
and remembrance. Most of the articles that follow, however, are devoted to country or regional studies that illustrate the variety of political confrontations about
history and remembrance. While the specifics differ greatly, with few exceptions
the reactions to public presentations of "inconvenient truths" about history are
suggestively similar.[2] These include substantial delays—foot-dragging—in confronting such elements of the past; challenging the motives, integrity, and/or loyalty of the messengers to discredit or brush aside the information they bring;
attempting to quarantine information damaging to established histories and to
relativize negative revelations ("there weren't that many people displaced in what
you call ethnic cleansing"; "don't call it genocide"; "were there really 6 million
Jews killed in the Holocaust?").

The two concluding articles discuss some ways of coping with problems
attending the past's persistence in the political, psychological, and pedagogic
aspects of life, and they touch on some of the normative and practical political
hurdles in the way of "solutions." We raise many questions and touch on many
problems but can offer few means to ameliorate the contentious relationships
within and between societies that flow from different constructions of the past,
conflicting memories, and, often, the threats to individual and collective identities and self-esteem that emanate from them.[3]

Politics of the Past

Howard Zinn, the dean of radical American historians, titled one of his most
prominent books *The Politics of History* (1990). There, as throughout his long
career, he questioned the claims to detached objectivity made by most historians; he
challenged his profession to engage history with questions about the implications of
events *for people*—the general public and especially the underrepresented and less
fortunate. Zinn provides revisionist interpretations of history and calls on historians
to change their methods. Like most radical historians, he highlights the (most often
conservative or status quo–affirming) political positions embedded in standard
accounts, especially textbooks. He notes that such positions are usually unacknowl-
edged and sometimes seemingly embraced without their authors' awareness. This
volume of *The Annals* also deals with the politics of history, but here the phrase
denotes two concerns different from, though not entirely unrelated to, those Zinn
has emphasized: *we focus on history as both the subject and the object of politics* and
frequently leave the narrative depiction of the past as well as the meta-theoretical
and methodological aspects of our scholarship in the background.

The title of this article contains a play on words: the double meaning of *currency* is intended to highlight two sides of the extraordinarily complex and elu-
sive nature of our subject. First, the past is present in our lives; its pervasiveness
and intrusiveness are evident in daily media reports. Second, like currency, the
past is often fungible; it can serve as a medium of exchange in relationships, both

within and between societies. Past suffering and misfortune may be converted into moral capital in negotiations for the resolution of a sixty-year-old conflict;[4] under some circumstances, reminders of centuries-old wrongs can generate shame on the part of the descendants of the perpetrators and benefits for the descendants of the victims (see, e.g., Barkan 2000, chaps. 7-13).

History as subject reflects growing preoccupations with narratives of past events in current political discourse in much of the world. Jay Winter notes in his foreword that the past has become a larger presence in public consciousness since—and in part as a consequence of—the First World War, and renditions of it are more likely to be disputed. History as object points to the present uses of the past for political ends, including attempts to control its framing, storytelling, and interpretations, and to shape (some would say manipulate) public or collective memories for current partisan, factional, national, or ideological advantage. History and memory are intertwined, so that attempts to articulate collective recollections are associated with purposive formulations of historical accounts (Novick 2007, 30). Richard Ned Lebow provides a richly illustrated and sophisticated explanation in his article of the politics of memory and history and the linkages between them. But memory may have sufficient autonomy to resist efforts to manipulate it through the recasting of history, as James Wertsch's research on Russian/Soviet history and collective memory shows.

The gist of the articles that follow is that altering collective memory and "amending" history through new, more clearly articulated, newly disclosed, or reinterpreted evidence is virtually never straightforward or unproblematic. Undertaking such changes usually leads to contention, sometimes even violence. The forces propelling such contention are varied and complex, and their virulence often fails to abate with the passage of time—at least not within several generations of the ostensible causes. The persistence of grievances and quarrels may be a function, at least in part, of the symbolic nature of the subjects involved. As I argue in my concluding article, there are not only important existential reasons adduced for resisting significant changes to narratives of the collective past but sometimes also morally conflicted arguments involving the collectivity's well-being, security, and even survival. Such resistance is virtually universal, even where few or no significant material consequences would follow (Torpey 2003, 7).

While such disputes and the sensibilities on which they touch are not exclusive to the modern world, there are reasons to think that most are connected to aspects of modernity, and especially democratization along several dimensions. Jay Winter points to one such connection: the democratization of warfare or, more accurately, of some of its consequences that put the general population (not only those in the military forces) at risk of becoming casualties and that exact substantial sacrifices for the common good from ordinary citizens.[5] Democratization as the leveling of formal standing or citizenship status has also increased the plausibility of legitimate claims for rectifying past wrongs. Thus, populations previously excluded from consideration—and often from history—now demand inclusion, including in history. Michael Kammen's elegant sweep of more than two hundred years of American history makes it possible to see that, over time and often accompanied by political games and controversy, it is possible to achieve such inclusion—in writing, if not always in life—but those games and controversies do not come to a halt.

Greater inclusiveness not only brought the consequences of war home to the general population; it also expanded the populations to be taken into account. This process, still very much ongoing, not only calls for constant adjustments or amendments to history, but also threatens to de-center collective self-concepts by undermining their moral assumptions. If, in 1948, large numbers of Palestinian Arabs lived on the land where Israel was established, then the power of the old Zionist mantra of "a land without people for a people without a land" as a justification for creating a Jewish state of Israel in Palestine is at least brought into question and likely substantially diminished (Brunner 1997). Democratization has fostered a number of protonorms regarding exclusion, nonrecognition, and other dimensions of relationships between groups and societies. Protonorms are not fully formed or specified norms; they operate by precluding or compromising the legitimacy of certain justifications, in this case, for the historical exclusion (and exclusions from history) of women and ethnic and religious minorities—all those not accorded a (positive) place in the story of the collectivity.

Where such exclusion is no longer deemed acceptable, societies, or at least their elites, may be called upon to adjust their stories. (In several instances, such calls have come from contributors to this volume.) Will they, as Rogers Smith (2003) expects, use acknowledgment of past shortcomings and efforts to rectify them to reinforce positive self-concepts, or will they challenge assertions of past wrongs by maligning the messengers, denying the message or simply lying, as Michael Walzer (1994) avers? While the cases reported here constitute a cross-section from democratic or democratizing countries, they are not a systematically representative cross-section. In the absence of much more comprehensive comparative research, we cannot determine whether Smith's or Walzer's views are closer to the mark in general.

The answer to the question, "How do societies deal with revelations of unpalatable actions in the past taken in their name?" has an important practical role in current political action. As Friedrich Kratochwil (2006, 6) recently reminded us, "The understanding of 'politics' requires a historical awareness that is *sui generis*. Politics is inherently *practical* since it deals with doing the right [i.e., situationally appropriate] thing at the right time in view of the particular historical circumstances." Thus, for example, the understanding from American history of what the United States stands for has been an important part of the background against which the government's actions in the war on terror and the conflict in Iraq have been projected—by civilian and military decision makers, opinion leaders, and the general public.

The premise that "the United States does not torture" derives from the narrative of "who we are." "We" do not torture because we have never done that, because that is not who we are. Therefore, the argument goes, accusations and visible evidence of torture by Americans are either false or aberrations—by presumption and perhaps definition, the "un-American" actions of a few. This is one manifestation of the power of pride to which Nietzsche points.

Here we encounter another dimension of democratization, more recent and probably even more important than the extension of the effects of war to general populations: the reach of modern media of communication and the "information revolution." The number of people who have seen the surreptitiously made photographs of the abuse of prisoners at Abu Ghraib is probably greater than the combined number of people directly affected by all the wars of the past century. While "photographs may lie" (in that they can be manipulated), they can also engender disbelief in contrary assertions, or at least insinuate serious doubts, regarding the presumptions derived from the historical narrative of what the United States is and stands for. And thus pride is challenged and perhaps wounded.

The consequences reverberate both inside and outside the country. For example, if access to information were no more extensive or readily obtainable in China or South Korea than it was sixty years ago, the problem-laden relationships between those countries and Japan, stemming from the latter's actions during the war on the mainland of Asia in the 1930s and 1940s, might have remained "elite business." In the twenty-first century, however, the history of Japanese behavior in China and Korea during the Asian war is now addressed by the citizens of those countries, through civil society groupings; through appeals to their own governments to demand acknowledgment of abuses—including the notorious and contentious issue of "comfort women"; by direct petitions to the Japanese government; and through not insignificant appeals to wider public opinion.

As Claudia Schneider and Hirofumi Hayashi show in their articles, grievances centered on Japan's actions in the Asian war have also given rise to domestic, Japanese, academic and civil society initiatives—initiatives Japanese elites now find impossible to ignore. Even an issue in a domain that a few decades ago would have been considered an exclusively domestic matter, the content of school textbooks, has been internationalized: several Japanese renditions of the Asian war are vigorously challenged by the country's East Asian neighbors for glossing over or recasting into less damaging language some of the atrocities of which it is accused.

Efforts to ignore or deny unpalatable elements that come to light about a collectivity's past actions can be interpreted as attempts to preserve the ideas that define it; negative stories can undermine the authority of elites or the broader regime of rule. But might denial ultimately be more damaging to authority? Some of the articles that follow suggest the important differences between negative stories focused on current or recent incumbents (e.g., the recently ousted government in Australia, discussed by Andrew Bonnell and Martin Crotty), or regimes (e.g., the communist regime in Romania or its successor, Vladimir Tismaneanu's focus; the Franco regime, or its republican predecessor, or the post-Franco regime, discussed in Carolyn Boyd's article), or the society as a whole.

What kinds of negative stories are likely to be most damaging, what kinds less, and to whom or what? Revelations that challenge the rectitude or credibility of the government-of-the-day or an earlier one need not undermine the regime or seriously damage the political society—if the latter can draw on broader support for or identification with the community as a whole. Are there more effective and less effective ways of acknowledging bad news and responding to their bearers? What is the effect of time? Does the proximity or remoteness in time of the revealed events make a difference, and if so, how and how much? We do not yet have clear, evidence-based grounds for answering these questions; but the contributors to this volume have provided a good beginning.

Normative Time

A major reason, though not the only one, for the contentiousness of the past is that some revelations threaten the authority of those in power (commonly including historically dominant groups and cultures, not only current holders of power) and the positive self-concepts of societies and groups within them. But the dynamics of the politics and, for that matter, the psychological and normative aspects of the past are complicated by differences in the normative worlds of then and now.[6] Unwholesome actions or events in the past that surface at a later time are perceived and judged through current normative optics, not those that prevailed when the actions or events took place. Here again, Kratochwil's (2006) call to consider the practical implications of the—in this case normative—historical context is crucial. My concern here is not whether to embrace or reject historicist arguments (see Kratochwil 2006) but, rather, to suggest that in modern societies—probably most societies in the twenty-first century—the general public as well as elites see it and perhaps want to have it both ways.

We are aware that the European settlement of the Western Hemisphere, Australia, New Zealand, and many other parts of the world—not to mention the imposition of colonial rule everywhere—entailed enormous violence and caused great suffering. There were many robust justifications for those actions at the time. But for more than half a century, a wide and probably still expanding consensus has rejected, with increasing vehemence, the ethnic cleansing, dispossession, forced religious conversion, pillage, torture, and mass murder associated with them. While, as Elazar Barkan (2000) and others have suggested, those actions in the distant past can be acknowledged with benefit for the present, it is possible for many people to relegate them to the past and, with or without atonement or restitution, to regret them in some fashion.

In many, perhaps most, instances it is difficult or extremely impractical to rectify wrongs done long ago. Claims based on those wrongs by the actual—but often only nominal or symbolic—descendants of those who suffered them are formulated in terms of today's norms. That could not be otherwise, but a dilemma persists nonetheless: while it may be possible to address (what are now deemed to have been) wrongs committed in the past, the costs of doing so may be great for those who undertake them, even if only symbolically. Nonetheless, as Martha Minow (1998), Elazar Barkan (2000), and others (e.g., Barkan and Karn 2006) convincingly argue, the effort is worth making.

[W]hile it may be possible to address (what are now deemed to have been) wrongs committed in the past, the costs of doing so may be great for those who undertake them, even if only symbolically.

Moving Forward

The complexity of the past cannot be reduced to a set of dicta, methods, or facts. No amount of research and scholarly analysis can produce renditions of history straightforward enough to preclude strong objections from some, perhaps many. A version of history that no one would consider one-sided or subjective or factually flawed would probably be rejected on the ground that it was vacant. We have deeply held beliefs about how we came to be who we are and about what elements of the past are indispensable to our collective and individual identities (Wiebe 2002). All societies have built more or less resilient, self-sustaining, and self-validating cognitive, social, religious, and political edifices on the foundations of their version of the past (see, e.g., Smith 2003). They have enmeshed their past in a narrative; concretized it (often literally) in memorials and rituals; and, at least in the past two or three centuries, made it into a fungible political commodity with a wide range of uses, principally but not only in the hands of elites, for creating or enhancing solidarity, differentiating groups or societies from each other, or advancing one ideology or worldview over others (see Alonso 1988).

But if historical narratives and attempts to update, correct, or modify them are likely to remain contentious, the objects of contention—or at least many of them—can be effectively addressed. This is especially so in the case of relatively recent transgressions or objects of contention.

Some have suggested that trials, truth and reconciliation commissions, and reparations may be useful (Minow 1998). Others (e.g., Barkan 2000) contemplate restitution, where feasible. But transgressions committed generations ago cannot engage the survivors, nor perhaps their direct descendants. As Barkan (2000, 306-7) notes, even where direct restitution or other forms of compensation may not be practical, engaging in substantive, ongoing discussion—including, most importantly, those who identify with the populations often wronged—can become "a process of mourning and affirmation in which the discussion goes a long way to examine public responsibility, delineate its boundaries, and play a significant role in public education."

Such discussions—political and ethical talk focused on the past, efforts to mold narratives and collective representations of it, seeking to evoke or influence particular emotional or identitive responses from it—can both foster greater feelings of solidarity—or it can sharpen divisions among people. The outcomes may be mutually contingent: enhanced solidarity in a population may only be possible at the cost of sharper differences between it and outsiders, while divisions between segments of a population often produce more cohesion within each segment.

Finally, perhaps most encouraging in the long run, are the history textbooks.[7] They are an important and obvious medium for linking past and present, one that can also help to bridge normative changes over time or at least frame their consideration. History textbooks not only provide narrative accounts of the past; they can also frame the past in its temporal and normative contexts. They can be readily updated to reflect new scholarship and to relate events to cultural or normative shifts.

As Claudia Schneider's article on Japanese textbook controversies shows, they often do not succeed in playing these roles or in playing them effectively, whether as a result of political pressures or for other reasons (Hein and Selden 2000; Schissler and Soysal 2005). But Falk Pingel's article and the work he has directed for many years through the auspices of the Georg Eckert Institute for International Textbook Research and its journal give reason for optimism regarding this medium for treating the past and reconciling contentious issues about the past.

The contentious nature of history reflects politics *par excellence*. Like history, indeed like both the scientific and humanistic pursuits of knowledge and understanding, it is and must remain open to new findings, revision, and reframing. But friction seems unavoidable even in the sciences (consider the advent of the theory of quantum mechanics, string theory, or the perennial confrontation of evolution and intelligent design) and the humanities (e.g., poststructuralism and postmodernism, constructivism feminist studies, and subaltern history), so it would be unrealistic and unwise to expect "settlement" or closure in the battles revolving around the past. For that reason, it is important to gain better understanding of the dynamic processes of those battles, that is, the politics of history.

Notes

1. My language here was influenced by Rogers Smith's seminal book, *Stories of Peoplehood: The Politics and Morals of Political Membership* (2003).

2. Perhaps the most often cited exception, discussed in a more rotund fashion by Jenny Wüstenberg and David Art in this volume, is West Germany, that is, the Federal Republic before German unification in 1990.

3. The penultimate article, by Falk Pingel, is an exception. He discusses a promising approach to reconciliation between parties to recent conflicts.

4. As this article was being completed, in November 2007, and as a conference on Middle East peace was being planned for the end of the month, an association of Justice for Jews from Arab Countries announced that it would meet in early November to annunciate once more their claim that Arab states expelled a larger number of Jews in the late 1940s than the number of Palestinians driven out of the new state of Israel. Coinciding with the sixtieth anniversary, on November 29, of the United Nations resolution on the partition of Palestine, the organization announced as its twofold aim the blunting of the ritual denunciation of Israel by the United Nations General Assembly on that date and providing a moral bargaining chip for the Israeli government at the upcoming peace conference on the issue of the right of return for Palestinian refugees (Hoge 2007). Earlier in 2007, in the course of negotiations on reforming the institutions of the European Union, the Polish government sought to use German aggression against Poland in World War II to justify its claims to a greater voice in the European Union.

5. Winter associates this development with World War I and subsequent conflicts in which the numbers of noncombatant victims of war equaled or exceeded combatant casualties. An evocative literature focused on the Second World War already assumes a generalized audience for the politics of constructing stories, memories, and memorials related to war (see, e.g., Lebow, Kansteiner, and Fogu 2006; Müller 2002; cf. Olick 2003, for discussions with a greater time horizon). On the relationship between warfare and democracy from classical antiquity through the Second World War, see Peter Manicas's (1989) important work. It can be argued that there has been an evanescence of the "democratic" impacts of war in some places in recent years and the emergence of what could be termed postmodern war, at least for advanced industrial countries, since risks seem once more to be borne largely by the professional military, and few if any sacrifices are called for by war leaders of any but their families. Thus, the current American war in Iraq might be termed a postmodern war.

6. I have discussed the temporal dimension of similar normative considerations elsewhere (Heisler 2001) and return to it in the concluding article in this volume.

7. Systematic presentations of scholarship-based history through other media, such as film, television, software, and the Internet can play parallel roles, but the school setting and the imprimatur of the formal authority of educational authorities are important contributors to the effectiveness of textbooks.

References

Alonso, Ana María. 1988. The effects of truth: Re-presentations of the past and the imagining of community. *Journal of Historical Sociology* 1 (1): 33-57.

Barkan, Elazar. 2000. *The guilt of nations: Restitution and negotiating historical injustices.* New York: Norton.

Barkan, Elazar, and Alexander Karn, eds. 2006. *Taking wrongs seriously: Apologies and reconciliation.* Stanford, CA: Stanford University Press.

Brunner, José. 1997. Pride and memory: Nationalism, narcissism and the historians' debates in Germany and Israel. *History and Memory* 9 (1-2): 256-300.

Hein, Laura, and Mark Selden, eds. 2000. *Censoring history: Citizenship and memory in Japan, Germany, and the United States.* Armonk, NY: M. E. Sharpe.

Heisler, Martin O. 2001. Now and then, here and there: Migration and the transformation of identities, borders, and orders. In *Identities, borders, orders: Rethinking international relations theory,* ed. Mathias Albert, David Jacobson, and Yosef Lapid, 225-47. Minneapolis: University of Minnesota Press.

Hoge, Warren. 2007. Group Spotlights Jews Who Left Arab Lands. *New York Times,* November 5, p. A6.

Kratochwil, Friedrich. 2006. History, action and identity: Revisiting the "second" great debate and assessing its importance for social theory. *European Journal of International Relations* 12 (1): 5-29.

Lebow, Richard Ned, Wulf Kansteiner, and Claudio Fogu, eds. 2006. *The politics of memory in postwar Europe.* Durham, NC: Duke University Press.

Manicas, Peter T. 1989. *War and democracy.* Cambridge, MA: Basil Blackwell.

Minow, Martha. 1998. *Between vengeance and forgiveness: Facing history after genocide and mass violence.* Boston: Beacon.

Müller, Jan-Werner, ed. 2002. *Memory and power in post-war Europe: Studies in the presence of the past.* Cambridge: Cambridge University Press.

Nietzsche, Friedrich. 1989. *Beyond good and evil*. New York: Prometheus Books.

Novick, Peter. 2007. Comments on Aleida Assmann's lecture. *Bulletin of the German Historical Institute* 40 (Spring): 27-31.

Olick, Jeffrey K., ed. 2003. *States of memory: Continuities, conflicts, and transformations in national retrospection*. Durham, NC: Duke University Press.

Schissler, Hanna, and Yasemin Nuhoglu Soysal, eds. 2005. *The nation, Europe and the world: Textbooks and curricula in transition*. New York: Berghahn Books.

Smith, Rogers M. 2003. *Stories of peoplehood: The politics and morals of political membership*. Cambridge: Cambridge University Press.

Torpey, John. 2003. Introduction: Politics and the past. In *Politics and the past*, ed. John Torpey, 1-34. Lanham, MD: Rowman & Littlefield.

Walzer, Michael. 1994. *Thick and thin: Moral argument at home and abroad*. Notre Dame, IN: University of Notre Dame Press.

Wiebe, Robert. 2002. *Who we are: A history of popular nationalism*. Princeton, NJ: Princeton University Press.

Zinn, Howard. 1990. *The politics of history*. 2nd ed. Urbana: University of Illinois Press.

The author compares and contrasts the public discourse over memory in Western Europe and North America. The greater awareness in continental Europe of memory as a political resource and site of contestation has profound implications for elite behavior and mass responses. It also has the potential to alter the dynamics by which collective and institutional memory is created, recalled, and altered.

Keywords: memory; future of memory; institutional memory; collective memory

The Future of Memory

By
RICHARD NED LEBOW

In this article, I speculate about some of the ways in which greater public awareness of memory as a political resource and source of contestation is likely to influence elite and mass behavior. Changes of behavior in turn have the potential to affect the dynamics by which memory is created, recalled, and altered. If knowledge of memory influences the practice of memory, which in turn negates, at least in part, the validity of any understanding of the interaction between institutional, collective, and individual memories, we are talking about an infinite regress—something that would surely put a smile on Max Weber's face.

My inquiry is premised on three related assumptions. The first, an empirical one, is that elite and public opinion in at least some countries has become increasingly aware of memory as something that is problematic and often a source of contestation. My second assumption,

Richard Ned Lebow is the James O. Freedman Presidential Professor of Government at Dartmouth College. His most recent books are A Cultural Theory of International Relations *(Cambridge 2008) and* Conflict, Cooperation and Ethics *(Routledge 2006). Recent coedited volumes include* The Politics of Memory in Postwar Europe *(Duke 2006),* Unmaking the West: "What-If" Scenarios That Rewrite World History *(Michigan 2006), and* Theory and Evidence in Comparative Politics and International Relations *(2007).*

DOI: 10.1177/0002716207310817

theoretical in nature, is that elite and public opinion in at least some countries has become more receptive to the implications of this information. My third assumption, also empirical, is that growing awareness by the elite and the ordinary public of both the malleability and politicization of memory will have important consequences for future efforts to influence and control memory at institutional, collective, and individual levels.

My first assumption has two components: awareness of memory as something that is not necessarily accurate, unchanging, and recallable; and recognition that groups with competing agendas often struggle to shape and control memory on at least the institutional level. What evidence is there to support this claim? This is not an easy question to answer in the absence of good survey data. A simple poll could provide useful data about how the public regards memory along several relevant dimensions.

A follow-on and more elaborate study would devise measures to determine the degree of public exposure to discourses that problematize memory and treat it as a source of contestation (the independent variable) and would then survey the public in a sample of countries that score high and low on the independent variable to see the percentage of people in each who acknowledge memory to be problematic and contested (the dependent variable). A high correlation between greater public exposure to conflicts over memory and greater public awareness of memory as a source of contestation, and a lower correlation in countries where public exposure was less, would help establish this claim. In the absence of such studies, I must fall back on less scientific, impressionistic arguments.

The discourse on memory takes place in the scholarly literature and more popular media. In the historical profession, in North America and Europe, there is undeniably a "memory boom" under way. Searches on Amazon under the heading of "memory politics" or "politics of memory" get almost four thousand results of publications in English alone. A cursory examination of major historical journals over the past two decades also indicates a growing interest in the subject. Jay Winter (2000) went so far as to claim that memory is the new paradigm of history, overpowering and restructuring other frames of reference like class and gender. In the United States, academic debates take place in a rarefied atmosphere and, with few exceptions, have little impact on wider publics. In Western Europe, especially in Germany and Italy, the media cover controversial political issues, and in Europe these have not infrequently concerned questions of historical memory and memorialization. Examples include the Touvier and Papon trials in France, the Waldheim affair in Austria, U.S. pressures on Swiss banks, official recognition of the Jedwabne massacre in Poland, and the design and location of the Holocaust memorial in Berlin (Golsan 1996; Bloxham 2001; Lebow, Kansteiner, and Fogu 2006). All of these issues brought up past events, often crimes in which the state was complicit and that official versions of institutional memory sought to hide.

Until recently, Eastern Europe had a different trajectory. In the Soviet Union and other communist states there was no open debate about the past and its memorialization, only efforts to impose official interpretations of history through the educational system and the media. The heavy-handed nature of such social-ization, and the extent to which it was so much at odds with more national rep-resentations of the past, made people more aware than they would have been otherwise of the importance of memory and the extent to which it was a political resource. The fall of communism has had the same effect, although for the oppo-site reason. The "right to memory" has been asserted by peoples everywhere east of the former Oder-Neisse Line and has served as a catalyst for the revival of national histories, but also for efforts to confront the past in ways inimical to those propagating or supporting self-congratulatory national histories (Brossat 1990; Judt 1992; Wyrda 2007, 227-30). In the past decade, debates about the past, and about the politics of memory itself, have been at least as prominent in Eastern Europe as in the West (Orla-Bukowska 2006). During this period, the countries of Eastern Europe have at times been under pressure from both Russia and the West to approach memory in particular ways. Applications for entry into the European Community provided some leverage to the West in this regard, and there were pressures on Eastern European countries in the 1990s to consider their past more openly and honestly, pressures that strengthened the hand of indigenous intellectuals and politicians who were similarly inclined. Moscow was exerting its influence in the direction of retaining and respecting Soviet war memorials that were present throughout the region. More recently, the destruc-tion of a Soviet war memorial in Talinn, Estonia, provoked riots by ethnic Russians, a conflict with Russia, and a growing public debate in Estonia (BBC News 2007; Mälksoo 2007).

The United States is something of an outlier here, as it is on so many issues. As a victor in World War II, it had little incentive to reconsider its past. This arose ini-tially from the internment of Americans of Japanese descent, which was declared unconstitutional after the war was over and widely recognized as morally repre-hensible some decades later (Ng 2002). Attempts to problematize World War II outside of the scholarly realm have not been noticeably successful. The contro-versy over the cancellation of Martin Harwit's planned *Enola Gay* exhibit at the National Air and Space Museum in April 1995 indicates that service organizations, the military, and conservative congressmen remain unwilling to reconsider the ethics of Hiroshima and Nagasaki (Harwich 1996; Kohn 1996). Although a loser in Indochina, the United States was still powerful enough to shrug off its defeat, and there was very little effort outside of the academic community to rethink the country's national security policy on the basis of this experience. The Persian Gulf War of 1990 to 1991 and the invasion of Iraq in 2003 evoked memories of the Vietnam War and of the trauma arising from the American defeat. It produced a display of yellow ribbons on cars, houses, and trees, many of them with the motto "support our troops." In 2007, in keeping with their commitment to "stay the course" in Iraq, right-wing revisionists began publicizing the myth that America would have won the Vietnam War if public opinion had supported the forces engaged in combat (Lembcke 1998; Turner 1996; Hixon 2000).

That memory has become at all problematic in the United States has more to do with the phenomenon of "repressed" or "recovered" memory. The concept

was originated by Freud, later rejected by him, and remains one of the controversial subjects in psychiatry (Freud 1896/1923, 187-221). A repressed memory,
usually associated with trauma, is one that is not available to the conscious mind.
Some therapists contend that memories of this kind recur in dreams and may be
recovered years after the event. Other health professionals deny their existence.
Repressed memory was popularized in the 1980s and 1990s by the media, some
feminist groups, and a small number of psychologists. It featured in numerous
criminal and civil trials, many of them involving alleged sexual abuse of children.
In some states, the presumed existence of repressed memories provided the
grounds for extending the statute of limitations in child abuse cases (for research
skeptical of recovered memory, see Whitfield 1995; Brandon et al. 1998). Many
of these trials have been widely discussed in the media, including those where
recovered memory has been discredited, as in the case of Cardinal Joseph
Bernadin, who was charged with sexual abuse by a former seminarian who subsequently withdrew his allegation (on the Bernadin case and related cases, see
Simmons 1994).

*That memory has become at all
problematic in the United States has more to
do with the phenomenon of "repressed" or
"recovered" memory.*

During this period, repressed memories became the subject of popular books
and a frequent talk show topic (Bass 1988). They have long provided plot lines
for feature films, including *Spellbound* (1945), *Tommy* (1975), *The Butterfly
Effect* (2004), and *Serenity* (2005), as well as for video games and comic books.
In the movie *Serenity*, the lead character's mental health is restored once he is
made aware of a repressed traumatic memory. In the video game *Final Fantasy
VII*, the protagonist has false memories of his military service because his "real"
memories have been suppressed by brainwashing. Alien abduction is another
major theme that features repressed memories of encounters, often aboard
spaceships, which cause nightmares and other problems until they are recovered
(Matheson 1998; for a true believer, see Mack 1994).

   This foregrounding of repressed memory can reasonably be expected to have
sensitized the American public to the importance of memory, but in a very different way than in Europe. The discourse of memory in the United States has

been comparatively apolitical as it is focused largely on personal trauma. While the phenomenon of recovered memory has been extremely controversial, I have not found any data on how credible it is in the eyes of the American public. I surmise that it is high given the state-level legislation for which it is responsible. As for alien abduction, it is estimated that 3.7 million Americans claim to have been abducted by aliens, and a 2002 Roper poll indicates that one in five Americans believe in alien abduction (cited in Wilson 2007). For those who reject recovered memory, the concept of memory itself cannot help but become more problematic. Just the reverse is true for those who give credence to recovered memory because it suggests that memories can be repressed but are "real" and remain remarkably resistant to efforts to reshape their content.

My second assumption is that elite and public opinion in at least some countries has become more receptive to evidence indicating the malleability of memory. In other words, many people not only recognize memory as a resource that groups in their society attempt to exploit, but believe in the feasibility of this enterprise. This understanding of memory could profitably be examined in many different countries, but I will restrict myself to Europe, where the memory boom—in scholarly literature and popular media—has arguably been the most pronounced.

Earlier, I noted the connection between memory and identity. As memory is considered by most people to make them who they are, they are most likely to safeguard and defend their memories—individual, collective, and official—when they are confident about and content with their identities. They will defend their memories with a particular vengeance if they feel beleaguered. A dramatic case in point was the Protestant commitment during the so-called "troubles" in Northern Ireland to march through Catholic neighborhoods on Orange Day to commemorate the Protestant victory over Catholics at the Battle of the Boyne in July 1690. The march reaffirmed Protestant identity and political power and was accordingly resisted, often violently, by Catholics, for whom the Battle of the Boyne was a marker of subjection. When identity becomes problematic, which it can for many reasons, people are likely to be less committed to memories and commemorations on which existing identities are based or from which they derive justification. Some of those memories and commemorations may become inconvenient if they stand in the way of changing or reformulating identities. For reasons that are widespread and idiosyncratic, identity was problematic in much of Europe after World War II, and it is so again in the aftermath of the cold war and collapse of the Soviet Union.

The paradigmatic case in postwar Europe was the Federal Republic of Germany. National identity, previously strong, became uncomfortable for many Germans by reason of the country's Nazi past and the postwar division (on identity, memory, and the two memories, see Herf 1997; the best work on the Federal Republic is Kansteiner 2006). Few Germans wanted to identify with Nazi Germany, but many found it difficult to define their identities in terms of either successor state. Some citizens of the Federal Republic sought to strengthen their attachments to the regions or to develop a new, or at least supplemental, identity as Europeans. In Germany, *Heimat* (referring to the territory, people, and customs of a region) had historically preceded *Vaterland* (the national state) as an identity and had remained a viable and respected secondary identification. Germans also had some earlier experience with transstate identities. In the nineteenth century, *Deutschland* and *Deutschtum* referred to the community of Germans and German speakers regardless of their political unit (e.g., Prussia, Austria, Bavaria). These preexisting identities made postwar substate and suprastate identities more accessible and acceptable.

Regional and European identities for Germans were also welcomed by their neighbors and Americans. Regional identities—Prussia aside, and that was in the German Democratic Republic—appeared to them relatively benign and raised the prospect of centrifugal tendencies that might restrain the still not trusted federal government. Supranational identities were built around European integration, of which the Franco-German alliance was the core, and were encouraged as a means of integrating Germany more fully into the Western community. Both kinds of identity—and they are by no means exclusive—had to be built on memories. In June 2004, Germany was invited for the first time to the D-Day commemoration at the invasion beaches in France. German Chancellor Gerhard Schroeder used the opportunity to align Germany with the allies, telling his audience that D-Day was not a "victory over Germany, but a victory for Germany" that led to its liberation from Nazi rule. Schroeder's speech raised some eyebrows at home but was very favorably received by other European leaders and public opinion (BBC News 2004). This unprecedented move toward a common, celebratory understanding of a former battle stands in sharp contrast to the continuing division in Northern Ireland over the Battle of the Boyne, or in Poland, the Baltic countries, and Russia over Russia's "liberation" of Eastern Europe in 1944 and 1945.

Another indication of receptivity to the idea that memory is malleable is the burgeoning of counterfactual history, academic and popular. In North America and Europe, it is no coincidence that the rise of counterfactual history has paralleled the memory boom. Popular counterfactual history is based on the premise that the present is highly contingent and that with only surgical interventions in the tissue of history—what Max Weber called "minimal rewrites"—different presents can readily be conjured up. Counterfactual novels often address the outcome of wars, like the American Civil War and World War II, that are central to contemporary problems of identity and memory. They highlight, even call into question, the connection between identity and history by revealing the contingent nature of both. More scholarly efforts at counterfactual history have sought to undermine essentialist narratives and counteract the certainty of hindsight bias. They have also sought to expose the generally unspoken assumptions on which historical interpretations are based and, by extension, the identities they support (Tetlock and Lebow 2001, 829-43; Tetlock, Lebow, and Parker 2006; Lebow forthcoming).

Implications

My third assumption is that growing awareness of memory as malleable and as a source of political contestation will have serious longer-term implications for the practice of memory. It will affect the importance of memory for identity, the ease by which memory is reshaped or renegotiated, the means by which this is accomplished, and ultimately, the shape and membership of communities. In this connection, I offer a series of observations, some of them in the form of hypotheses. All refer to developments that have not occurred, if indeed they ever will. They cannot yet be evaluated empirically but are intended to serve as guides for future research. Some of the propositions may appear contradictory because they predict opposing developments. However, change not infrequently transforms normal distributions into highly skewed ones.

1. Increased resistance to institutional memory. To the extent that people become conscious of any socialization process, they have greater potential to free themselves from it. This is more likely to happen in circumstances in which socialization is vocally contested by others. It not only makes people aware of a process that might otherwise have gone unnoticed but also provides alternative perspectives and choices. It can also shed light on the possible motives of those advancing the competing perspectives. This has happened in the course of the so-called culture wars in the United States and in the extensive debates in many European countries over their responsibility for and roles in World War II. Resistance can take the form of aloofness to all narratives that encode institutional memories, that is, awareness of them but not acceptance. Such resistance will inevitably have consequences for identity, making it more problematic at the national and supra-national levels where it relies so heavily on institutional memories. If so, subnational and other forms of identity (e.g., professional, generational, religious, or family identities that cut across national boundaries) will become correspondingly more important, as will the collective memories on which they rest.

2. Increased receptivity to self-congratulatory national narratives. In mechanics, every action provokes an equal and opposite reaction. In politics, reactions are also inevitable, but not necessarily equal. Vocal and largely successful challenges of traditional narratives of American history that present it as unalloyed progress toward wealth and freedom; ignore or gloss over the brutal treatment of Native Americans and slaves; and downplay, or downright exclude, the contributions of Blacks, women, and ethnic minorities to America's democracy and economic and cultural development provoked a strong backlash from conservatives. In Europe, attempts to rewrite history to acknowledge imperialism and its consequences; root fascist or Nazi regimes in their countries' pasts; and acknowledge collaboration, ethnic cleansing, and complicity in the Holocaust elicited similar reactions from nationalists committed to uncritical historical narratives that generally define the nation, if not explicitly in genetic terms, then with reference to those who lived on its territory for countless generations—what Germans formerly called *blut* and *boden* (blood and land).

3. The shaping and contestation of institutional memory. National narratives are subsumed under the category of institutional memory because they have traditionally been the prerogative of the state exercised through its control of the educational system and other vehicles for shaping mass opinion. These narratives are frequently challenged by individual groups who oppose the current government or regime. In the West, these conflicts have drawn in a wider segment of the national community when they have been featured in the media. Newspapers, films, and television can propagate officially sanctioned narratives but can also offer versions of the past at odds with institutional memory. This can occur even in countries where governments retain considerable control, or at least influence, over the media, as in Poland when the Lanzmann documentary *Shoah* was televised (Orla-Bukowska 2006).

4. International influences on institutional memory. The post-1945 period was distinguished by efforts of states and groups of states to shape the construction of official and collective memory in other states. American occupation policies in Germany and Japan had this as one of their avowed goals. In Germany, local populations were compelled to visit recently liberated concentration camps, while the Nuremberg Trials, and the evidence they unearthed concerning Nazi crimes, were widely disseminated in German-language newsreels and newspapers (Tent 1982; Smith 1996). More recently, Washington has put pressure on Switzerland and its banks to acknowledge their theft of assets deposited by subsequent victims of the Holocaust and make efforts to locate and compensate their families (Ludi 2006). Members of the European Union have individually and collectively encouraged the countries of Eastern Europe to confront their past more honestly; and China, Korea, and the Philippines have called upon Japan to acknowledge its war crimes, including the Rape of Nanjing, medical experimentation on prisoners of war and civilians, and the pressing of young women into involuntary service as sexual servants for Japanese troops. Outside pressures of this kind always meet resistance, but they have succeeded to a surprising degree in Europe. Change of the desired kind in official narratives appears to hinge on the leverage of outside parties; the existence of groups within the target countries whose agendas are served by responding positively to external pressures; and the ability of these groups to convince the wider public, or at least key officials, that they must respond because of overriding political or national interests.

International involvement can take the more benign form of foreign aid and other assistance to countries to aid in historical revision and reconstruction. These activities can take the form of research, seminars, training of scholars, and collaborative projects that range from textbooks to documentation of atrocities. China and Japan have a joint textbook project under way and, despite the various difficulties that have arisen, hope to produce a companion volume for school curricula. The Venice Peace Foundation (Fondazione della Pace Venezia), with the support of Venice International University, the city of Venice, and several banks, is organizing a joint exploration of memory of World War II and its aftermath by Italy and other countries along the Adriatic littoral. Collaborative projects of this kind are likely to become increasingly common and, if successful, have the potential to serve as useful catalysts for national reconciliation.

Change of the desired kind in official narratives appears to hinge on the leverage of outside parties; the existence of groups within the target countries whose agendas are served by responding positively to external pressures; and the ability of these groups to convince the wider public, or at least key officials, that they must respond because of overriding political or national interests.

---

5. *Institutional memory as a form of reassurance.* In April 2005, the College of Cardinals elected a German pope—Cardinal Joseph Ratzinger—who had been a member of the Hitlerjugend and briefly served in the Wehrmacht. The new pope is controversial in Europe—but for his ultraconservative religious views, not for his German past. As the College of Cardinals was deliberating, Chinese demonstrators, egged on by their government, were throwing stones at the Japanese embassy in Peking and consulates elsewhere in China, attacking Japanese businesses, and generally protesting Japan's efforts to obtain a permanent seat on the United Nation's Security Council. The demonstrators, and the Chinese government, were doubly enraged by the nearly simultaneous publication of a Japanese textbook that sought to downplay or discredit the atrocities that Japanese occupation forces had committed in China and elsewhere in Asia. The textbook, like most in Japan, also put a favorable gloss on Japan's invasions of China and Southeast Asia, describing them as acts of anticolonialism and as economically beneficial for those who were occupied (Onishi 2005a, 2005b; Kahn 2005c; Young 2005; French and Kahn 2005).

These two events in two different regions of the world were closely related, even if diametrically opposed in their symbolic value. The election of a German pope, and one, moreover, who had worn a military uniform, would have been hard to imagine in the absence of a serious effort over the decades of successive German governments to come to terms with the past and accept their responsibility for the horrendous suffering the Nazis inflicted on Europe. The Chinese government was not shy about making this counterfactual argument. Chinese officials praised Germany for acknowledging its Nazi past, for paying billions of dollars in reparations to victims or their families, and for the forthright approach of its school curriculum. They noted the visits of Prime Minister Willy Brandt and President Richard Weizsäcker to Auschwitz and the seemingly heartfelt apologies they made for Germany's crimes. If the Japanese had behaved this way, one official said, China would view them and their claims for a Security Council seat differently (Kahn 2005a, 2005b). The March 2007 public apology of Japanese Prime Minister Shinzo Abe for the suffering of women exploited for sex during World War II only appears to have added oil to the fire because senior members of his administration continue to deny that the Japanese military organized a brothel system that pressed foreign women into service (Wallace 2007). Abe himself has stonewalled U.S. congressional efforts to encourage Japan to own up to and apologize for these actions (McCurry 2007).

Germany has set a precedent, which the Germans themselves realize. In the 1990s, they took the lead in encouraging the countries of Eastern Europe who sought membership in NATO and the EU to address their pasts more openly and honestly, and Germany has invested heavily in civic education projects in the region. The German media were openly critical of the Kaczynski government in Poland for backsliding in this regard (*Die Tageszeitung* 2006 triggered a diplomatic incident between the two countries). Russia has been noticeably reluctant to address its past; the efforts Gorbachev initiated with his policy of *glasnost* have stalled under President Vladimir Putin. Putin's return to nationalism and more authoritarian rule and Russia's recent cyberwar against Estonia have been taken by many as evidence that it is unpredictable and possibly hegemonic in its ambitions (*The Economist* 2007; Traynor 2007). German Chancellor Angela Merkel has been much more outspoken in her criticism than her predecessor, publicly rebuking the Russian government on multiple occasions for its perceived violation of democratic norms (for a recent instance, see Penketh 2007, 30). To reassure the West, Russia would not only have to alter its policies but also confront its past. It is not far-fetched to predict that post-Bush and post–Iraq War efforts by the United States to regain the trust of its Western allies will depend not only on its resumption of more multilateral policies but also efforts to acknowledge its responsibility for bringing chaos and widespread death and destruction to the Middle East.

6. Shared remembrance. The Napoleonic Wars and World War I were remembered separately by victors and losers for many decades, if not longer in the case of the Napoleonic Wars. It was only in 2005 that France joined Britain at ceremonies led by the Queen commemorating the British naval victory at Trafalgar (Wyatt 2005). World War II repeated this pattern. Periodic celebrations of the D-Day landings in June 1944 were limited to the allies who had landed soldiers on the beach (the United States, United Kingdom, Canada, and France) and the occasional Soviet observer until 2004, when Germany was invited to participate. A public opinion poll in France revealed widespread support for the move—fully 86 percent of the respondents thought it a good idea, a figure, moreover, that did not vary significantly by age (*Le Figaro* 2004, 1). Just as remarkable were the joint commemorations of the Battle of Gettysburg (July 1863), generally described as a turning point in the American Civil War and the well-known site of Lincoln's eponymous address. On two anniversaries of the battle, in 1913 and 1938, the Grand Army of the Republic and the United Confederate Veterans held a joint reunion where they camped out together and shared reminiscences of the battle. These reunions were a symbol of and catalyst for the rapprochement of North and South.

Events of this kind are a sign not only that hostile relations and the enmity they generate have been overcome, but that unilateral commemoration is now perceived as dissonant with the current state of amicable relations. Joint celebrations allow former enemies to recast their meaning in a manner that reduces dissonance and sustains the partially common identities former adversaries have come to develop. They require interpretations of the past that somehow turn the battles in question, if not into some kind of victory for both sides, as Chancellor Schroeder attempted to do with the Normandy landings, then into an event with positive associations for all participants. To the extent that relations improve between Russia and the West; Russia and the countries of Eastern Europe; Japan, Korea, and China; the United States and Mexico; or any other long-standing historical division—and I am not predicting that they will—joint commemorations of past battles, or of other events previously characterized by clashing national narratives, are likely to symbolize and further facilitate such reconciliation.

7. *The proliferation of collective memory communities.* Institutional memory helps to shape the identities of citizens who identify with their state, but few states are coterminous with nationalities. In these countries—Japan and Iceland are the great exemplars—collective memories are nested within the state, and the permeability of collective to institutional memory, and vice versa, should be reasonably high. As both political systems have high legitimacy, institutional and collective memory are likely to be more mutually reinforcing than elsewhere. In states that include multiple nationalities or ethnic groups, institutional and some collective memories are more likely to clash to the extent that institutional memory excludes or deprecates these other nationalities or ethnic groups. In the nineteenth and twentieth centuries, much of domestic and foreign policy revolved around ethnic conflicts, which were the major source of intrastate and interstate violence and war.

Such conflicts continue to disrupt the peace, but other forms of community have also become prominent. They include communities that are international in membership and organized around religious, confessional, or professional affiliations. Since 9/11, the former has received growing attention, and there is widespread recognition that religious identities frequently compete with national ones and are sustained by their own historical narratives. This is true for many Muslims in the Middle East, India, and Indonesia; Hindus in India; and various Christian sects, primarily in North America. At the secular end of the spectrum, business, professional, and academic communities are increasingly international in their membership and identification. In Europe, and to a lesser extent in North America and the Pacific Rim, executives, professors, and businesspeople are multilingual, work, or have spent time in countries other than those in which they grew up. For all these reasons, they often tend to identify with their peers more than they do with their fellow nationals. With globalization, cross-cutting identities of this kind are almost certain to become a more widespread phenomenon. Such communities also need collective memories to sustain themselves, and it will be interesting to see the extent to which they form and on what they are based.

In states that include multiple nationalities or ethnic groups, institutional and some collective memories are more likely to clash to the extent that institutional memory excludes or deprecates these other nationalities or ethnic groups.

In eighteenth-century Europe, communities and the memories that sustained them were hierarchal. Continental elites spoke French, intermarried, and on the whole identified with one another more than they did with the nonaristocratic inhabitants of the lands in which they resided. Nationalism largely did away with this hierarchical community; aristocrats learned local languages and increasingly came to identify with national communities. Memory construction at the official and collective levels facilitated and justified this shift in identification. Globalization has the potential of creating not one but multiple hierarchical communities and of bringing about another great shift in the structure of collective memory. As before, such a shift will have profound implications for social and political behavior. One way of tracking any progress in this direction is by observing the emergence of new communities of collective memory and their understanding of identity.

8. *The penetration of local collective memory by corporations and nonprofit organizations.* Collective memory has always been to some extent penetrated by institutional memory, and this has been part and parcel of efforts by political authorities who have sought to build national states. Today, collective memory is increasingly molded by institutions that are to varying degrees independent of the state. The film and television industries may be the most important nonstate influences on collective memory, and both readily cross national and linguistic barriers. For the most part, state control over the entertainment industry takes the form of the veto. State bureaucracies can exercise censorship of all kinds, a common practice in almost all authoritarian regimes. Democratic states play this game as well. In a clear effort to defend institutional memory, the French government sought to prevent *Le Chagrin et la pité* (*The Sorrow and the Pity*) from being produced, first for television, and then as a film. When French director Marcel Ophüls raised money abroad for a film production, the French government kept it from being shown in French theaters even after it was released in West Germany, Switzerland, the Netherlands, and the United States. Negotiations with French television to show the film in France were blocked in accordance with what Ophüls labeled "censorship through inertia." Finally released in April 1971 in a small movie house in the Latin Quarter, and later in a larger theatre on the Champs Élysées, the film in the end attracted more than six hundred thousand viewers, in part because of the notoriety it had achieved by virtue of its censorship (Golsan 2006).

Like institutional memory, collective memory often has physical sites associated with it. They include religious shrines, ruins, museums, buildings, and other locations associated with memorable events. In the developed world, ownership of these sites is occasionally contested, although more often contestation concerns how they are used to represent the past and the cultures to which they refer. The Musée de l'histoire de Judiasme—the Jewish Museum of Paris—offers a nice example of the latter kind of conflict. Its rooms and exhibits tell the story of Jews in France and display an impressive collection of religious objects and other memorabilia. A state museum, whose exhibits and accompanying narratives are the product of the relevant ministry, it reflects an officially sponsored narrative that emphasizes France's openness and assimilation of its Jewish inhabitants and their historical willingness in turn to become French. Only minimal space is devoted to the fate of Jews in the Vichy regime and occupied France, and when I toured the museum a few years ago, there was no mention of French collaboration in the deportations of Jews to death camps. The bookstore on the ground floor, run by the Parisian Jewish community, is filled with books and other materials on wartime France. The contrast between the display space and the books, and their respective messages, could not be more striking.

In less wealthy countries, the sites of collective memory have increasingly become contested. Local groups have been losing control to states and corporations. In part, this is a response to tourism and the money that is to be made from it. It also reflects efforts by UNESCO and like-minded organizations with the well-intentioned goal of preserving major cultural sites, especially those threatened by commercial or other kinds of development. At the same time, new technologies and changes in the politics of representation have encouraged individuals and groups to see themselves as the most legitimate curators of their own memory. This claim often pits groups against their own governments and international nonprofit organizations. These conflicts are likely to intensify and over time become part of and possibly strengthen collective memories, even if the groups in question lose control over the sites they are seeking to retain.

In the developed world, official memories are fragmenting, and in less developed countries, collective memories are under siege. We need to track how memory struggles in these two worlds evolve and the degree to which globalization will affect them by creating ever more links between them and the still largely separate arenas in which they currently take place.

9. *Collective versus institutional memory.* For reasons I have noted, institutional memory can be expected to become less monolithic and more problematic. This is already evident in democratic countries and is likely to become more apparent in authoritarian regimes as it becomes increasingly difficult to maintain a monopoly over the flow of information. Collective memory communities proliferate when states lose the ability to impose institutional memories on their populations. They also become more important when they sustain multiple identities that have the potential to reduce the overall importance of national identity to populations. In Europe, multiple identities have proliferated and increased in importance, although national identities have not undergone a significant decline (on this subject, see Cederman 2001; Herrmann, Risse, and Brewer 2004). We need to know more about this relationship and the circumstances under which multiple identities make national ones less important. Regardless of this relationship, the very proliferation of identities and their increasing importance for individuals should make the collective memories that create and sustain these identities an increasingly important source of contestation.

The ability to influence memories at the collective versus the institutional level requires a different set of resources and strategies. As one size does not fit all, governments that want to influence collective memory must direct their efforts at specific memory communities. They must become more like businesses and political movements that use large databanks and sophisticated algorithms to identify and target selected groups of consumers and voters. Nongovernmental keepers of collective memories will develop their own methods—cultural spam filters—to protect themselves from unwanted outside messages. We might also expect to see more informal and formal cooperation among collective memory communities to advance their respective interests and to protect themselves. Under the right conditions, they might also work with governments, corporations, and international organizations to advance their goals. Given the proliferation of multiple identities, individuals are likely to belong to multiple memory communities, making contact and cooperation across these communities more feasible. The next decade may accordingly witness alliances among different memory communities, strengthening their collective power.

Conclusion

In *Through the Looking Glass*, Alice complains that she cannot remember things before they happen, provoking the Queen to respond that "it's a poor sort of memory that only works backwards" (Carroll 1872/1982, 171; for this quote I am indebted to Bell 2006). We know, of course, that memory works forward as well in the sense that our individual behavior and many governmental policies are based on memories of what worked or failed in the past. The ability to influence these memories and, thus, their putative behavioral and policy implications, is one means of achieving influence in the present over the future. As Alice recognizes, we have no memories of the future, but we do have imagined memories of the future. We routinely build scenarios with good or bad outcomes based on the lessons we think we have learned from the past and use them to work our way through life and policy choices or, rhetorically, to try to sell our preferences to others. Future "memories" of this kind are just as important for building and sustaining identities as memories of the past—and many of the latter are, of course, also imaginary. Proselytizers of religion and nationalism have painted equally rosy and grim pictures of the future allegedly dependent on the success of their missions. Artists and writers have depicted these outcomes as if they had already come to pass, or were in the process of happening. Hieronymus Bosch's *Last Judgment* triptych and Dante's *Inferno* are cases in point. Both encourage viewers or readers to come away with memories of the future.

[W]e have no memories of the future, but we do have imagined memories of the future. We routinely build scenarios with good or bad outcomes based on the lessons we think we have learned from the past and use them to work our way through life and policy choices or, rhetorically, to try to sell our preferences to others.

The scholarship on memory has focused almost entirely on reconstruction of the past. There are undoubtedly two reasons for this: it largely mirrors the conduct of the actual politics of memory, and it is a field dominated by historians.

There is no particular reason to think that future memory politics may be more future-oriented than in the past, but it is a possibility worth exploring. Either way, future memory is an important and neglected component, especially of individual and collective memory, and one worthy of serious investigation. For Alice's queen and philosophers, past and future are logically equivalent. This stands in sharp contrast to conventional understandings, which is why we find the Queen's comment so amusing. Perhaps it is time for scholars and practitioners alike to take her majesty more seriously.

References

Bass, Ellen. 1988. *Courage: A guide for women survivors of childhood sexual abuse*. New York: Perennial Library.

BBC News. 2004. Leaders and veterans mark D-Day. June 6. http://news.bbc.co.uk/1/hi/world/europe/3780381.stm.

———. 2007. Estonia removes Soviet memorial. April 27. http://news.bbc.co.uk/1/hi/world/europe/6598269.stm.

Bell, Duncan. 2006. Introduction: Memory, trauma and world politics. In *Memory, trauma and world politics: Reflections on the relationship between peace and present*, ed. Duncan Bell, 1-32. London: Palgrave-Macmillan.

Bloxham, Donald. 2001. *Genocide on trial: War crimes and the formation of Holocaust history and memory*. Oxford: Oxford University Press.

Brandon, S., J. Boakes, D. Glaser, and R. Green. 1998. Recovered memories of childhood sexual abuse: Implications for clinical practice. *British Journal of Psychiatry* 172:296-307.

Brossat, Alain. 1990. *A L'Est, la mémoire retrouvée*. Paris: Éditions la Découverte.

Carroll, Lewis. 1872/1982. *The complete illustrated works of Lewis Carroll*. London: Chancellor Press.

Cederman, Lars Erik. 2001. *Constructing Europe's identity: The external dimension*. London: Lynne Rienner.

Die Tageszeitung. 2006. Polens neue Kartoffel [Poland's new potato]. June 26.

The Economist. 2007. A cyber riot. May 10.

French, Howard W., and Joseph Kahn. 2005. Thousands rally in Shanghai, attack Japanese Consulate. *New York Times*, April 16.

Freud, Sigmund. 1896/1923. The etiology of hysteria. In *The standard edition of the complete psychological works of Sigmund Freud*, vol. 3 (1893-1899), *Early psycho-analytic publications*. London: Hogarth Press.

Golsan, Richard, ed. 1996. *Memory, the Holocaust and French justice: The Bosquet and Touvier affairs*. Hanover, NH: University Press of New England.

———. 2006. The legacy of World War II in France: Mapping the discourses of memory. In *The politics of memory in postwar Europe*, ed. Richard Ned Lebow, Wulf Kansteiner, and Claudio Fogu, 73-101. Durham, NC: Duke University Press.

Harwich, Martin. 1996. *An exhibit denied: Lobbying the history of Enola Gay*. New York: Springer-Verlag.

Herf, Jeffrey. 1997. *Divided memories: The Nazi past in the two Germanies*. Cambridge, MA: Harvard University Press.

Herrmann, Richard, Thomas Risse, and Marilynn Brewer, eds. 2004. *Transnational identities: Becoming European in the EU*. Lanham, MD: Rowman & Littlefield.

Hixon, Walter L. 2000. *Historical memory and representations of the Vietnam War*. New York: Garland.

Judt, Tony. 1992. The past is another country: Myth and memory in postwar Europe. *Daedalus* 4:83-118.

Kahn, Joseph. 2005a. Chinese pushing and supporting Japanese protests. *New York Times*, April 15.

———. 2005b. If 22 million protest at UN, Japan won't. *New York Times*, April 1.

———. 2005c. No apology from China for Japan protest. *New York Times*, April 18.

Kansteiner, Wulf. 2006. *In pursuit of German memory: History, television, and politics after Auschwitz*. Athens: University of Ohio Press.

Kohn, Richard H. 1996. History at risk: The case of the Enola Gay. In *History wars: The Enola Gay and other battles for the American past*, ed. Edward T. Blumenthal and Tom Engelhard, 140-71. New York: Henry Holt.

Lebow, Richard Ned. Forthcoming. *Forbidden Fruit: Counterfactuals and international relations*. Princeton, NJ: Princeton University Press.

Lebow, Richard Ned, Wulf Kansteiner, and Claudio Fogu. 2006. *The politics of memory in postwar Europe*. Durham, NC: Duke University Press.

Le Figaro. 2004. June 6, p. 1.

Lembcke, Jerry. 1998. *The spitting image: Myth, memory, and the legacy of Vietnam*. New York: New York University Press.

Ludi, Regula. 2006. Past as present, myth, of history? Discourses of time and the Great Fatherland War. In *The politics of memory in postwar Europe*, ed. Richard Ned Lebow, Wulf Kansteiner, and Claudio Fogu, 210-48. Durham, NC: Duke University Press.

Mack, John. 1994. *Abduction: Human encounters with aliens*. New York: Scribner's.

Mälksoo, Maria. 2007. The "Bronze Soldier" and the memory politics of World War II in Estonia. Paper presented to the Centre of International Studies Staff Research Colloquium, May 15, University of Cambridge, UK.

Matheson, Terry. 1998. *Alien abduction: Creating a modern phenomenon*. New York: Prometheus Books.

McCurry, Justin. 2007. Japan rules out new apology to "comfort women." *Guardian*, March 5.

Ng, Wendy. 2002. *Japanese-American internment in World War II: A history and study guide*. Westport, CT: Greenwood.

Onishi, Norimitsu. 2005a. In Japan's new texts, assertions of rising nationalism. *New York Times*, April 17.

———. 2005b. Protests over history texts. *New York Times*, April 6.

Orla-Bukowska, Annamaria. 2006. New threads on an old loom: National memory and social identity in postwar and post-communist Poland. In *The politics of memory in postwar Europe*, ed. Richard Ned Lebow, Wulf Kansteiner, and Claudio Fogu, 177-209. Durham, NC: Duke University Press.

Penketh, Anne. 2007. Merkel and Putin clash over summit demonstration. *The Independent*, May 19, p. 30.

Simmons, Philip S. 1994. Lawyers and memory: The impact of repressed memory. *Institute for Psychological Therapies* 6. http://www.iptforensics.com/journal/volume6 /j6_3_6.htm.

Smith, Arthur L. 1996. *The war for the German mind: Reeducating Hitler's soldiers*. Providence, RI: Berghahn Books.

Tent, James F. 1982. *Mission on the Rhine: Reeducation and denazification in American-occupied Germany*. Chicago: University of Chicago Press.

Tetlock, Philip E., and Richard Ned Lebow. 2001. Poking counterfactual holes in covering laws: Cognitive styles and political learning. *American Political Science Review* 95 (December): 829-43.

Tetlock, Philip E., Richard Ned Lebow, and Geoffrey Parker. 2006. *Unmaking the West: "What-if" scenarios that rewrite world history*. Ann Arbor: University of Michigan Press.

Traynor, Ian. 2007. Russia accused of unleashing cyber war to disable Estonia. *The Guardian*, May 17.

Turner, Fred. 1996. *Echoes of combat: The Vietnam War in American memory*. New York: Anchor.

Wallace, Bruce. 2007. A qualified Abe apology. *Los Angeles Times*, March 27.

Whitfield, Charles L. 1995. *Memory and abuse: Remembering and healing the effects of trauma*. Deerfield Beach, FL: Health Communications.

Wilson, Amy. 2007. One in five Americans believe in alien abductions. *UFO Digest*, May 16.

Winter, Jay. 2000. The generation of memory: Reflections on the "memory boom" in contemporary historical studies. *Bulletin of the German Historical Institute* 27:69-92.

Wyatt, Caroline. 2005. France accepts Trafalgar legacy. BBC News, June 27. http://news.bbc.co.uk/2/hi/uk_news/4627469.stm.

Wyrda, Harold. 2007. *Communism and the emergence of democracy*. Cambridge: Cambridge University Press.

Young, Jim. 2005. A hundred cell phones bloom. *New York Times*, April 25.

The American Past Politicized: Uses and Misuses of History

This article examines some of the major ways in which
American history has been written, revised, and reinterpreted from partisan perspectives and for political
purposes. It takes note of the Revolutionary founders'
concerns about the ways in which their pivotal era
(1765-1789) was likely to be misunderstood or distorted; how several of the most central events in the
national narrative, such as the sectional conflict and
Civil War, came to be misremembered for politically
self-serving reasons; how presidents have misread or
misrepresented American and international history to
justify their policies; how the Supreme Court (and
lower courts) has used history selectively to achieve
outcomes (often desirable) that the justices felt were
necessary; and finally, how the so-called culture wars of
the early 1990s caused innocent words like "interpretation" and "revisionism" to become fighting phrases and
the basis for shrill and often small-minded polemics
between progressive and conservative agendas.

Keywords: revisionism; patriotic history; "lessons of the
past"; sanitized history; "law-office history";
presidential history; history standards
(1992-1995)

By
MICHAEL KAMMEN

The novelist Anatole France once quipped
that "all the historical books which contain no
lies are extremely tedious" (Bartlett, 1968, p. 801).
We would nonetheless like to believe that honest history can be heuristic as well as engaging;
but for quite some time now, scholars have

*Michael Kammen is the Newton C. Farr Professor of
American History and Culture at Cornell University,
where he has taught since 1965. He is an elected member
of the American Academy of Arts and Sciences and past
president of the Organization of American Historians
(1995-1996). He is the author of* People of Paradox: An
Inquiry concerning the Origins of American Civilization
(1973 Pulitzer Prize for History), A Machine That Would
Go of Itself: The Constitution in American Culture
(1987 Francis Parkman and Henry Adams prizes), and
Mystic Chords of Memory: The Transformation of
Tradition in American Culture *(1991).*

NOTE: The author wishes to thank the following for
their thoughtful and constructive readings of this article in draft form: Martin Heisler, Carol Kammen,
Walter LaFeber, Richard Polenberg, and Joel Silbey.

DOI: 10.1177/0002716207310816

been intrigued by the ways in which the past has so often been written and revised for partisan policy purposes, a phenomenon that is hardly unique to the United States. The role of court historians required to record events in a manner pleasing to their masters is by now a long-familiar pattern. Alfonso the Great of Aragon, king of Naples in the fifteenth century, kept two historians in his service: they gave him history lessons and wrote the history of his reign in a highly satis- factory way.

Two other disparate examples should suffice. In seventeenth- and eighteenth- century India, Mughal illustrations were used opportunistically to legitimize cur- rently acceptable interpretations of the past. When a text fell from favor because of dynastic change, or a historical chronicle was considered outdated because a new interpretation of events was needed, illustrations would be removed expedi- ently and later reused in new contexts regarded as "up-to-date" and politically cor- rect. Second, in South Africa until 1990, if history textbooks mentioned Nelson Mandela at all, he was referred to as a terrorist and an enemy of the nation. When he became the country's revered president, the story of his life had to be radically revised in a worshipful way.

Comparable developments in the United States have sometimes been more subtle, yet notable and revealing nonetheless. The subject deserves a substantial book. In this article, which cannot be comprehensive, I will take note of the Revolutionary founders' anxieties about the ways in which their deeds might be misunderstood or distorted; how several of the most pivotal events in the national narrative came to be misremembered for politically self-serving reasons; how the Supreme Court has often relied upon "law-office" history in support of outcomes the justices (and sometimes the plaintiffs) wished to achieve; how prominent politicians have misread or misused history in making major policy decisions and in writing their memoirs; and finally, how the so-called "history wars" of the early 1990s caused innocent words like "interpretation" and "revisionism" to become fighting phrases and the foundation for shrill, often small-minded polemics.

Inscribing and Distorting the Revolutionary Era and the Sectional Conflict

Among the founders, no one worried more than John Adams about how the Revolution would be recorded. "The history of our Revolution," he wrote, "will be one continued lie from one end to the other. The essence of the whole will be that Dr. Franklin's electric rod smote the earth and out sprang General Washington. That Franklin electrified him with his rod, and thenceforward these two conducted all the policy negotiations, legislatures, and war" (Cunliffe 1960, 23). Beginning in 1809, Dr. Benjamin Rush of Philadelphia pleaded with Adams to write his own account of the Revolutionary era, believing that Adams could do so with greater accuracy and candor than anyone else. Adams responded in 1811 with characteristic despair: "I do believe that both tradition and history are already corrupted in America as much as they ever were in the four or five first centuries of Christianity, and as much as they ever were in any age or country in the whole history of mankind" (Schutz and Adair 1966, 151, 186-87).

In 1813 Adams exchanged views with Thomas Jefferson about the politicization of Revolutionary history and poured out his built-up bile against an array of historians. A few extracts convey a clear sense of his concern. He noted that so little of the rich correspondence from that era had been published.

> I have wondered for more than thirty Years that so few have appeared: and have constantly expected that a Tory History of the Rise and progress of the Revolution would appear. And wished it. I would give more for it than for Marshall, Gordon, Ramsay and all the rest. . . . Gordon's and Marshall's Histories were written to make money: and fashioned and finished, to sell high in the London Market. I should expect to find more Truth in a History written by Hutchinson, Oliver or Sewell [Tories]. And I doubt not such Histories will one day appear. . . . Your Character in History may be easily foreseen. Your Administration, will be quoted by Philosophers, as a model, of profound Wisdom; by Politicians, as weak, superficial and shortsighted. Mine, like Popes Woman will have no Character at all. The impious Idolatry to Washington, destroyed all Character (Cappon 1959, 349).

A generation later the French Revolution was being unfavorably compared by Americans with their own because the former was known to have been so bloody and politically destabilizing. By contrast, the American Revolution came to be romanticized as comparatively bloodless, as more of a reform movement, in fact, than a tumultuous revolution, and one that achieved a unifying consensus among the American people (Kammen 1978, 73-74). Bitter feuding between Patriots and Loyalists followed by bickering between Federalists and Anti-Federalists managed to be minimized, along with the fierce internecine political conflicts of the 1790s, which rank among the nastiest in all of American history.

Subsequently, when sectional differences threatened national cohesion, innovative and revisionist versions of how and when the Union technically began were offered up as valid history by statesmen ranging from Chief Justice John Marshall and John Quincy Adams to Abraham Lincoln. The historical issue at stake was whether the states (and hence their sovereignty) preceded the Union. Common sense (and historical realities) would suggest that they did because the Union as it would be known in antebellum times surely dated only from 1787 to 1788 when the Constitution was written and ratified, giving rise to the federal government. Moreover, James Madison had insisted in the *Federalist Papers* that the states would retain much of their sovereignty (Stampp 1978, 6, 10, 15-16, 27, 29).

On the contrary, according to northern statesmen committed to their notion of a "Perpetual Union," a genuine Union really began when the Second Continental Congress gathered in 1775 and called the states into being, thereby predating the creation of sovereign states that only began to receive their legitimate status when the Declaration of Independence referred to "these united colonies" a year later in 1776 (Stampp 1978, 6; Morris 1981). If the Union preceded the states, then it enjoyed "perpetual" status and supremacy. Therefore, states could not nullify an act of Congress and certainly could not simply secede when they found themselves unhappy with policies formulated in Washington. Victory in 1865 would validate the unhistorical claims of the nationalists, but that simply meant a triumph of political power over truth.

Similarly, the Civil War would for many generations be remembered as a great conflict primarily involving the preservation of that Union, with slavery as a political and social issue being minimized as a cause of the four-year bloodletting (Pressly 1954). Not until well after the Civil War centennial did most historians and the public begin to acknowledge the centrality of slavery and its potential expansion as primary issues that triggered hostilities in 1860 and 1861 (Foner 1990). During the first half of the twentieth century, the years of Reconstruction (1865-1877) came to be remembered by historians and the lay public alike as a calamitous time in the South when radical Republicans, bent on vengeance, perpetuated a regime of harsh misrule in collaboration with buffoonish freedmen ill prepared for the responsibilities of government (Franklin 1961; Foner 1988).

When the United States went to war with Spain in 1898, President McKinley offered the public three fundamental reasons to justify this militaristic intervention between the Cuban rebels and imperial Spain: humanitarian grounds to safeguard the citizens of Cuba from tyranny; protection of American "commerce, trade, and business of our people" as well as "the wanton destruction of property and devastation of the island"; and then, noting the mysterious explosion of the U.S. battleship *Maine* in Havana's harbor, McKinley declared that "the present condition of affairs in Cuba is a constant menace to our peace, and entails upon this Government an enormous expense" (Gould 1980, 85).

McKinley failed to mention that he and the Congress did not want the Cuban revolutionaries to end up in control of the island. He feared that they very well might if the United States remained neutral during the summer rainy season in 1898. American opposition to Cuban independence had very deep historical roots, and as Louis Pérez (1998) has written, a free Cuba "raised the specter of political disorder, social upheaval, and racial conflict: Cuba as a source of regional instability and inevitably a source of international tension." In addition, the growing desire to expand American markets overseas also went unmentioned as a major stimulus for war (pp. 12-13).

Governmental Agencies "Make" History

During the twentieth century, several new governmental agencies came into existence that increasingly provided official versions of key episodes and aspects of American history. In notable instances they gradually rewrote or reinterpreted the public's perception of the national past. The National Park System, for example, was created in 1916 and initially had primary responsibility for such natural wonders as Yellowstone, Yosemite, and other scenic areas set aside by Theodore Roosevelt during his term as president. In 1933, however, Horace Albright, the

second director of the Park Service, persuaded Franklin Roosevelt to transfer all
historic battlefields from the custodianship of the War Department to management
by the Park Service. At that point the latter became deeply invested in historical
properties and their interpretation (Bodnar 1992, 175-76, 201-5).

The Park Service had recently authorized and accepted two sites that soon
became problematic because of their inauthenticity: the highly suspect replica of
George Washington's birthplace at Wakefield, Virginia (which burned to the
ground in 1779), and the re-creation of a spurious cabin in Hodgenville,
Kentucky, supposedly the birthplace of Abraham Lincoln. Both became instant
shrines, and the latter was even enclosed within a Greek revival temple, thereby
heightening its lack of veracity. With the passage of time, both sites became genuine embarrassments in a country that only began to regard its architectural heritage with genuine professionalism when the National Trust for Historic
Preservation was chartered by Congress in 1949. It is exceedingly difficult for the
Park Service to de-accession sites that have been incorporated into the system.
Even spurious venues have their venerating stakeholders (Hosmer 1981, 478-93;
1965, 141, 145-46).

Issues involving historical interpretation and revisionism based upon new
knowledge or altered ways of thinking about the past have plagued the Park
Service as well as other institutions. When a movement got under way in the
1980s to rename the Montana site long known as the Custer Battlefield National
Historical Park, champions of George Armstrong Custer, who still regarded him
and his men as martyrs, mounted a bitter protest. One leader of the Little Big
Horn Association, a group devoted to the worshipful memory of Custer, offered
this typical testimony before a congressional committee: "Totalitarian states practice historical revisionism. They simply tear down monuments and rewrite their
history. But democratic societies do not change their history." Senator Malcolm
Wallop of Wyoming also expressed sentiments widely shared among the lay public: "We could avoid the whole problem and confusion by simply living with history as it was originally written." During the so-called "history wars" of the later
1980s and 1990s, politicians repeatedly expressed their disdain for "revisionist
history," which in reality simply meant providing different perspectives on our
understanding based upon new information, insights, and cultural perspectives
(Linenthal and Engelhardt 1996, 116-17, 131, 135, 213).

Presidential Revisionists Justify Their
Policies and Problems

Scholars have devoted a fair amount of attention to the uses and misuses of
history by presidents and their critics, noting that they too often engage in "revisionism," sometimes unwittingly but most often deliberately to persuade others
to support their policy preferences and retrospective judgments. Although
Theodore Roosevelt, Woodrow Wilson, and John F. Kennedy studied and wrote

history before ascending to the White House, the focus of inquiry ever since Franklin Delano Roosevelt has tended to concentrate on presidential invocations of the past and their skeptics.

Scholars have devoted a fair amount of attention to the uses and misuses of history by presidents and their critics, noting that they too often engage in "revisionism," sometimes . . . to persuade others to support their policy preferences and retrospective judgments.

It seems to be well remembered that Harry Truman read American history avidly, and that doing so helped to inform some of his most important decisions. Historian Ernest May, however, has presented a strong critique of Truman and his advisors for facing the cold war using inappropriate analogies based upon events from the 1930s and World War II (May 1973, 51, 81-82, 84). It is undeniable that the "lessons of Munich," meaning the appeasement of Hitler in 1938, were very much on Truman's mind in 1950 when North Korea invaded the South. Truman and Dean Acheson never doubted that aggression had to be met with strong resistance. Historian Otis Graham has observed of that period and beyond that "policymakers were not good at utilizing history, but they were hopelessly addicted to doing so" (Graham 1983, 7).

As for Truman's much lauded knowledge of American history, for which he claimed (and received) much credit in his memoirs, scholars have often pointed to his inflexible commitment to versions of events that he misunderstood. As historian George Mowry (1966) remarked, "Few Presidents, perhaps, have ever been as forthright in publicly reading their present passions into the past." As an example of Truman's historical carelessness, he oddly credited Thomas Jefferson with the famous remark *allegedly* made by Andrew Jackson in response to an unfavorable Supreme Court decision handed down by Chief Justice John Marshall, condemning Georgia for arresting white missionaries who worked with the Cherokees (1832): "John Marshall has made his decision, now let him enforce it" (Mowry 1966, 7, 9-10, 15).

John F. Kennedy and Lyndon B. Johnson took far greater interest in history than Dwight Eisenhower had, yet there is now abundant evidence that both of the 1960s presidents misused arguments derived from history in questionable ways to justify the deepening American engagement in Southeast Asia. Because both men were highly intelligent, however, and believed that they had a strong sense of presidential history, they were under no illusions about the need for success in foreign policy if their domestic agendas were to prevail. LBJ confided the following to a confidante who later helped to write his memoirs: "I knew that Harry Truman and Dean Acheson had lost their effectiveness from the day that the Communists took over China. I believed that the loss of China had played a large role in the rise of Joe McCarthy. And I knew that all these problems, taken together, were chickenshit compared with what might happen if we lost Vietnam" (Mowry 1966, 7, 12-13; Neustadt and May 1986, 86).

Richard Neustadt, an influential political scientist and presidential advisor, teamed up with foreign policy historian Ernest May to write the most astute analysis of how a sense of the past shaped the views of Kennedy and Johnson, especially concerning Vietnam. When LBJ and his associates considered committing American ground forces, the authors observed, "they did so with faith buttressed by remembered victories: The United States always won. . . . And when Johnson's people thought of peace, they recalled that the North Koreans and Chinese had eventually negotiated an end to the Korean War. They recalled as well that other limited wars, elsewhere and earlier, had also ended in compromise" (Neustadt and May 1986, 137, 161-66).

When we turn to presidential memoirs in modern times—the irresistible desire to set *my* historical record straight—we encounter sins of omission more frequent and serious than sins of commission. Problematic major episodes and judgments are either glossed over or else explained away in self-serving terms. In the case of Harry Truman's *Memoirs* (2 vols., 1955-1956), they are useful at times in revealing his motivations but inadequate in terms of his understanding of the Soviets or the real situation in Korea at the time of conflict in 1950. Lyndon Johnson wanted his memoirs, *The Vantage Point* (1971), to be statesmanlike, so unlike Truman's they are devoid of human interest and come across as a sanitized and lifeless account of his presidency. From the perspective of Arthur Goldberg, who served LBJ in several capacities and knew him well, they are disingenuous. As one biographer has observed, Johnson pressured his team of writers into "making it a bland exercise in self-congratulation that received negative reviews and reached only a small audience" (Unger and Unger 1999, 522-24; Dallek 2004, 364).

From the time he left office in 1974, Richard Nixon worked tirelessly—one might almost say heroically—to rehabilitate his reputation, and eventually published nine works following his presidency, most of them devoted to his encounters with foreign leaders, advice concerning international relations, written in what appeared to be a judicious tone. When he completed the initial manuscript of his memoirs in 1977, it was so massive that it had to be cut by two-thirds. Published in 1978 as *RN: The Memoirs of Richard Nixon*, the kinder assessments declared them "readable but unreliable." Many others, intensely predisposed against the former president, simply declared the project "Lies." All of the reviews noted how much had been omitted and complained that the whole Watergate episode had been minimized as an unfortunate but minor blip in an administration filled with achievements, above all in foreign policy. Watergate was dismissed as a bungled attempt to obtain information, as others had done before, but with barely a word about the cover-up and obstruction of justice (Ambrose 1991, 513, 516, 573-74; Doyle 1999, chap. 6).

The rehabilitation of Nixon's reputation during the final decades of the twentieth century was not entirely of his own making. He enjoyed considerable help from surprisingly generous biographical studies by such historians as Joan Hoff, Herbert Parmet, journalist/historian Tom Wicker, and even the final volume of Steven Ambrose's huge trilogy. All of them felt so disillusioned by the ideological conservatism of the Reagan and Bush presidencies that they increasingly viewed Nixon as some sort of liberal. By the time Nixon died in 1994, memories of Watergate had dimmed and its historical significance seemed markedly reduced (Greenberg 2003, chap. 8).

Although Bill Clinton's elephantine memoir, *My Life* (2004), sold well enough to repay his multi-million-dollar advance, critics responded with many of the same kinds of criticisms that had greeted Johnson's and Nixon's works. He was charged with glossing over the issues that really mattered: the failure of his health care initiative, the unintended consequences of his administration's decisions to pressure Sudan to expel Osama bin Laden in 1996 (thereby driving bin Laden to Afghanistan where he was more difficult to track), or to launch cruise missile attacks against targets in Sudan in retaliation for the embassy bombings in East Africa in 1998 (an act that some terrorism experts believe fueled the conviction among terrorists that the United States was an ineffectual giant that relied upon low-risk, high-tech responses). The overwhelming reaction to this nine-hundred-page saga was that less might have been more: much less about boyhood travails, meetings, meals, and travels; and much more about key policy issues. As Michael Langan wrote in the *Boston Globe*, "Clinton's fabled photographic memory sometimes goes dark when it is not in his interest to be too specific (June 24, 2004).

Interestingly, there is a common pattern to the way all of these presidential histories got composed, from Truman to Clinton half a century later. A team of researchers is assembled to pour through hundreds of thousands of pages of documents, make selections, impose order, create drafts, and then permit the statesman to set a certain tone and filter the information selectively. Invariably, what we get is history as though painted by numbers, yet the picture set forth always remains incomplete. What varies most is the degree of impersonality that comes through, ranging from Johnson's sadly distanced work to Clinton's undeniably personable volume.

It may be instructive here, for purposes of perspective, to recall what happened a century and a half ago when a prominent American politician was determined to appeal for a policy initiative on substantive albeit highly selective historical grounds. In 1859 Senator Stephen A. Douglas, Democrat from Illinois and a presidential aspirant, determined to write a brief on behalf of popular sovereignty concerning slavery in the territories. In April he wrote to the most prominent historian in the United States at that time, George Bancroft, explaining his plan to prepare an address "upon the right of the people of the Territories to govern themselves in all their domestic relations, without the interference of the federal government." Arrangements for publication were made in secret with *Harper's Magazine* because this would be an extraordinary innovation in the publishing history of American literary magazines (Johannsen 1959, 611-16).

Interestingly, there is a common pattern to the way all of these presidential histories got composed, from Truman to Clinton half a century later. . . . Invariably, what we get is history as though painted by numbers, yet the picture set forth always remains incomplete.

Douglas turned to early American history in search of precedents for his concept of popular sovereignty, pulling all sorts of primary and secondary sources from the Library of Congress. He clearly believed that the colonists claimed an exclusive right to legislate "in respect to their internal polity, slavery included." Bancroft (also a Democrat) obliged Douglas with copies of numerous colonial documents, explaining that "the entire control of the question of slavery by the respective colonial legislatures appears still more clearly from the laws relating to emancipation. . . . All such matters were always decided as the [individual] colonies pleased" (Johannsen 1959, 613, 614). Other friends with historical interests sent the senator additional information to support his case. The long, tedious, and contrived essay appeared in *Harper's* in September, but basically preached to the choir in terms of Douglas's presidential ambitions. The next year he broke with the southern Democrats, received only the nomination of the northern wing, carried just two states, and died shortly after the outbreak of war in 1861.

The Supreme Court and "Law Office" History

The kind of historical treatise that Douglas wrote provides a fine example of what we commonly refer to as "law-office" history, namely, history based upon a carefully selected body of information that omits anything germane that might be prejudicial to the case being argued. The most significant venue in the American experience for that kind of history is the Supreme Court, so we should turn to that institution for prime examples of law-office history created not only in some of the Court's most important decisions, but in the preparation of briefs to be argued before the Court in some notable cases. When constitutional history and precedent run contrary to a desired outcome, the Court has indeed been known to ignore both, appealing instead to the principle of an *evolving* Constitution, one that has to be adapted to conditions that the framers could not possibly have envisioned in 1787 when they met in Philadelphia (Rakove 1996).

One of the most notorious examples of justices looking selectively to the founding of the nation for a rationale in decision making occurred in the case of *Dred Scott v. Sandford* (1857), for which Chief Justice Roger B. Taney wrote the Court's principal opinion. The outcome in that case was directly opposed to Stephen A. Douglas's self-determination dogma because it involved the status of a slave who had been taken by his master from a slave state to a free state. Did doing so thereby liberate the slave? Taney had earlier advanced a principle that would endure for more than a century, namely, that the Court should not intervene in highly charged political questions. In the case of *Dred Scott*, however, it proceeded to do just that, in part because the country seemed to have reached a stalemate over the slavery issue. Taney argued that the Declaration of Independence did not apply to enslaved Africans and that "they were not regarded as a portion of the people or citizens of the government then formed [in 1787]." Looking at the Constitution as it was ratified a year later, Taney observed that "the only two provisions which point to them [slaves] and include them, treat them as property, and make it the duty of the government to protect it; no other power, in relation to this race, is to be found in the Constitution; and as it is a government of special, delegated powers, no authority beyond these two provisions can be constitutionally exercised. The government of the United States has no right to interfere for any other purpose but protecting the rights of the owner" (Kutler 1977, 153).

As Alfred H. Kelly, a distinguished constitutional historian, concluded in 1965, Taney's effort to prove that the Constitution was exclusively a "white man's document" rested on flagrantly flimsy grounds, "especially in his attempt to discount the Declaration of Independence." At that point, in his opinion, Taney lapsed into the "a priori, fiat technique. His conclusion was already effectively disproved at the time he offered it" (p. 126). The South rejoiced in Taney's decision, of course; but there were almost as many opinions handed down as there were justices. The lack of consensus in the Court in terms of the historical basis for this decision left the issue fundamentally unresolved politically, thereby assisting the swift ascent of the Republican Party and meaning Civil War just a few years later. The country had not been well served by law-office history designed to rationalize a desired and prejudicial outcome.

In more recent times, however, there are numerous instances of history being invoked to support an outcome for which most Americans are grateful. When Thurgood Marshall prepared the NAACP Legal Defense Fund case that resulted in *Brown v. Board of Education* (1954), his director of research for the project,

Professor John A. Davis of Lincoln University, invited two distinguished historians to help by providing contextual material: C. Vann Woodward of Johns Hopkins University and Marshall's old friend John Hope Franklin of Howard University. Franklin readily accepted the urgent invitation; but Davis's correspondence with Woodward is illuminating. Woodward responded to the letter of recruitment that he was glad to help, but "I should feel constrained by the limitations of my craft. . . . I would stick to what happened and account for it as intelligently as I could. . . . You see, I do not want to be in a position of delivering a gratuitous history lesson to the Court. And at the same time I do not want to get out of my role as historian" (Kluger 1975, 623).

Davis then had to face a difficult question. Could historians dedicated to the most objective version of truth possible, "and lawyers, presumably seeking to shape as forceful and partisan a case for their clients as possible," really collaborate in an effort such as the NAACP brief to the Supreme Court? One member of Marshall's team observed that "all history is a distortion of sorts, depending on the historian's myopia and precepts" (Kluger 1975, 623). So Davis responded to Woodward, "Your conclusions are your own. If they do not help our side of the case, in all probability the lawyers will not use them. If they do help our argument, the present plan is to include them in the overall summary argument and to file the whole work as a brief in an appendix. No matter what happens, your work will be of real educational value to the men who must argue before the Court" (Kluger 1975, 623-24).

When the Court ordered that the case be reargued in 1953 and 1954, it essentially went on a fishing expedition. It asked the plaintiffs whether there was any evidence that the Congress that passed the Fourteenth Amendment (and the state legislatures that ratified it in 1868) understood that the amendment would abolish segregation in the public schools. If not, the Court wondered whether it was possible to interpret the Fourteenth Amendment as empowering any federal agency to do so (Franklin 2005, 156-57).

By the end of the summer of 1953, John Hope Franklin had prepared a virtual monograph on "the way in which the Southerners defied, ignored, and worked against every conception of equality laid down in the Fourteenth Amendment and subsequent legislation." Inclusion of that monograph in the final NAACP brief came as a stinging rebuke to the segregated states. South Carolina's brief called it "this catalogue of inflammatory labels [sic]." Woodward, meanwhile, encountered no difficulty in doing the requisite research, and his essay along with Franklin's argued that the original equalitarian intentions of the post–Civil War amendments had been eroded in ensuing decades by political and economic pressures and extralegal tactics in the South. The precise intent of those who framed the Fourteenth Amendment remains unclear to this day, but few Americans regret that the Supreme Court accepted the historical and sociological arguments provided by Thurgood Marshall's team of researchers and advisors (Kluger 1975, 624, 638).

During the 1960s the Court issued a series of monumentally important and highly welcome decisions that essentially required and hinged upon law-office history. Ever since the early twentieth century, urbanization took place at an increasingly rapid rate in the United States. Because the states controlled the apportionment of voting districts, by midcentury there was a discernible imbalance of power in the state legislatures and Congress, with underpopulated rural districts being overrepresented as compared with urban areas. The desire for what was referred to as "one person, one vote," led the Court to take the momentous step of intervening in what was essentially a *political* issue involving state constitutions and accepted usage over time, something that many since Chief Justice Taney had recommended the Court should avoid. Doing so, in fact, had become an established Court tradition. But as Justice William Brennan explained at the very outset of his opinion on behalf of the Court in *Baker v. Carr* (1962), "We hold that this challenge to an apportionment presents no nonjusticiable 'political question.' The cited cases do not hold the contrary" (Kutler 1977, 586). What he really meant, but would not say in so many words, was that an undemocratic injustice had been allowed to fester for more than half a century. If the states were unwilling to do anything about it, then the federal government would simply *have* to do so. This meant a major reversal on the part of the Court in terms of precedent.

Moreover, as legal historian Charles A. Miller has pointed out, in this case and in several that promptly followed, the Court made claims that cannot be supported by the historical record, for example, that the Founding Fathers had intended in 1787 that the Constitution require equally populated congressional districts. The sequential cases that dealt with closely related issues, such as congressional apportionment, *Wesberry v. Sanders* (1964) and *Reynolds v. Sims* (1964), once again misconstrued the intent of the founders, prompting Miller (1969) to conclude that "it is ironic that the Court was less justified by the facts when it did resort to history than when it did not." Associate Justice Hugo Black was so determined to believe that the Fourteenth Amendment "incorporated" or made the Bill of Rights applicable to the states, despite the absence of hard evidence from the time of its passage, that he essentially relied upon historical "evidence" that did not exist (pp. 127, 129)

Despite such dissenters as associate justices Felix Frankfurter and John Marshall Harlan, whose sense of constitutional history was especially acute and who served as a source of restraint, the liberal Warren Court handed down other decisions that most of us applaud because they accord with our notions of social justice and common sense. This was true of Arthur Goldberg's opinion in *Bell v. Maryland* (1964), which upheld the rights of blacks who engaged in restaurant sit-ins to demand service. The majority opinion, written by Justice Brennan, upheld the plaintiffs' right to be served on nonconstitutional grounds. Goldberg along with William O. Douglas preferred to invoke history in constitutional arguments, attempting to assert that it was the contemporary understanding of the Fourteenth Amendment that African Americans were to be guaranteed nondiscriminatory treatment at places of public accommodation. The historical sources that Goldberg used simply did not sustain his opinion—yet another instance of a socially desirable outcome that could not be sustained on historical grounds (Miller 1969, 103-7).

The same held true a year later when the justices resuscitated the long-ignored "penumbra" aspect of the ambiguous Ninth Amendment in the case of *Griswold v. Connecticut* (1965) to overturn an 1879 state law making it a crime for a physician to supply a married woman with information about birth control. Once again Justice Goldberg argued that the framers envisioned certain non-specified rights that extended beyond any specific enumeration. (The Ninth Amendment simply reads, "The enumeration in the Constitution of certain rights shall not be construed to deny or disparage others retained by the people.") By then linking such nonspecified rights to the "liberty" guaranteed by the Fourteenth Amendment, he perceived a right of marital privacy. Justices Warren and Brennan joined him, and that decision would lead in turn to a series of cases, culminating in *Roe v. Wade* (1973), that hinged upon privacy rights for which there were no constitutional or historical precedents. Along with Justice Hugo Black, Goldberg's historical foundations for pivotal decisions have been found wanting by careful students of the Court (Kelly 1965, 149-55).

By . . . linking such nonspecified rights to the "liberty" guaranteed by the Fourteenth Amendment, [Justice Goldberg] perceived a right of marital privacy. . . . That decision would lead in turn to a series of cases, culminating in Roe v. Wade (1973), that hinged upon privacy rights for which there were no constitutional or historical precedents.

Politicizing the Past in American Schools

Our final example of American history being contested and politicized erupted with a bang in 1994 to 1996 when a major project, based at UCLA with funding from the National Endowment for the Humanities (NEH) beginning in 1992, produced new National History Standards designed to improve the quality of history education in primary and secondary schools. The authors creating these standards were committed to a more inclusive view of the American past that placed greater emphasis upon the role of women and minorities. The standards had received input from thousands of teachers across the country, had been reviewed by many scholars and committees, and perhaps most important, were not mandatory even though supported by federal funds.

From the moment they were released, Lynne Cheney, who had been the supportive chair of NEH in 1992, deemed them unpatriotic and published a hostile screed in the *Wall Street Journal* in October 1994 that activated attacks by highly vocal conservatives. Rush Limbaugh declared on his widely heard radio program that "history is real simple. You know what history is? It's what happened. The problem you get into is when guys like this try to skew history by [saying], 'Well, let's interpret what happened because maybe we can't find the truth in the facts, or at least we don't like the truth as it is presented. So let's change the interpretation a little bit so that it will be the way we wished it were.' Well, that's not what history is" (Nash, Crabtree, and Dunn 1997, 6).

Many of the shrill critics who inveighed against the new National History Standards had never actually seen the volumes; and for those few who had, the offending examples were drawn from suggested activities and illustrative cases rather than from the standards themselves. Much ado was made, for example, of the infrequency with which George Washington's name appeared and the contrasting frequency of Harriet Tubman's. The role of the Founding Fathers and the framing of the Constitution seemed insufficiently treated, and too many illustrations of injustice or majoritarian failure seemed to permeate the standards. In January 1995 the U.S. Senate was manipulated into voting 99-1 to condemn these voluntary criteria, and later that year, when Senator Bob Dole attacked them, the Clinton administration, most notably the secretary of education, who had been supportive, rejected the standards—a candid acknowledgment that politics took precedence over history (Nash, Crabtree, and Dunn 1997, 246-47).

Meanwhile, the *Congressional Quarterly Researcher*, which prepares in-depth reports on major issues in Washington, devoted twenty-two pages to this contretemps, reminding readers that U.S. history "has sparked controversies for almost as long as history has been taught in schools." It reviewed the new scholarship in social history since the later 1960s that had so expanded our understanding of the American past and described a "search for consensus" to resolve this highly visible dispute that had involved so many people in an effort to engage students with new material, new approaches, and new questions (Nash, Crabtree, and Dunn 1997, 248).

Many of the ongoing conservative attacks had a familiar ring, as when Senator Kay Bailey Hutchinson of Texas declared that "when we revise our history, we devalue our culture." But eventually a blue-ribbon, bipartisan commission was created to review the standards one more time and make recommendations. Its carefully considered report noted that most of the criticisms had not been directed against the standards themselves but against some of the teaching examples and activities. So it urged that the latter be deleted from the final edition, that certain subjects receive expanded treatment, that some concepts be clarified, and that ethnic and gender issues be more effectively connected to their historical contexts. A news release indicated that the project would fundamentally be vindicated, and within a year numerous changes had been made, reviewed, and approved (Nash, Crabtree, and Dunn 1997, 248-57).

With remarkable speed, the newly published National History Standards were being adopted and widely used. The realization began to sink in, even among politicians who had not looked at the standards or the information available about them, that they had never been meant to be mandatory. The government was not dictating what American children must learn, or how. It was only that tests had clearly demonstrated a dramatic need for improvement. State education officials had for the most part been levelheaded all along. The Wisconsin state superintendent, for example, remarked that his office had never assumed that the standards were "official," and then expressed his concern "about the many ways in which educational issues are becoming politicized" (Nash, Crabtree, and Dunn 1997, 258).

Thereafter the whole brouhaha swiftly died down; but what took place between 1994 and 1996 was far more than a tempest in a teapot. It caused an entire nation to consider and reconsider how its history should be taught and understood to be meaningful and valued. It has not, unfortunately, put to rest the meaning and use of "historical interpretation" and "revisionism" as pejorative words in the minds of many politicians. Nor has it diminished their anxiety about the public's access to revealing information. At the Senate confirmation hearings held in 1997 for George Tenet to become the new director of the CIA, he was asked about the long-delayed declassification and release of historical documents. His symptomatic response fudged: "It's dangerous to look back over your shoulder."

References

Ambrose, Stephen E. 1991. *Nixon*, vol. 3, *Ruin and recovery, 1973-1990*. New York: Simon & Schuster.
Bartlett, John. 1968. *Bartlett's familiar quotations*. 14th ed. Boston: Little, Brown.
Bodnar, John. 1992. *Remaking America: Public memory, commemoration, and patriotism in the twentieth century*. Princeton, NJ: Princeton University Press.
Cappon, Lester J., ed. 1959. *The Adams-Jefferson letters: The complete correspondence between Thomas Jefferson and Abigail and John Adams*. 2 vols. Chapel Hill: University of North Carolina Press.
Clinton, Bill. 2004. *My life*. New York: Alfred A. Knopf.
Cunliffe, Marcus. 1960. *George Washington: Man and monument*. Boston: Little, Brown.
Dallek, Robert. 2004. *Lyndon B. Johnson: Portrait of a president*. New York: Oxford University Press.
Doyle, William. 1999. *Inside the Oval Office: The secret White House tapes from FDR to Clinton*. New York: Kodansha International.
Foner, Eric. 1988. *Reconstruction: America's unfinished revolution, 1863-1877*. New York: Harper & Row.
———. 1990. Slavery, the Civil War, and Reconstruction. In *The new American history*, edited by E. Foner, 73-92. Philadelphia: Temple University Press.
Franklin, John Hope. 1961. *Reconstruction: After the Civil War*. Chicago: University of Chicago Press.
———. 2005. *Mirror to America: The autobiography of John Hope Franklin*. New York: Farrar, Straus and Giroux.
Gould, Lewis L. 1980. *The presidency of William McKinley*. Lawrence: The Regents Press of Kansas.
Graham, Otis L. 1983. The uses and misuses of history: Roles in policymaking. *The Public Historian* 5 (2): 5-19.
Greenberg, Donald. 2003. *Nixon's shadow: The history of an image*. New York: Norton.

Hosmer, Charles B., Jr. 1965. *Presence of the past: A history of the preservation movement in the United States before Williamsburg*. New York: Putnam.

————. 1981. *Preservation comes of age: From Williamsburg to the National Trust, 1926-1949*. 2 vols. Charlottesville: University Press of Virginia.

Johannsen, Robert W. 1959. Stephen A. Douglas, *Harper's Magazine*, and popular sovereignty. *Mississippi Valley Historical Review* 45 (1): 606-31.

Johnson, Lyndon. 1971. *The vantage point: Perspectives on the presidency, 1963-1969*. New York: Holt, Rinehart, and Winston.

Kammen, Michael. 1978. *A season of youth: The American Revolution and the historical imagination*. New York: Knopf.

Kelly, Alfred H. 1965. Clio and the Court: An illicit love affair. *Supreme Court Review*, 119-58.

Kluger, Richard. 1975. *Simple justice: The history of Brown v. Board of Education and black America's struggle for equality*. New York: Knopf.

Kutler, Stanley I., ed. 1977. *The Supreme Court and the Constitution: Readings in American constitutional history*. 2nd ed. New York: Norton.

Langan, Michael D. 2001. Hype aside, missteps mark "My Life." *Boston Globe*, June 24, D1.

Linenthal, Edward T., and Tom Engelhardt, eds. 1996. *History wars: The Enola Gay and other battles for the American past*. New York: Henry Holt.

May, Ernest R. 1973. *"Lessons" of the past: The use and misuse of history in American foreign policy*. New York: Oxford University Press.

Miller, Charles A. 1969. *The Supreme Court and the uses of history*. Cambridge, MA: Harvard University Press.

Morris, Richard B. 1981. The Union came first. *New York Times*, January 31, 23.

Mowry, George E. 1966. The uses of history by recent presidents. *Journal of American History* 53 (2): 5-18.

Nash, Gary B., Charlotte Crabtree, and Ross Dunn. 1997. *History on trial: Culture wars and the teaching of the past*. New York: Knopf.

Neustadt, Richard E., and Ernest R. May. 1986. *Thinking in time: The uses of history for decision-makers*. New York: Free Press.

Pérez, Louis A., Jr. 1998. *The war of 1898: The United States and Cuba in history and historiography*. Chapel Hill: University of North Carolina Press.

Pressly, Thomas J. 1954. *Americans interpret their Civil War*. Princeton, NJ: Princeton University Press.

Rakove, Jack N. 1996. *Original meanings: Politics and ideas in the making of the Constitution*. New York: Knopf.

Schutz, John A., and Douglass Adair, eds. 1966. *The spur of fame: Dialogues of John Adams and Benjamin Rush, 1805-1813*. San Marino, CA: The Huntington Library.

Stampp, Kenneth M. 1978. The concept of a perpetual union. *Journal of American History* 65 (2): 5-33.

Truman, Harry. 1955-56. *Memoirs*. Two volumes. Garden City, NY: Doubleday.

Unger, Irwin, and Debi Unger. 1999. *LBJ: A life*. New York: John Wiley.

Blank Spots in Collective Memory: A Case Study of Russia

By
JAMES V. WERTSCH

The dynamics of collective remembering are examined by analyzing what happens when a "blank spot" in history is filled with information that had previously not been available or publicly acknowledged. Taking Russian accounts of the secret protocols of the Molotov-Ribbentrop Pact of 1939 as a case study, it is argued that "schematic narrative templates" that shape deep collective memory give rise to a tendency to maintain this memory and help it overcome the "narrative rift" that occurs when embarrassing episodes from the past are publicly acknowledged. Schematic narrative templates are set forth as underlying strong conservative forces that resist change in collective memory at a deep level. It is suggested that debates grounded in formal history may help overcome this resistance to change but that such efforts will be limited as long as the forces of deep collective memory are not recognized.

Keywords: collective memory; national narrative; Russia; Molotov-Ribbentrop Pact

T he Soviet Union was well known for treating certain episodes and personalities in its history as "blank spots." In some cases, these were literally blank, as in photos where people's images had been painstakingly airbrushed out of existence (King 1997); in other instances, the notion was more figurative, having to do with what could—and could not—be discussed in a public setting. Regardless of their form, these blank spots were understood by Soviet citizens as involving something that could not be mentioned—even when they dealt with someone

James V. Wertsch is Marshall S. Snow Professor of Arts and Sciences at Washington University in St. Louis, where he is also director of the McDonnell International Scholars Academy. His current research is concerned with language, thought, and culture, with a special focus on collective memory, national narratives and identity, and culture. His most recent book is Voices of Collective Remembering *(Cambridge University Press, 2002).*

NOTE: An earlier version of this article was presented at the conference "Memory and War" at the Massachusetts Institute of Technology in January 2003. The statements made and the views expressed are solely the responsibility of the author.

DOI: 10.1177/0002716207312870

who had been at the center of public discourse just the day before. During the last few decades of the Soviet Union's existence, these blank spots in history became the object of increasing debate and protest, at least in private settings. Indeed, some people thought, perhaps naively, that if these blank spots could only be publicly acknowledged and filled with accurate information, truth would then replace falsehood and omission once and for all.

For many people living in the Baltic region of the former Soviet Union, the most obvious blank spot in history was the Molotov-Ribbentrop Pact of 1939. For decades there had been little doubt in their minds that this infamous pact included secret protocols that lay behind the forced annexation of Estonia, Latvia, and Lithuania by Soviet forces in 1940. However, the existence of these protocols was officially denied by Soviet leaders, including Mikhail Gorbachev, up until the final years of the USSR's existence. While enjoined from discussing this matter in public, many Estonians, Latvians, and Lithuanians were insistent, at least in private, that this was an episode of forced annexation and violence, the memory of which would not be lost, and the true story of which would eventually come out.

In what follows, I shall examine Russian accounts of the Molotov-Ribbentrop Pact. In particular, I shall be concerned with the pact's secret protocols in which Hitler and Stalin agreed to carve up Eastern Europe, and I shall argue that in post-Soviet Russia, the transformation of the memory of this pact did not occur in a single step yielding a final, fixed account. Instead, it involved a process of change that has undergone two stages, and this change has given rise to an account that is clearly not what the people of the Baltic countries remember. I shall also argue that to account for the dynamics of this transformation it is useful to invoke the notions of "schematic narrative templates" and "deep collective memory."

I base my analysis on an examination of high school history textbooks from Soviet and post-Soviet Russia. As I have noted elsewhere (Wertsch 2002), textbooks are only one reflection of a wider set of cultural and political processes involved in defining official history, and as such they compete with other sources of information, like film and the popular press, for impact on young generations. They provide a good starting point, however, for examining official, state-sanctioned accounts of the past.

The first question to pose about these accounts is whether they really are about history, at least history in any strict sense of the term. Instead of speaking of blank spots in *history*, it will become obvious that it may be more appropriate to speak of blank spots in *collective memory*. In reality, "history" instruction in Soviet and post-Soviet schools—as well as in virtually every other country in the world—involves a complex mixture of what professional historians would consider to be a sound interpretation of past events based on the objective, balanced review of evidence on one hand, and an effort, on the other, to promulgate collective memory, or a usable past, as part of a national identity project. In this context, notions of history and collective memory clearly overlap. Both ways of representing the past deal with events occurring before the lifetime of the people doing the representing, and in both cases there is the assumption that the accounts being presented are true. Furthermore, both rely on narratives as "cultural tools" (Wertsch 1998). The upshot is that it is often difficult to separate history from collective memory, and what we routinely call "history" textbooks almost always involve a mixture of the two.

This, however, does not mean that no useful distinction can be made between history and collective memory. Indeed, it is essential to distinguish between them. The father of modern collective memory studies, Maurice Halbwachs[1] (1980, 1992) made this point in the 1920s in his discussion of "formal history" and how it differs from collective memory. Before Halbwach's time it came up in other discussions; for example, it was an object of debate in the nineteenth century in writings by the philosopher Ernest Renan (1882/1990), who viewed serious historical research as often posing a threat to popular efforts at collective remembering.

In contemporary debates, this discussion has continued in historiography, where history and collective memory are often viewed not just as different, but as being in basic conflict. The reason for this is the different aspirations of the two modes of relating to the past. For its part, history aspires to provide an objective and distanced (i.e., non-"presentist") account of the past, even if this means giving up favored and often self-serving narratives. In contrast, collective remembering inevitably involves some identity project in the present—remembering in the service of constructing a preferred image of a group—and is resistant to change even in the face of contradictory evidence. As Assmann (1997, 9) noted, in collective remembering "the past is not simply 'received' by the present. The present is 'haunted' by the past and the past is modeled, invented, reinvented, and reconstructed by the present."

In short, formal history and collective memory must be kept distinct for several reasons. Collective memory tends to reflect a single, subjective, committed perspective of a group in the present, whereas formal history strives to be objective and to distance itself from the present and any particular perspective currently in favor. In addition, collective memory leaves little room for doubt or ambiguity about events and the motivations of actors (Novick 1999), whereas formal history strives to take into account multiple, complex factors and motives that shape events.

A final property that characterizes collective remembering is that it tends to be heavily shaped by "schemata" (Bartlett 1932/1995), "implicit theories" (Ross 1989), or other simplifying organizational frameworks. To be sure, such frameworks also shape formal history, but in the case of collective memory they take on a particularly important role, meaning that accounts of the past often are quite schematic and include little in the way of detailed information, especially information that conflicts with the basic narrative that supports an identity project. In collective remembering, such conflicting evidence is often distorted, simplified, and ignored.

The Molotov-Ribbentrop Pact: A Soviet Account

This brief review of the difference between formal history and collective memory has several implications for understanding the transformation in the Russian view of the Molotov-Ribbentrop Pact. As will become apparent, most of what I have to say about this view reflects the pressures of collective memory.

However, the key to overcoming some of the problems that emerge from these pressures may lie with formal history.

[F]ormal history and collective memory must be kept distinct for several reasons. Collective memory tends to reflect a single, subjective, committed perspective of a group in the present, whereas formal history strives to be objective and to distance itself from the present and any particular perspective currently in favor.

I begin my analysis of the Molotov-Ribbentrop Pact with the official Soviet account from that period. From the perspective of this account, there is nothing to say about the secret protocols of the pact since they simply did not exist: the fact that the Baltic countries became part of the USSR had nothing to do with spheres of influence or any other form of external coercion. Instead, their annexation grew out of uprisings by the workers and peasants in these countries who desired to be part of the Soviet Union. In *A Short History of the Communist Party of the Soviet Union* (1970), for example, the "nonaggression pact" was presented as follows:[2]

> [I]n August 1939 Hitler's government proposed a non-aggression pact to the Soviet Government. The Soviet Union was threatened with war on two fronts—in Europe and the Far East—and was completely isolated. The Soviet Government, therefore, agreed to make a pact of non-aggression with Germany. Subsequent events revealed that this step was the only correct one under the circumstances. By taking it the USSR was able to continue peaceful construction for nearly two years and to strengthen its defenses. (P. 247)

Given that there were no secret protocols in this version of the events of 1939, the subsequent inclusion of the Baltic countries in the Soviet Union was not treated as being part of the story of the nonaggression pact. Instead, it was an event that arose due to a completely independent set of forces grounded in quite different motives. As outlined in that same text:

> In 1940, when the threat of German invasion loomed over Lithuania, Latvia, and Estonia, and their reactionary governments were preparing to make a deal with Hitler, the peoples of these countries overthrew their rulers, restored Soviet power and joined the USSR. (P. 247)

From this perspective, the fact that the Baltic countries became part of the USSR in 1940 was part of a Marxist-Leninist story of class struggle, a story that ended with the restoration of Soviet power. Indeed, this passage suggests that the period of independence in Estonia, Latvia, and Lithuania in the 1920s and 1930s was somehow unnatural and that once oppression had been removed, the people in these countries returned to their natural progressive path, joining the international march of socialist countries.

Narrative Rift as Step 1 in Post-Soviet Revision

With perestroika—and especially Gorbachev's admission in 1989 that the secret protocols had been part of the Molotov-Ribbentrop Pact, the old Soviet version of the events of 1939 and 1940 could no longer serve as an official account. It had to be revised, a process that had already begun in the final years of Soviet power. For example, in a 1989 high school history textbook (one that still took the USSR as its object of study), Korablëv, Fedosov, and Borisov (1989) wrote,

> The territorial composition of the country changed. Its borders were extended to the west. In 1939 the land and populations of Ukraine and Belorussia underwent reunification. In 1940 Romania returned to the composition of the USSR Bessarabia, which had been torn away in 1918. This led to the formation of the Moldovian SSR instead of an autonomous republic. As a result of complex processes of international and internal development Soviet power was established anew in Latvia, Lithuania, and Estonia, which entered the composition of the USSR in 1940.
>
> However, in the new regions entering the USSR, breaches of the law characteristic for those years of the abuse of power were tolerated along with democratic revolutionary transformations.
>
> All of this made the situation more complicated in these regions. It had a negative effect on people's psychological state and at the same time on the military preparedness of the USSR. (P. 348)

The first and perhaps most striking feature that distinguishes this from previous Soviet accounts is that the absorption of Latvia, Lithuania, and Estonia into the USSR was no longer formulated in Marxist-Leninist terms. There is no mention of "reactionary rulers" and so forth. Indeed, there is a great deal that is critical—at least implicitly—of Soviet power. Mention of "breaches of the law characteristic for those years of the abuse of power" is something that was simply unimaginable in official Soviet accounts. Instead of focusing on the glories of the Soviet Union through the desired vision of the party, this account allows that mistakes were made.

Another striking feature of this account is its awkwardness and ambiguity. It contains formulations that are so clumsy as to make the evasions obvious, if not laughable. In particular, the extensive use of the passive voice made it possible to avoid specifying as to who was responsible for the actions. By refusing to assign agency, the authors created an account in which things just seemed to happen on their own.

For people of the Baltic countries, expressions like "as a result of complex processes of international and internal development Soviet power was established" or "the territorial composition of the country changed" amount to evasion and attempts to avoid telling the truth. From this perspective, statements such as "all of this made the situation more complicated in these regions" are certainly true, but the prevarication involved is so great that the comments raise more questions than they answer.

The obvious awkwardness in this passage derives from a fundamental contradiction in the official Soviet account of the late 1980s in the USSR. On one hand, there was a need to acknowledge that events, the existence of which had previously been denied, had in fact occurred. It was no longer possible, for example, to deny the existence of the secret protocols of the Molotov-Ribbentrop Pact. On the other hand, there was no agreement on what the larger story was now supposed to be. How would the basic "narrative truth" (Mink 1978) of an official Soviet account change now that it could no longer be built around the claim that the party was always right in leading the march to a glorious future for international socialism? Would newly released archival evidence force Russia to create a new narrative that would cast the USSR as an imperialist power not unlike pre-revolutionary Russia?

Answers to such questions were still very unclear in 1989, and officials were apparently nervous at that time about making statements that could come back to haunt them. As a result, they seem to have arrived at an unsatisfactory compromise: they would include newly acknowledged information in official Soviet accounts of history but would not rewrite the basic narrative. The result was that new information appeared in a way that was inconsistent with the general flow of the text. It was as if this new information concerning the secret protocols of the Molotov-Ribbentrop Pact had appeared out of nowhere in the official account and that the authors had no idea how to weave it into the text. The fact that the meaning of events is largely shaped by the narrative in which they are enmeshed (Mink 1978), however, made this compromise unlikely to be satisfactory or stable, and this was indeed the case.

Narrative Repair as Step 2 in Post-Soviet Revision

Awkwardness and disjointedness characterized the first step in moving beyond Soviet accounts of the secret protocols of the Molotov-Ribbentrop Pact; during the second stage a kind of "narrative repair" emerged to reestablish coherence based on a new narrative. As was the case in step 1 of the revision process, this new version moved beyond official Soviet accounts in that it made no attempt to deny the existence of the secret protocols of the Molotov-Ribbentrop Pact. Indeed, it freely admitted them. It also moved beyond the awkward and evasive formulation that characterized the narrative rift in step 1.

The narrative repair that occurred at this stage involved a story that might be titled "Stalin's Difficult Choice." This narrative took several forms in the emergence of post-Soviet Russian collective memory of the Molotov-Ribbentrop Pact, and in fact several of its elements had long been part of the discussion of Stalin's actions leading up to World War II. Hence, using it in the late Soviet period amounted to dusting off some existing "off-the-shelf" narrative tools and putting them to new use in official discourse.

An early post-Soviet version of "The Difficult Choice" narrative can be found in a 1998 history textbook for ninth-graders by Danilov and Kosulina.

> **A difficult choice.** . . . While not giving up on a resolution of the "Polish question" through force, Hitler also proposed to the USSR to begin negotiations toward concluding an agreement of non-aggression and dividing up spheres of influence in Eastern Europe. Stalin was confronted with a difficult choice: either reject Hitler's proposal, thereby agreeing to have German forces move to the borders of the USSR in case Poland was defeated in a war with Germany, or conclude an agreement with Germany that would provide the possibility for pushing borders back from its west and avoid war for some time. . . . And thus the agreement was signed. On August 23, 1939 the entire world was shocked by the news that the USSR and Nazi Germany had signed a treaty of nonaggression. This was also wholly unexpected for the Soviet people. But no one knew the most important fact—secret protocols had been added to this treaty. In these secret protocols Moscow and Berlin divided up Eastern Europe among themselves into spheres of influence. . . . In the fall of 1939 the Soviet Union concluded treaties of mutual assistance with Estonia, Latvia, and Lithuania. In accordance with these treaties Soviet forces were introduced into these countries. In the summer of 1940 the Soviet leadership, using propitious external conditions, demanded that the Baltic countries accede to the introduction of additional forces, a replacement of governments, and emergency parliamentary elections. . . . The new organs of power, which had been selected under the control of Soviet representatives, turned to the Supreme Soviet of the USSR with the request to receive Lithuania, Latvia, Estonia, and Besarabia into the composition of the Soviet Union. This request was of course granted, and on the map of the USSR there appeared new union republics: the Latvian, Lithuanian, Estonian, and Moldavian Republics. In this fashion, almost all the western provinces that had earlier been in the Russian empire, with the exception of Poland and Finland, were returned. (Pp. 324-26)

In contrast to official Soviet accounts of the Molotov-Ribbentrop Pact, this text does not deny the existence of the secret protocols. Indeed, it highlights them. And in contrast to the narrative rift characteristic of step 1, there is relatively little awkwardness or prevarication in this case, although some, to be sure, remains. Instead, the events are represented in such a way that the motives that lay behind them are no longer an embarrassment to Russian collective memory.

"The Difficult Choice" story made it possible to explain events that had previously either been omitted or had given rise to awkwardness and a narrative rift in official Soviet accounts. The secret protocols of the Molotov-Ribbentrop Pact were presented as a decision forced on the Soviet Union by the fact that Germany was about to attack Poland, allowing the German army to approach the borders of the USSR. And the choice is presented as somehow easier by the fact that the USSR was returning to borders that had previously defined the Russian Empire. But the main thrust of such accounts is that even though the Soviet Union was reluctant to expand its borders, it was simply forced to do so to ensure the defeat of a German nation that was a threat to the entire world.

Before turning to the forces that gave rise to the narrative repair in step 2, it is worth emphasizing that "The Difficult Choice" story is by no means the only one that can be imagined about these events. For example, one Baltic version of the Molotov-Ribbentrop Pact has disputed the assertion that it lessened the chance of war between Germany and the Soviet Union, arguing instead that "it was one of the direct causes of World War II" (Vizulis 1988, vii). And Kestutis Girnius (1989) has argued that instead of seeking to create a buffer against German invasion, the pact was motivated by long-standing tendencies of Russian territorial expansionism.

> There is little doubt that the Soviet government hoped to profit from the growth of tensions in Eastern Europe to regain land that was formerly part of the Russian empire. The Soviet Union made clear its interest in the Baltics in the early stages of its negotiations with France and Great Britain. Soviet negotiators were so insistent on the matter that they were willing to risk a breakdown in the talks rather than renounce their aims. German willingness to satisfy demands that the Western democracies would not countenance seems to have been an important factor in determining Moscow's decision to cooperate with the Nazis. (P. 2)

Interpretations such as these are what people in the Baltic countries hoped would emerge and be widely accepted once the secret protocols of the Molotov-Ribbentrop Pact were made public. However, the narrative repair in post-Soviet Russian collective memory clearly did *not* move in this direction. It instead moved steadfastly toward one or another version of "The Difficult Choice" story.

The "Expulsion of Foreign Enemies" Schematic Narrative Template

Some observers would attribute this turn of events in the revision of official Russian collective memory to transparent and defensive self-interest. But the process involved is more subtle and deep-seated than a conscious effort to avoid facing new evidence, and recognizing this will be key to transcending the endless disputes over the past that emerge in such cases.

The process of revision in this instance reflects underlying forces connected with a "schematic narrative template" (Wertsch 2002) that is an essential part the national identity and worldview of Russia. The narrative in this case is schematic in the sense that it exists at an abstract level involving few details about specific actors, times, places, and so forth; it is a template in the sense that this abstract form provides a pattern for interpreting multiple episodes from the past. Schematic narrative templates stand in contrast to "specific narratives" (Wertsch 2002) that name concrete dates, actors, locations, and so forth. The textbook passages cited above are examples of specific narratives.

The notion of a schematic narrative template stems from writings in folklore (Propp 1968), psychology (Bartlett 1932/1995; Ross 1989), and other disciplines. Interpretations of the past are heavily shaped by the abstract meaning of structures and schemas associated with cultural tools used by members of a collective. This means that detailed information, especially that which contradicts a general perspective, is distorted, simplified, and ignored, something that stands in contrast to formal history, or at least its aspirations (Wertsch 2002).

Arguing in the tradition of Vygotsky (1981, 1987), Bakhtin (1986), and others, I take schematic narrative templates to be structures that emerge out of the repeated use of a standard set of specific narratives in history instruction, the popular media, and so forth. The narrative templates that take shape in this process are especially effective in organizing what we can say and think, both because they are largely unnoticed by, or "transparent" to, those employing them and because they are a fundamental part of the identity claims of a group. The result is that these templates act as powerful "coauthors" when we attempt to tell what "really happened" in the past (Wertsch 2002).

---

*[N]arrative templates that take shape
in this process are especially effective in
organizing what we can say and think,
both because they are largely unnoticed by,
or "transparent" to, those employing them
and because they are a fundamental part
of the identity claims of a group.*

The schematic narrative template at work in the case of the Molotov-Ribbentrop Pact is one that occupies a central place in Russians' understanding of crucial historical episodes. It can be titled the "Expulsion of Foreign Enemies" narrative template, and it imposes a basic plot structure on a range of specific characters, events, and circumstances. This narrative template includes the following elements:

1. An initial situation in which Russia is peaceful and not interfering with others.
2. The initiation of trouble in which a foreign enemy treacherously and viciously attacks Russia without provocation.
3. Russia almost loses everything in total defeat as it suffers from the enemy's attempts to destroy it as a civilization.
4. Through heroism, and against all odds, Russia triumphs and succeeds in expelling the foreign enemy, thus justifying its claims of exceptionalism and its status as a great nation.

At first glance it may appear that there is nothing peculiarly Russian about this narrative template. For example, by replacing "Russian" with "American," at least the first two elements would seem to be consistent with American collective memory of the Japanese attack on Pearl Harbor in 1941. The claim is not that this narrative template is used only by members of the Russian mnemonic community or that it is the only one available to them. However, there are several indications that it plays a particularly important role and takes on a particular form in this case.

The first of these concerns its ubiquity. Whereas the United States and many other societies have accounts of past events that are compatible with this narrative template, it seems to be employed more widely in the Russian tradition than elsewhere. In this connection, consider the comments of Musatova (2002) about the cultural history of Russia. In a passing remark about the fate of having to learn "the lessons of conquests and enslavement by foreigners" (p. 139), she lists several groups who are viewed as having perpetrated similar events in Russia's history: "Tatars, Germans, Swedes, Poles, Turks, Germans again" (p. 139). This comment suggests that while the particular actors, dates, and setting may change, the same basic plot applies to all these episodes. They are all stamped out of the same basic template.

Some observers would go so far as to say that the "Expulsion of Foreign Enemies" narrative template is *the* underlying story of Russian collective remembering, and this provides a basic point of contrast with other groups. For example, it is strikingly different from American items such as the "Mystique of Manifest Destiny" (Lowenthal 1994, 53) or a "Reluctant Hegemon" story (Kagan 2006). The "Expulsion of Foreign Enemies" narrative template plays a central role in Russian collective memory, even in instances where it would not seem relevant, at least to those who are not native speakers (Lotman and Uspenskii 1985) of this tradition. For example, in post-Soviet Russia communism has often been portrayed as a foreign enemy that invaded Russia and had to be expelled after nearly destroying the nation.

All this is not to say that this narrative template has no grounding in actual historical experience. It clearly does reflect traumatic events and experiences from Russia's past. At the same time, however, it is important to recognize that this is a cultural and cognitive construction, a particular way of pursuing what Bartlett (1932/1995) called the "effort after meaning," and hence not the only possible way to interpret events such as signing the secret protocols of the Molotov-Ribbentrop Pact. As already noted, people from places like Estonia, Latvia, and Lithuania have quite different interpretations of this event, and the basic tenets of these alternative interpretations directly contradict many of those in the Russian version.

This Russian effort after meaning appears to have had a powerful hand in shaping narrative repair in the case of the secret protocols of the Molotov-Ribbentrop Pact. The acknowledgement of these protocols initially was an embarrassment to official narrative, but this did not lead to the kind of fundamental and permanent transformation that had long been envisioned by people in the Baltic countries. Instead, after an initial period of confusion and prevarication, characterized by narrative rift, this schematic narrative template reasserted its power and gave rise to "The Difficult Choice" story, an account that among other things seems to be aimed at precluding alternative interpretations of events such as those based on Russian expansionism.

Conclusion: The Conservatism of Collective Memory

In looking at the secret protocols of the Molotov-Ribbentrop Pact, I have purposefully chosen a case where one might expect a fundamental revision in collective memory. People in the Baltic countries, as well as elsewhere, had expected—or at least hoped—that making these secret protocols public would be a sufficiently powerful embarrassment to existing Russian accounts to lead to such a revision. What turned out to be the case, however, was something quite different. After an initial period of relatively superficial disruption in the official narrative (i.e., the narrative rift of step 1), an account emerged that smoothed over the awkwardness and prevarication of the narratives of that period.

I have argued that this narrative repair in step 2 was heavily shaped by a cultural tool that mediates deep collective memory in Russia, namely, the "Expulsion of Foreign Enemies" schematic narrative template. Like schematic narrative templates in any society, this one reflects a particular worldview and interpretative perspective in the effort after meaning. The power of this perspective is obvious to those with competing interpretations of the Molotov-Ribbentrop Pact. However, because schematic narrative templates operate at a nonconscious level and are especially transparent to their users, members of the Russian mnemonic community usually operate on the assumption that they are simply telling what really happened rather than coauthoring an account with a narrative tool.

The fact that the Expulsion of Foreign Enemies storyline is so jarring to others provides a reminder of the strong emotional attachment and identity commitments typically associated with such narrative templates. They are by no means neutral cognitive instruments. Instead, they are cultural tools deeply embedded in the more general project of developing and maintaining an image that supports a collective identity.

All this is not to deny the noticeable change in textbook accounts of the Molotov-Ribbentrop Pact during the late Soviet and post-Soviet years, beginning with a period of apparent unease over how to rewrite the narrative in light of the acknowledgment of the secret protocols. However, this initial step did not last long, and perhaps more important, the new version of the secret protocols that eventually emerged was not the sort of basic revision in an official account that people in the Baltics had hoped for. Instead, the narrative repair that characterizes step 2 amounted to patching over the rift created by acknowledging the secret protocols. It did this by embedding them in an effort after meaning, the general underlying pattern of which was already well established.

These developments suggest that deep collective memory is very conservative and resistant to change, something that runs counter to observations about the radically new public versions of the past that emerged with the breakup of the USSR. It is indeed important to recognize that post-Soviet Russian history text-books include assertions that would have landed their authors in prison a few decades earlier. However, focusing on this alone fails to take into account the important difference between a surface level of narrative organization, where radical changes in specific narratives may be found, and the schematic narrative templates that mediate deep collective memory. While the specific narratives about the Molotov-Ribbentrop Pact may have changed in some surprising and seemingly radical ways, the underlying schematic narrative has been a very conservative force.

This would appear to be sobering if not depressing news for those dedicated to overcoming differences and resolving conflict between groups. Are people in countries like Estonia and Russia doomed to continued, intractable opposition over interpretations of the past? Is this the case for places like India and Pakistan or Turkey and Armenia as well? Efforts by historians in these and other such troubled cases suggest that one way forward may be to switch the discussion away from collective memory and toward a heavier reliance on formal history. As noted earlier, official accounts found in history textbooks are typically a mixture of the two, but the relative contributions from each may vary widely. When trying to resolve differences over the interpretation of past events, one useful means may be to introduce a heavier dose of objectivity and complexity into such textbooks.

Professional historians such as Romila Thapar (2005) in India and Taner Aksam (2007) in the case of Turkey have stepped forward in recent years to argue that professional historians must reassert control of at least part of the public discourse about the past. This would involve shifting the discussion away from narratives that support emotionally laden identity claims toward narratives whose standing rests on a more balanced, objective consideration of evidence. This suggests a different role for historians than is often assumed in academic discourse, and some historians resist precisely because they fear that it could lead to the elision of the distinction between collective memory and formal history that they have been so assiduous in maintaining.

Principled and courageous attempts to introduce the rigor of formal history into discussions about the past do seem to provide some hope for moving debates between opposing perspectives to a calmer and more productive plane. However, this is hardly a panacea, given that historians themselves often cannot agree over what narrative applies to past events. As Cronon (1992) has noted, two competent professional historians can use the same basic archives and "facts" to arrive at quite different historical accounts, and this reflects the basic claim by philosophers of history such as Mink (1978) that no amount of objective evidence can alone reveal the narrative that must be told about the past.

Hence, a move toward formal historical analysis may be an important step in overcoming intractable differences between groups' understanding of the past, but an appreciation of the deep memory of each group may be another necessary component. A failure to recognize the powerful conservative forces of narrative templates as an inherent part of the process may mean that even the best efforts to resolve differences based on formal historical analysis are destined to fail.

Principled and courageous attempts to introduce the rigor of formal history into discussions about the past do seem to provide some hope for moving debates between opposing perspectives to a calmer and more productive plane.

If the events surrounding the Molotov-Ribbentrop Pact show anything, they show that people are not likely to arrive at a common understanding of the past simply because they are exposed to a common body of objective information. Given how central deep memory is to collective identity, this should be no surprise. So the best hope we may have is to recognize the existence and power of the narrative templates as a first step and then proceed to harness formal history in an effort to adjudicate differences over "what really happened" in the past.

Notes

1. The two major works by Halbwachs in English, *On Collective Memory* (1992) and *The Collective Memory* (1980), are compilations of French publications from the 1920s, 1930s, and early 1940s. Halbwachs died in Buchenwald concentration camp shortly before the end of World War II.

2. Note that Stalin and associates like Molotov were out of official favor in 1970 and hence no longer appeared in such accounts.

References

Aksam, Taner. 2007. *A shameful act: The Armenian genocide and the question of Turkish responsibility.* New York: Holt.

Assmann, J. 1997. *Moses the Egyptian: The memory of Egypt in Western monotheism.* Cambridge, MA: Harvard University Press.

Bakhtin, M. M. 1986. The problem of speech genres. In *Speech genres & other late essays*, 60-102. Translated by Vern W. McGee, edited by Caryl Emerson and Michael Holquist. Austin: University of Texas Press.

Bartlett, F. C. 1932/1995. *Remembering: A study in experimental and social psychology*. Cambridge: Cambridge University Press.

Cronon, W. 1992. A place for stories: Nature, history, and narrative. *Journal of American History* 78 (4): 1347-76.

Danilov, A. A., and L. G. Kosulina. 1998. *Istoria Rossii. XX Vek. Uchebnik dlya starshikh klassov obshcheobrazovatel'nykh uchrezhdenii. Rekomendovano ekspertnym sovetom Ministerstva obrazovaniya Rossiskoi Federatsii* [The history of Russia. Twentieth century. Textbook for older classes of general education institutions. Recommended by the expert soviet of the Ministry of Education of the Russian Federation]. Moscow: Izdatel'skii dom Yakhont.

Girnius, K. 1989. The historiography of the Molotov-Ribbentrop Pact. *Lituanus* 34 (2).

Halbwachs, M. 1980. *The collective memory*. Translated by Francis J. Didder Jr. and Vida Yazdi Ditter. New York: Harper & Row.

———. 1992. *On collective memory*. Edited, translated, and with an introduction by Lewis A. Coser. Chicago: University of Chicago Press.

Kagan, R. 2006. *Dangerous nation: America's place in the world from its earliest days to the dawn of the twentieth century*. New York: Knopf.

King, D. 1997. *The commissar vanishes: The falsification of photographs and art in Stalin's Russia*. Preface by Stephen F. Cohen; photographs from the David King Collection. New York: Metropolitan Books.

Korablëv, Yu. I., I. A. Fedosov, and Yu. S. Borisov. 1989. *Istoriya SSSR. Uchebnik dlya desyatogo klassa srednei shkoly* [History of the USSR. Textbook for the tenth grade of middle school]. Moscow: Prosveshchenie.

Lotman, Yu. M., and B. A. Uspenskii. 1985. Binary models in the dynamics of Russian culture (to the end of the eighteenth century). In *The semiotics of Russian cultural history. Essays by Iurii M. Lotman, Lidiia Ia. Ginsburg, Boris A. Uspenskii*, ed. A. D. Nakhimovsky and A. S. Nakhimovsky, 30-66. Ithaca, NY: Cornell University Press.

Lowenthal, D. 1994. Identity, heritage, and history. In *Commemorations: The politics of national identity*, ed. J. R. Gillis, 41-57. Princeton, NJ: Princeton University Press.

Mink, L. O. 1978. Narrative form as a cognitive instrument. In *The writing of history: Literary form and historical understanding*, ed. R. H. Canary and H. Kozicki, 129-49. Madison: University of Wisconsin Press.

Musatova, M. 2002. *Sviatogorskii Uspenskii monastyr': Mikhailovskaia shkol'naia pushkiniana* [Sviatogorsky Uspensky Monastery: Mikhailov school of Pushkin studies]. Pskov, Poland: Pskovskaia oblastnaia tipografiia.

Novick, P. 1999. *The Holocaust in American life*. Boston: Houghton Mifflin.

Propp, V. 1968. *Morphology of the folktale*. Translated by Laurence Scott. Austin: University of Texas Press.

Renan, E. 1882/1990. What is a nation? In *Nation and narration*, ed. H. K. Bhabha. London: Routledge.

Ross, M. 1989. Relation of implicit theories to the construction of personal histories. *Psychological Review* 96 (2): 341-57.

A short history of the Communist Party of the Soviet Union. 1970. B. N. Ponomarev and others. Translated from the Russian by David Skvirsky. Moscow: Progress Publishers.

Thapar, R. 2005. *Somanatha: The many voices of history*. London: Verso.

Vizulis, I. 1988. *The Molotov-Ribbentrop Pact of 1939: The Baltic case*. New York: Praeger.

Vygotsky, L. S. 1981. The instrumental method in psychology. In *The concept of activity in Soviet psychology*, ed. J. V. Wertsch. Armonk, NY: M. E. Sharpe.

———. 1987. The collected works of L.S. Vygotsky. Vol. 1, Problems of general psychology. Including the volume *Thinking and speech*, ed. and translated by N. Minick. New York: Plenum.

Wertsch, J. V. 1998. *Mind as action*. New York: Oxford University Press.

———. 2002. *Voices of collective remembering*. New York: Cambridge University Press.

Using the Past in the Nazi Successor States from 1945 to the Present

By
JENNY WÜSTENBERG
and
DAVID ART

This article examines the political uses of memory in the three successor states of the Third Reich. The focus is on how political elites offered stylized histories of the Nazi past in the service of broader political goals, both domestic and international. After reviewing key junctures in the politics of memory, the authors discuss contemporary debates about history, particularly in Germany, the country often viewed as the model for coming to terms with a traumatic past. Despite the massive and growing literature about confronting the Nazi past, the authors note that there are few studies that link ideas about history to broader political outcomes and suggest that this represents a fertile area for future research. The article concludes by considering whether German memory politics will serve as a model for European memory.

Keywords: Germany; Austria; memory; European Union; Holocaust

G ermany has earned an international reputation for its critical and ongoing examination of its own crimes. As Timothy Garton Ash (2007) noted, "The enterprise in which the Germans truly are Weltmeister is the cultural reproduction of their country's versions of terror. No nation has been more brilliant, more

Jenny Wüstenberg is a doctoral candidate in government and politics at the University of Maryland, College Park. Her dissertation examines the long-term impact of the "history movement" and the role of civil society activism in German memory politics more generally. She has published articles in German Politics and Society *and the* Central European University Political Science Journal *and held a fellowship at the American Institute for Contemporary German Studies in Washington, D.C.*

David Art is an assistant professor of political science at Tufts University. He is the author of The Politics of the Nazi Past in Germany and Austria *(Cambridge University Press, 2006) and is completing a book manuscript titled* How Radical Right Parties Organize *(under contract with Cambridge University Press). He is the coconvener of the European Consortium of Political Research's Standing Group on Extremism and Democracy.*

DOI: 10.1177/0002716207312762

persistent, and more innovative in the investigation, communication, and representation—the re-presentation, and re-re-presentation—of its own past evils." Most other states with massive human rights violations in their not-too-distant pasts are regularly chastised for either whitewashing these events or denying them outright. But Germany's process of "coming to terms" with the Holocaust is usually compared favorably with the two other direct successor states of the Third Reich: the German Democratic Republic (GDR, or East Germany) and Austria. Decades after the end of World War II, East German communist leaders still saw themselves on the victorious side of history—a position that simultaneously justified imposing dictatorship on the untrustworthy masses and prevented taking responsibility for Nazism. Meanwhile, until the mid-1980s Austrians continued to portray their nation as the victim of, rather than coconspirator in, Nazi crimes. West Germans, on the other hand, beginning in the 1960s, have made public contrition a central element of domestic politics and statecraft. West Germany (and later united Germany), then, often serves as the positive standard against which other societies are evaluated.

Given the massive literature on the politics of the past in Germany, and the growing literature on memory in Austria and the GDR, it is worthwhile reconsidering these stylized histories. In this article, we critically review the politics of memory in the three Nazi successor states. We argue that though these societies confronted the Nazi past in profoundly different ways, their political elites ultimately had one thing in common: they sought to interpret and present the Nazi catastrophe in ways that legitimated their actions both to domestic and international audiences.

While scholars of memory often emphasize the moral, judicial, and cultural imperatives of remembering and restitution, we draw attention to how the past can be and has been used to buttress "hard" state and elite interests. In the cases of the Federal Republic of Germany (FRG, or West Germany) in the early years, and Austria and the GDR much longer, those interests were so powerful that they largely prevented an honest confrontation of Nazism and the Holocaust. When this dominant version of history was called into question in West Germany, the state was at first challenged and arguably weakened until it adopted a new "usable" past. Today, in the united Germany, the direct and democratic confrontation with the Nazi legacy is an everyday normality. At the same time, the state has skillfully found ways to use this version of history to support foreign and domestic policy choices.

We then consider the extent to which the literature on the Nazi past relates to core questions within comparative politics and international relations. We note that comparativists have, by and large, paid little attention to historical memory as a causal variable in domestic politics. Scholars of international relations, particularly those operating within the constructivist paradigm, have done more in this regard and offer a theoretical apparatus for understanding the diffusion of German memory to the European level. We close by briefly considering whether Germany's confrontation with the Nazi past has been so successful that it may serve as a model for other societies.

The Histories of Memory in the Nazi Successor States

German *Vergangenheitsaufarbeitung* ("working through the past") was a tortured process, fraught with scandals, setbacks, and resistance from large portions of society. After careful wartime planning, the Allies implemented a comprehensive program of de-Nazification, internment of Nazi functionaries, reeducation of the population, and war crimes trials. For the two German states founded in 1949, the legacy of this occupation policy was twofold. On one hand, they effectively dismantled and discredited Nazism, thus largely preventing its organizational and ideological resurgence. The Allies thereby created a precedent and foundation for confronting the past that could be drawn upon in later decades. On the other hand, the majority of Germans resented the Allies' measures. German politicians catered to and magnified such sentiment in the early years of independence, particularly during elections. Widespread feelings of the unjust imposition of "victor's justice" reinforced the solidarity of a *Volksgemeinschaft* (a Nazi term for "people's community") among postfascist Germans (Frei 1997).

The cold war produced two separate German states. Though the official goal of unification remained, the systemic competition between the two governments and their respective struggles to regain sovereignty within each geopolitical camp made this increasingly unlikely. The reckoning with Nazism, the Holocaust, and the interpretation of history more generally became a pivotal component of the ideological contest. Attitudes about the Nazi past, and policy responses to it, developed along different but interrelated trajectories. In both Germanys, the Nazi past played a crucial role in the struggle to regain legitimacy in the aftermath of humiliating defeat. As the cold war raged on, each state attempted to present itself in contradistinction to the other by claiming to embody the correct lessons learned from the recent disaster as well as a positive national tradition derived from previous democratic movements (Assmann and Frevert 1999). As Jeffrey Herf (1997) has shown, the instrumentalization of the past prevented honest remembering on both sides: the GDR fashioned itself as an antifascist state and repositioned itself on the victorious side of history, while the FRG used anticommunism and the need for reintegration into the West as a justification for neglecting justice and historical truth.

Memory politics in the German Democratic Republic

The GDR reintegrated many Nazi perpetrators and fellow travelers into public life while suppressing the memory of noncommunist victims and outlawing their organizations. At the same time, the East German state was founded on the myth that the population had united in communist resistance to fascism. This narrative precluded any form of moral accounting or material restitution to victims of the Nazi regime, while simultaneously legitimizing the regime both domestically and internationally in contradistinction to its "fascist and imperialist" Western counterpart. Unlike the FRG, unified and aggressive history politics were a priority in the GDR even in the early resource-scarce years. To this end, the state founded a new national museum of history and erected a range of representative memorials to celebrate communist and German achievements. Apart from the icons of the communist movement such as Rosa Luxemburg and Karl Liebknecht, the communist resistance to Nazism took center stage.

> *[T]he East German state was founded on the myth that the population had united in communist resistance to fascism . . . legitimizing the regime both domestically and internationally in contradistinction to its "fascist and imperialist" Western counterpart.*

The GDR blamed capitalism for the catastrophe and largely ignored German fascism's racist and anti-Semitic components (Reichel 2001). Communists and workers were regarded as the primary victims of Hitler, and reverence to them became the central ritual legitimizing the dictatorship. The Buchenwald concentration camp memorial was created very early on (though of course there was silence about the crimes committed there by the Soviet secret police after 1945), and it became one of the most important memory spaces reinforcing the new state identity (Assmann and Frevert 1999). Jewish and other racially persecuted groups were marginalized, and many victims were forced to assimilate and repress their memories, so as not to be accused of "Zionism" or oppositional activity. In foreign policy, the GDR neither paid compensation to nor established friendly relations with Israel.

The paradoxical combination of antifascist rhetoric and denial of responsibility for the Holocaust, as well as the stylized rites of remembrance, remained relatively unchanged for the duration of the East German regime. Only in the course of the 1980s was there a certain opening of the mnemonic discourse and the slow recognition of Jewish suffering. In November 1988, for the first time, the anti-Semitic pogroms of 1938 were publicly recalled more prominently than the 1918 German revolution.

Memory politics in the Federal Republic of Germany

The progression of Vergangenheitsaufarbeitung in West Germany was far more complex than in the East. From the outset, dominant trends were interrupted by dissenting individuals and groups, such as Aktion Sühnezeichen Friedensdienste (Action Reconciliation Service for Peace), underlining the more pluralistic character of this society. Though the FRG government undoubtedly pursued specific strategies of memory politics, there was never a unified state policy, as was the case in the GDR. In the West, political elites responded to popular resentment of Allied policy by rolling back de-Nazification and the pursuit of justice to the point that convicted war criminals were released from prison. Norbert Frei (1997) has argued that this almost indiscriminate exoneration was driven by a societal consensus that rejected the purported imposition of collective guilt, as well as by the negative electoral implications of forcing a confrontation with the past. The amnesty granted to war criminals enabled the new leaders to emphasize the break with the occupation period and harness the support of the population—all in the name of democracy (Frei 1997; see also Frei 2005). According to Herf (1997, 389), the first chancellor, Konrad Adenauer, "struck a bargain with compromised Germans: in exchange for his reticence about the Nazi past, they would agree to accept the new democracy, or at least not try to destroy it." This arrangement was seen by Western Allies as a tolerable price to pay for the FRG to be firmly rooted in the anticommunist camp.

The early period of the FRG, then, was dominated by what philosopher Hermann Lübbe (1983) called a "communicative silence" about recent history that extended the solidarity of Nazi society into the democratic state but that also made possible its survival. However, the idea of silence about the past is somewhat misleading. West Germans in the 1950s were more than vocal about the war when it came to portraying themselves as victims. In particular the "expellees" of the eastern part of the Third Reich were effectively represented in government, society, and culture (Schulze 2001; Moeller 2001; Ahonen 2003). In contrast to Jewish and other victims of Nazism, German war casualties enjoyed a broad range of commemorative recognition. Concentration camps and other sites of terror were not instrumentalized as in the GDR but rather were mostly neglected.

With the foundations laid by the Allies and isolated individuals, the reckoning with the Nazi past in West Germany was gradually transformed in the 1960s and 1970s. Several developments explain this change. First, a number of legislative and societal debates, most importantly those on extending the statute of limitations on the crime of murder (and therefore on many acts committed under the Nazi regime), as well as new trials against war criminals, carried the moral, judicial, and political issues concerning the Nazi past into the public sphere. Second, a generational shift was under way that moved those who were not involved in the Nazi regime, but who were influenced by their parents' and grandparents' selective remembering of the past, into prominent societal and political positions. For this generation, the shortcomings of the immediate postwar decade helped to mobilize students and intellectuals in a general critique of the "Adenauer restoration." For the first time, there was an electoral majority in favor of confronting the past (Herf 1997). When Chancellor Willy Brandt fell to his knees in front of the memorial to the uprising at the Warsaw Ghetto in 1970, he thereby powerfully expressed the government's new approach to the Nazi past.

Despite this shift from "communicative silence" to open confrontation, the debate revolved around structural theories of Nazism that were mainly concerned with capitalist interests and the profiteers of fascism. There were few attempts to trace concrete perpetrators, their motives, and the historical context. This changed in the 1980s, triggered in large part by a "media event" of unprecedented importance: the screening in 1979 on public television of the fictional miniseries *Holocaust*, which exposed 20 million viewers to the everyday experience of persecution and genocide, as well as individual responsibility and resistance, under the Nazis. This new interest in history was harnessed by a developing grassroots movement of history workshops and citizens initiatives that organized all over the FRG to study local and neglected pasts and publicize their findings in exhibitions (Böge 2004). Though these activists did not intend from the start to erect memorials, they unearthed sites of persecution and resistance that they worked to recognize publicly. The result was a decentralized landscape of small memorials that is arguably unique to Germany today.

This grassroots activism happened in the context of (and often in opposition to) the newly aggressive history politics of the Kohl administration. The chancellor sought—through a series of foreign policy and domestic moves—to redefine German history as positive and "usable" and the Nazi period as only one chapter in the larger story of Germany. Kohl's message was that Germany deserved to move back onto the international stage unhindered by its past. However, he met with considerable opposition to his program, not only from the history activists on the left, but also from a growing number of elites across the political spectrum (Art 2006). A prominent instance of this is President Richard von Weizsäcker's 1985 speech on the fortieth anniversary of the Allied liberation, in which he stated, "Anyone who closes his eyes to the past is blind to the present. Whoever refuses to remember the inhumanity is prone to new risks of infection." The 1980s were, in sum, the high point of the critical examination of the Nazi past that shifted historical responsibility into the spotlight.

The end of the cold war and the unification of the two Germanys by no means ended the discussion over the Nazi past—in fact, the past two decades have seen a veritable "memory boom" (Winter 2000). However, the reckoning with the past has been complicated by the merging of the eastern and western cultures of memory, by the growing need to confront other pasts (such as the communist dictatorship, German colonial history, and German suffering during the Second World War) and by the realization that the experiential generation is fading. The years since 1990 have witnessed many intellectual and emotional debates about the meaning of history and are a testament to the fact that Germans continue to be fascinated by the past. The discussions about the exhibition about crimes of the German army, Goldhagen's (1996) thesis about Hitler's "Willing Executioners," the Holocaust memorial in Berlin, and the filmic interpretation of Hitler are only some of the most prominent instances of recent German memory culture. The Holocaust memorial is an especially poignant example of how Germans have managed to combine contrition with favorable public relations.

It is clear that the meaning of history has become a central tenet of German political culture: while the Nazi past is no longer necessarily the only focus, it remains the lens through which other episodes of German history must be evaluated. The routine taking of responsibility for Nazism and the Holocaust in public life has not diminished its usefulness for politicians. Since unification, German leaders have stressed that their good record of memory proves their reliability as an international partner and their legitimate presence in the halls of power.

The years since 1990 have witnessed many intellectual and emotional debates about the meaning of history and are a testament to the fact that Germans continue to be fascinated by the past.

Memory politics in the Austrian Republic

To paraphrase an old joke, the Austrians succeeded in convincing themselves—and the outside world—that Hitler was a German and Beethoven an Austrian. As Tony Judt (1992) has argued, every European state—including, as we have seen, the Germans—erected "founding myths" that sought to absolve the state and the general population from sins of omission and commission during the war. The Austrians were fortunate enough to have their own particular myth handed to them in the form of the Moscow Declaration of 1943. The Allied powers described Austria as "the first free country to fall victim to Hitlerite aggression," although they reminded Austria that "she has a responsibility for participation in the war on the side of Hitlerite Germany." The Austrians seized on the first passage and disregarded the second. The Austrian Declaration of Independence of 1945 referred to the country as "Hitler's first victim," a designation that would not be challenged by any significant actor in Austrian politics or society for more than forty years. Given the long tradition of political anti-Semitism in Austria (Pauley 1981), the popular support for the *Anschluss* (Bukey 2000), and the overrepresentation of Austrians among SS officers and death camp personnel, the Austrian republic's founding narrative was clearly at odds with historical reality.

As in both the FRG and the GDR, historical narratives of the Nazi past served concrete political goals in Austria. Classifying Austrians as the victims of the

Germans helped Austria's founders to disentangle their nation's identity from that of their northern neighbors. The lack of a strong Austrian national identity was viewed as one of the chief weaknesses of the First Austrian Republic (1918-1938), widely derided as "the republic no one wanted." The defense that Austrians were, like Jews, victims of Nazism was used to parry claims from Jewish groups for restitution. As Robert Knight's (1988) study of Austrian cabinet meetings demonstrates, the government adopted a deliberate policy of "dragging the matter out" and largely avoided paying significant reparations until recently. The victim myth also paved the way for the reintegration of half a million former Nazis into politics and society. The two large parties (the Socialists [SPD] and the People's Party [ÖVP]) openly courted these voters after the general amnesty of 1947, but most of them would find their way to the Federation of Independents (VdU), which became the Austrian Freedom Party (FPÖ) in 1956. Thereafter, the Socialists in particular reached out to former Nazis in their battles with the ÖVP. This policy reached its apotheosis under the chancellorship of Bruno Kreisky, a Jew who appointed several former Nazis to his cabinet and reacted bitterly to suggestions that such individuals were beyond the political pale.

Unlike in West Germany, there was virtually no public debate in Austria for forty years about the Nazi past. In 1986, however, allegations that former Secretary General of the United Nations and ÖVP presidential candidate Kurt Waldheim had covered up his Nazi past precipitated an intense national discussion about Austria's complicity in Nazi crimes, thus breaking "the great taboo" (Pelinka and Weinzerl 1987). The debate involved several international actors, including the World Jewish Congress, the *New York Times*, and the United States, and generated a nationalistic, and oftentimes anti-Semitic, reaction from Waldheim's defenders (Mitten 1992; Wodak et al. 1999). These politicians, journalists, and public intellectuals argued that Waldheim, and by extension Austria, had nothing to apologize for and was the victim of an international smear campaign. This "new victim discourse" proved effective as Waldheim cruised to an easy victory. On the other hand, a small number of Green politicians, artists, and intellectuals began to demand that Austria critically examine its Nazi past and accept some responsibility for Nazi crimes. Austrian academics produced a number of scholarly works that examined, and challenged, the victim narrative (Uhl 1992; Wasserman 2000). The Waldheim debate, however, hardly produced a new historical consensus. Both left and right continued to view the Nazi past differently, and both regularly accused the other of using history for partisan political gain.

Fourteen years after the Waldheim affair, Austria again became the subject of international attention when the ÖVP formed a coalition government with the FPÖ in February 2000. The leader of the FPÖ, Jörg Haider, had established a reputation for openly flirting with historical revisionism, implying on various occasions that there were positive aspects of Nazism and that members of the Waffen SS had defended the homeland from Bolshevism. Following a conference on the Holocaust in Stockholm, the fourteen other members of the European Union (EU) placed symbolic diplomatic sanctions on Austria. Although these sanctions, like the international criticism in the Waldheim affair, produced a rally-round-the-flag effect and strengthened the ÖVP-FPÖ government, they also forced Austria to take measures to improve its image. Only days after the formation of the new government, Chancellor Wolfgang Schüssel (ÖVP) appointed a task force to investigate Nazi slave labor in Austria. The government eventually agreed to pay 438 million euros to the approximately 150,000 surviving slave laborers. It also returned art and property seized from Jewish families. Indeed, under pressure from the international community, the ÖVP-FPÖ government did more than any previous Austrian government to address the Nazi past. Austria's degree of complicity is still disputed, and some politicians on the right still refuse to view the country as anything other than a victim. Still, under pressure from the European Union, as well as domestic civil society and historians, Austrians now seem to have joined Germans in pursuing a more honest reckoning with their Nazi past.

Wulf Kansteiner (2006) has recently contended that the fading of the generation that directly experienced the Second World War and the Holocaust has led to the professionalization and routinization of memory. The Hocaust is now studied self-confidently as any other subject of historical inquiry, and the institutions that remember it are a relatively noncontroversial component of the symbolic landscape in both Germany and Austria. Furthermore, the debates about dealing with the Nazi past have acquired a highly self-reflexive nature; that is, any discussion is always at least partially about what a given type of commemoration means in the larger political, artistic, societal, and even global context. On the whole, the Nazi successor states seem to be on their way to an exemplary approach to confronting their past. And yet this positive development seems diminished by the suspicion that there are ulterior motives behind public morality. Can the payment of restitution or the erection of a prominent memorial be hailed as a moral achievement when it was done at least partially to prove the government's trustworthiness to international partners?

The Nazi Past in Domestic and International Politics

Politicians clearly use narratives of the past to achieve a variety of goals. Yet it would be a mistake to assume that such narratives are necessarily absorbed, or internalized, by ordinary citizens (Confino 2006; Wolfgram 2007). While mass attitudes on the Nazi past appear to reflect elite discourse (Art 2006), and while education has led to more Holocaust awareness in both Germany and Austria (Levy and Dierkes 2002), individual ideas about the Nazi past are clearly varied and complex. It is also unclear to what extent they are connected to other political orientations. Does discussion of past atrocities foster democratic political attitudes, as some scholars have contended (Sa'adah 1998; Nino 1998), and as Willy Brandt implicitly suggested when he challenged Germans to "dare more democracy" by critically examining the Nazi past? Or might such a discussion decrease support for democracy, particularly in nations with a fledgling democracy, as

Lübbe (1983) argued in the German context? Although some scholars have tried to address this question (Langenbacher 2002; Langenbacher and Dandelet 2005), it remains open. It may remain forever so, given that the historical window for such an analysis has probably closed. A study similar to Gibson's (2004) quasi-natural experiment of the effect of the South African Truth and Reconciliation Committee on tolerance is clearly no longer possible in Germany or Austria.

The lack of empirical evidence connecting views of the Nazi past to support for democracy in the cases that have been most extensively studied points to a larger issue in the field of collective memory studies: the lack of theorizing about, and testing of, memory's causal effects on politics. To a large extent, the (inter-disciplinary) literature on memory has developed outside the mainstream of political science. Much of it is imbued with psychoanalytic concepts that have fallen out of favor within the discipline. Much of it is normative rather than empirical. Much of it falls within the realm of cultural studies or sociology. These are not criticisms of these approaches, but the fact remains that despite a real-ization among political scientists that "memory matters" (Müller 2002, 1), there are few studies that treat ideas about history as an independent variable and link it to distinct political outcomes. There are some exceptions. In an edited volume titled *The Politics of Memory—Transitional Justice in Democratizing Societies*, the authors attempted to link the issue of remembering to long-term processes of democratization. The concrete focus of these country studies is on the actions of civil society organizations rather than political leadership (Barahona de Brito, Aguilar, and Gonzaléz-Enríquez 2001). By contrast, Consuelo Cruz (2000), in her study of political development in Nicaragua and Costa Rica, examined how polit-ical elites use their understandings of the past to construct a menu of possibilities for the future. Nancy Bermeo (1992) argued that consideration of the abuses of dictatorship can lead to political learning among elites and is a potentially impor-tant factor in restoring democracy. In drawing such "lessons" from the past, it is often the rejection of certain possibilities that are most striking and easiest to trace. For example, Art (2006) argued that the construction of a culture of con-trition in (western) Germany has rendered elites especially vigilant against radi-cal right political ideas and movements, and their actions largely explain the failure of such parties to consolidate themselves in the German party system. However, the lack of this "culture in contrition" in Austria and in eastern Germany (Art 2004) has allowed radical right parties to succeed there.

If the study of memory is still in its infancy within comparative politics, stu-dents of international relations have had relatively more to say. Postwar German foreign policy—particularly the willful embedding of German power within mul-tilateral institutions—has provided an excellent case study for those seeking to demonstrate the theoretical lacunae of realist or neoliberal paradigms (Banchoff 1999; Katzenstein 1997; Berger 1998; Markovits and Reich 1997). Constructivist scholarship in general, with its attention to the formation of state identity through mechanisms such as collective memory formation, has been more deeply engaged with the politics of history than other paradigms of international relations. It might also help explain a recent phenomenon that may become more important in the coming decade—the diffusion of the German model of confronting the past to the European Union.

The lack of empirical evidence
connecting views of the Nazi past
to support for democracy in the cases
that have been most extensively studied
points to a larger issue in the field
of collective memory studies: the lack of
theorizing about, and testing of, memory's
causal effects on politics.

Martha Finnemore and Kathryn Sikkink (1998) argued that international norms often begin their life as domestic norms that "norm entrepreneurs" carry to the global stage. Since memory can be an important component of how domestic norms are framed and foreign policy is legitimized, it cannot be disregarded as a factor in international relations. According to Finnemore and Sikkink, norms are more likely to become institutionalized internationally if they are promoted by successful states. It is thus possible that as Germans regained sovereignty, slowly faced up to their past, and simultaneously pushed forward the process of European integration, they succeeded in promoting their brand of memory in the European arena. There is evidence that an honest confrontation with national history is now an unwritten accession criterion for the European Union. Polish leaders, for example, took pains to stress that their memory work with respect to the massacres in Jedwabne signified Poland's status as a modern European state (Wüstenberg 2007). Turkey's failure to confront the genocide of Armenians has repeatedly been cited as a reason to deny EU membership (Leggewie 2006).

The 2000 Stockholm International Forum on the Holocaust could be regarded as the first significant attempt at institutionalizing European memory. State representatives and scholars came together to vow that racism and anti-Semitism would not be tolerated in a united Europe. The high-profile attendance of the conference (as long as cameras were rolling) suggests that European leaders indeed regard the Holocaust as a suitable basis for historical legitimation of national and supranational institutions. Immediately after the conference, fourteen member states of the European Union sanctioned the fifteenth, Austria, for including the radical right FPÖ in its new government. In so doing, the EU member states were symbolically establishing the commonality of values based on the Holocaust as the universal reference point for European self-understanding. The journalist Michael Jeismann (2000, 2001) has pointed out that the participants of the Stockholm Forum had concrete political reasons to support such an initiative. German chancellor Gerhard Schröder used the event to emphasize his commitment to Holocaust remembrance, which had been questioned due to his fickle support for the Berlin "Memorial to the Murdered Jews of Europe." Swedish premier Goran Persson had similar needs after Swedish neutrality during the war had been called into question. Both the French and the Belgians, facing significant radical right parties at home, sought to make clear to their own voters the consequences of such parties coming to power.

While most European societies
have recently debated the layered meanings
of memory between victim, perpetrator,
and bystander perspectives,
East Central Europeans must confront
a more complex past in which the
Holocaust and the war are seen
through the prism of more than
forty years of communist rule and the
experience of the Gulag and famine,
which were silenced for just as long.

In contrast to such instrumentalist interpretations, scholars such as Dan Diner (2000) have argued that the formation of a genuine European collective memory is under way. Aleida Assmann (2007) has recently adopted Diner's notion of the Holocaust as the negative foundational moment for Europe and has proposed a set of guidelines for the establishment of "Europe as a Community of Memory." On the other hand, historian Stefan Troebst (2006) contended that Europe—far from developing one collective memory—is divided into "zones of memory" associated with the Second World War that are almost incommensurable: they range from the strong memory of liberation and resistance in the West, to the trauma of aerial bombardments and the experience of German and Soviet occupation, all the way to the overwhelming dominance in the public psyche in the former Soviet Union of the Red Army victory. These varying views of the past not only emerge from different historical experiences but are also determined by various political and societal processes of transformation that have taken place since 1945 (Troebst 2006). Similarly, Lothar Probst (2003, 55) argued that political experiences continue to be "interpreted in terms of national history" and that "a European public . . . still does not exist." While most European societies have recently debated the layered meanings of memory between victim, perpetrator, and bystander perspectives, East Central Europeans must confront a more complex past in which the Holocaust and the war are seen through the prism of more than forty years of communist rule and the experience of the Gulag and famine, which were silenced for just as long. Thus, it would seem that constructing a unified European memory would require a remarkable shift in which national narratives that have been cultivated for decades are merged. Before this can become a reality, we believe, European leaders must make a concerted effort to build a joint usable past. In other words, the formation of a collective European memory will require well-organized norm entrepreneurs backed by "hard interests." The German experience may provide an indication as to how this can be accomplished.

Conclusion

As the European reaction to Austria's new government indicates, an institutionalized "Euro-memory" would probably not be without its taboos; nor would it no longer be used by politicians to legitimize both national and European policy. However, the instrumental usage of memory does not preclude its serving a higher moral purpose; in fact, morality supported by "hard" interests may well be more sustainable. In Germany, the fact that the continuous confrontation with the Nazi past has become not only a societal imperative but also a *raison d'état* arguably makes an honest reckoning with history less subject to the political vagaries of the day. It is very difficult to imagine, for example, a contemporary German chancellor using a trip to Poland or Israel to signal a change in German foreign policy or its relationship to the Nazi past. When Kohl attempted to do just that in 1984 by noting, in Israel, that Germans of his generation had been graced by the "mercy of late birth" and were therefore free of the burden of the Nazi past, he produced a countermobilization that only strengthened the German culture of contrition. This culture has proven to be remarkably resilient; even recent debates about German suffering have not displaced memory of the Holocaust as the hegemonic force in Germany's memory landscape (Langenbacher 2005). It is indisputable that there has been a routinization of Holocaust memory, and that many politicians adhere to an accepted narrative of the Nazi past only because not doing so would cost them their jobs. Yet if one believes that certain "gag rules" enable liberal democracy in general (Holmes 1995), and that proscriptions on historical revisionism are an extension of Germany's particular form of "militant" democracy, the triumph of a certain interpretation of the Nazi past over its competitors has been an extraordinary normative achievement.

Does the German experience represent a form of "best practice" in the process of coming to terms with a traumatic past, one that deserves to be emulated by the EU and others? In posing the question, we should not forget that a right-wing party (the NPD) is currently represented in two German state parliaments, that prominent German politicians have warned nonwhite foreigners that certain areas are no-go zones, and that police still protect synagogues and Holocaust memorials from neo-Nazis. Nor should we ignore the fact that German narratives of the Nazi past in the early postwar period emphasized German victimization and suffering rather than complicity and contrition. Yet the fact that *only* militant extremists diverge from the consensus view on the Nazi past, and that their strength is concentrated in the former GDR, is significant. Most observers agree that Germany is remarkable precisely because of the relative weakness of such far-right political forces and for the prominent role that memory plays in government and culture. Germany has established a culture of continuous debate that is highly self-critical, rejects nationalism, and is founded on careful historiographical scholarship. Transferred to the European level, this suggests that as European elites come to believe that they are in need of a common (usable) past, it will become more likely that a unifying European memory culture will emerge. Using Germany as a model would mean establishing an open and empathetic European dialogue in which "national histories [are seen] from a transnational perspective" and "external national borders [transformed] into internal European ones" (Assmann 2007, 22). Such a common memory, however, would also require the existence of a European civil society that guards against racism and anti-Semitism and keeps states and European institutions "honest." As we have seen in the German case, elites and governments should never be entrusted with history politics alone—a "successful" memory culture thrives only with citizen engagement. Thus, the diffusion of the German model may at present be taking place mainly in the minds of academics and policy makers, rather than "on the ground." Yet given the three case studies and the newer developments that we discussed here, its institutionalization in other societies and at the transnational level is certainly a realistic prospect.

References

Ahonen, Pertti. 2003. *After the expulsion: West Germany and Eastern Europe 1945-1990*. Oxford: Oxford University Press.

Art, David. 2004. The wild, wild east: Why the DVU does not matter and the NPD does. *German Politics and Society* 22 (4): 124-33.

———. 2006. *The politics of the Nazi past in Germany and Austria*. New York: Cambridge University Press.

Assmann, Aleida. 2007. Europe as a community of memory? Twentieth annual lecture at the German Historical Institute, Washington, D.C. 16 November 2006. *GHI Bulletin* 40:11-25.

Assmann, Aleida, and Ute Frevert. 1999. *Geschichtsvergessenheit—Geschichtsversessenheit. Vom Umgang mit deutschen Vergangenheiten nach 1945*. Stuttgart, Germany: Deutsche Verlags-Anstalt.

Banchoff, Thomas. 1999. *The German problem transformed*. Ann Arbor: University of Michigan Press.

Barahona de Brito, Alexandra, Paloma Aguilar, and Carmen Gonzaléz-Enríquez, eds. 2001. *The politics of memory—Transitional justice in democratizing societies*. Oxford: Oxford University Press.

Berger, Thomas. 1998. *Cultures of antimilitarism*. Baltimore: Johns Hopkins University Press.

Bermeo, Nancy. 1992. Democracy and the lessons of dictatorship. *Comparative Politics* 24 (3): 273-91.

Böge, Volker, ed. 2004. *Geschichtswerkstätten gestern—heute—morgen. Bewegung! Stillstand. Aufbruch?* München, Germany: Dölling und Galitz Verlag.

Bukey, Evan Burr. 2000. *Hitler's Austria: Popular sentiment in the Nazi era*. Chapel Hill: University of North Carolina Press.

Confino, Alon. 2006. *Germany as a culture of remembrance*. Chapel Hill: University of North Carolina Press.

Cruz, Consuelo. 2000. Identity and persuasion: How nations remember their pasts and make their futures. *World Politics* 52 (3): 275-312.

Diner, Dan. 2000. Haider und der Schutzreflex Europas. Österreichs neue Regierung stört den wachsenden europäischen Gemeinsinn. *Die Welt*, February 26.

Finnemore, Martha, and Kathryn Sikkink. 1998. International norm dynamics and political change. *International Organization* 52 (4): 887-917.

Frei, Norbert. 1997. *Vergangenheitspolitik—Die Anfänge der Bundesrepublik und die NS-Vergangenheit*. München, Germany: C.H. Beck Verlag.

———. 2005. *1945 und Wir—Das Dritte Reich im Bewusstsein der Deutschen*. München, Germany: C.H. Beck Verlag.

Garton Ash, Timothy. 2007. The Stasi on our minds. *New York Review of Books*, May 31.

Gibson, James. 2004. *Overcoming apartheid: Can truth reconcile a divided nation?* New York: Russell Sage Foundation.

Goldhagen, Daniel. 1996. *Hitler's willing executioners*. New York: Knopf.

Herf, Jeffrey. 1997. *Divided memory—The Nazi past in the two Germanys*. Cambridge, MA: Harvard University Press.

Holmes, Stephen. 1995. *Passions and constraints: On the theory of liberal democracy*. Chicago: University of Chicago Press.

Jeismann, Michael. 2000. Das Seelenbündnis. Der Schwur von Stockholm und der Fall Haider. *Frankfurter Allgemeine Zeitung*, February 14.

———. 2001. *Auf Wiedersehen Gestern—Die deutsche Vergangenheit und die Politik von morgen*. Stuttgart, Germany: Deutsche Verlags-Anstalt.

Judt, Tony. 1992. The past is another country: Myth and memory in postwar Europe. *Daedalus* 121 (4): 83-118.

Kansteiner, Wulf. 2006. Losing the war, winning the memory battle: The legacy of Nazism, World War II and the Holocaust in the Federal Republic of Germany. In *The politics of memory in postwar Europe*, ed. R. N. Lebow, W. Kansteiner, and C. Fogu. Durham, NC: Duke University Press.

Katzenstein, Peter, ed. 1997. *Tamed power*. Ithaca, NY: Cornell University Press.

Knight, Robert. 1988. *"Ich bin dafür, die Sache in die Länge zu ziehen": die Wortprotokolle der österreichischen Bundesregierung von 1945 bis 1952 über die Entschädigung der Juden*. Frankfurt am Main, Germany: Athenäum.

Langenbacher, Eric. 2002. Memory regimes in contemporary Germany. Ph.D. diss., Georgetown University, Washington, DC.

———. 2005. Moralpolitik versus moralpolitik: Recent struggles over the construction of cultural memory in Germany. *German Politics and Society* 23 (3): 106-34.

Langenbacher, Eric, and Kyle Dandelet. 2005. Collective memory and democratization in Germany, Argentina and Chile. Paper prepared for the American Political Science Association annual meeting, August, Washington, DC.

Leggewie, Claus. 2006. Equally criminal? Totalitarian experience and European memory. *Eurozine*, June 1. http://www.eurozine.com.

Levy, Daniel, and Julian Dierkes. 2002. Institutionalizing the past: Shifting memories of nationhood in German education and immigration legislation. In *Memory and power in postwar Europe*, ed. Jan-Werner Müller. New York: Cambridge University Press.

Lübbe, Hermann. 1983. Der Nationalsozialismus im politischen Bewußtsein der Gegenwart. In *Deutschlands Weg in die Diktatur: Internationale Konferenz zur nationalsozialistischen Machtübernahme im Reichstagsgebäude zu Berlin*, ed. Martin Broszat. Berlin: Siedler Verlag.

Markovits, Andrei S., and Simon Reich. 1997. *The German predicament*. Ithaca, NY: Cornell University Press.

Mitten, Richard. 1992. *The politics of anti-Semitic prejudice: The Waldheim affair in Austria*. Boulder, CO: Westview.

Moeller, Robert G. 2001. *War stories—The search for a usable past in the Federal Republic of Germany*. Berkeley: University of California Press.

Müller, Jan. 2002. *Memory and power in postwar Europe*. New York: Cambridge University Press.

Nino, Carl. 1998. *Radical evil on trial*. New Haven, CT: Yale University Press.

Pauley, Bruce. 1981. *Hitler and the forgotten Nazis: A history of Austrian National Socialism*. Chapel Hill: University of North Carolina Press.

Pelinka, Anton, and Erika Weinzerl, eds. 1987. *Das Grosse Tabu: Österreichs Umgang mit seiner Vergangenheit*. Vienna, Austria: Edition S.

Probst, Lothar. 2003. Founding myths in Europe and the role of the Holocaust. *New German Critique* 90 (Autumn): 45-58.

Reichel, Peter. 2001. *Vergangenheitsbewältigung in Deutschland—Die Auseinandersetzung mit der NS-Diktatur von 1945 bis heute*. München, Germany: C.H. Beck Verlag.

Sa'adah, Anne. 1998. *Germany's second chance: Truth, justice and democratization*. Cambridge, MA: Harvard University Press.

Schulze, Rainer, ed. 2001. *Zwischen Heimat und Zuhause—Deutsche Flüchtlinge und Vertriebene in (West-)Deutschland 1945-2000*. Osnabrück, Austria: secolo Verlag.

Troebst, Stefan. 2006. Holocaust-Erinnerung und GULag-Gedächtnis: Memorialkonflikte im erweiterten Europa. Paper presented at the Zweite Sommeruniversität der Gedenkstätte Ravensbrück "Europäische Gedächtniskulturen," August 21-25, Berlin.

Uhl, Heidemarie. 1992. *Zwischen Versöhnung und Verstörung*. Vienna, Austria: Böhlau.

Wasserman, Heinz. 2000. *Zuviel Geschichte tut nicht gut!* Vienna, Austria: Studien Verlag.

Winter, Jay. 2000. The generation of memory: Reflections on the "memory boom" in contemporary historical studies. *Bulletin of the German Historical Institute* 27 (Fall): 69-92.

Wodak, Ruth, Peter Nowak, Johanna Pelikan, Helmut Gruber, Rudolf de Cillia, and Richard Mitten. 1999. *Wir sind alle unschuldige Täter!* Frankfurt am Main, Germany: Suhrkamp.

Wolfgram, Mark. 2007. The processes of collective memory research. *German Politics and Society* 25 (1): 102-13.

Wüstenberg, Jenny. 2007. Towards a new kind of legitimacy? Jan Gross's neighbors and Poland's reckoning with the past. *Central European University Political Science Journal—The Graduate Student Review* 2 (2): 152-74.

Through a Glass Darkly: Consequences of a Politicized Past in Contemporary Turkey

By
FATMA MÜGE GÖÇEK

The resolution of the three major political problems faced by the contemporary Turkish nation-state—namely, the massacres of the Armenians in the past, the treatment of the Kurds at present, and the contested partition of the island of Cyprus—has become increasingly urgent as these problems have started to impede Turkey's chances of joining the European Union and also of becoming more democratic. Yet, since the Turkish nation-state commences its own official historical narrative with either the Independence Struggle in 1919 or the subsequent establishment of the Republic of Turkey in 1923, it subsequently approaches these "Armenian, Kurdish, and Cyprus issues" as totally disparate and mutually independent, and in an ahistorical manner, resulting in increased entrenchment of the conflicts. The article argues that challenging the temporal boundaries of this Turkish official narrative by delving into its "prehistory," namely, the period preceding 1919 or 1923, reveals not only the common origin of all of these issues but also a possible peaceful solution to them all as well as for a more democratic Turkey.

Keywords: contemporary Turkey; Turkish Republic; Armenian issue; Kurdish issue; island of Cyprus; European Union; official narrative

In the contemporary era, when political legitimacy is predicated not on the unreachable sacredness of divine law but rather the precarious profanity of its human-made version, the nation-states' search for both sites of legitimacy and their control has become increasingly significant for their survival. The inherent political potential of alternate narratives of history to

Fatma Müge Göçek was born and raised in Istanbul, Turkey. She received her PhD from Princeton University before becoming a faculty member in the Sociology Department at the University of Michigan. She is the author of East Encounters West: France and the Ottoman Empire in the 18th Century *(Oxford University Press, 1988) and* Rise of the Bourgeoisie, Demise of Empire: Ottoman Westernization and Social Change *(Oxford University Press, 1996), and she is currently working on a book tentatively titled* Deciphering Denial: Turkish State and the Armenian Ethnic Cleansing of 1915.

DOI: 10.1177/0002716208314803

undermine the current status quo turns the past into such a site. It is therefore no accident that nation-states systematically develop their own official narratives of history in an attempt to sustain their present rule through the control of the past. I argue here that the subsequent political contestation over history makes the verse from the King James Bible (1 *Corinthians* 13:12) alluded to in the title of this article especially fitting in the case of contemporary Turkey. I hope to show in this article that the Turkish nation-state has created an imperfect and faulty perception of historical reality and in so doing has impeded its chances of becoming a truly participatory democracy.

This political contestation of the past is best exemplified by the three major political problems currently faced by the Turkish nation-state, namely, the past massacres of Armenians, the treatment of Kurds at present, and the contested partition of the island of Cyprus. The resolution of these problems has become increasingly urgent as they have started to impede Turkey's chances of joining the European Union (EU) and becoming more democratic. I demonstrate that the Turkish nation-state, acting within the temporal boundaries of its own official historical narrative that commences with either the Independence Struggle in 1919 or the subsequent establishment of the Republic of Turkey in 1923, currently presents and approaches these Armenian, Kurdish, and Cyprus issues as though they are totally disparate and mutually independent. In so doing, I argue that this tactic fails to make any significant progress in resolving any of them, and instead ends up getting increasingly more entrenched and embroiled in the ensuing conflicts. My contention here is that challenging the temporal boundaries of this Turkish official narrative by delving into what it considers "prehistory," that is, the period preceding 1919 or 1923, reveals not only the common origin of these issues, but also a possible peaceful solution to them that may advance a more democratic Turkey.

I proceed here by first discussing how the Turkish nation-state's official narrative currently presents the three major historical Armenian, Kurdish, and Cyprus issues as "fragments reflected through a glass darkly," that is, as totally disparate problems. The Turkish nation-state severely curtails the search for possible peaceful solutions to these issues through public discussion by its quick, easy, and successful deployment of the articles in the Turkish Penal Code that rebuke such discussion on the grounds that it may pose possible "insults to Turkishness." As a consequence, the Armenian, Kurdish, and Cyprus issues become more deeply entrenched, turning their successful resolution into a virtual impossibility. I then challenge the narrative control of the Turkish nation-state over the past by redrawing its temporal boundaries to demonstrate how these three major political issues were intimately connected to one another: all emerged simultaneously during the earlier struggles of the Ottoman Empire with political modernity. Specifically, it was the initial failure of the Ottoman state to provide equal rights to all its imperial subjects that generated both its demise and the subsequent "imperial legacy" of the Armenian, Kurdish, and Cyprus problems.

As the successor to the Ottoman Empire, the Turkish nation-state has been unwilling to acknowledge this historical precedence; it has treated these problems ahistorically, as discrete and disparate, and as a consequence, obfuscated and silenced the common factor responsible for producing them all, namely, the state's failure to provide equal political rights to all its constituents. In establishing a homeland for its future citizens, the Turkish nation-state placed its own preservation before all else and legitimated its political rule by predicating it on the dominance of the ethnic Turkish Sunni majority at the expense of the rest. These two measures led to the effective curtailment of the political rights of its citizens, a state of affairs that is empirically best documented through the persistent presence of Turkish penal articles such as the current Article 301 that punishes those who "insult Turkishness." These articles limit the freedom of expression of individual citizens since they are deployed, unlike similar legal articles in Western countries, repeatedly to successful ends (İdiz 2006). Their frequent employment is necessary to help defend and sustain the fragile political boundaries of Turkish nation-state legitimacy predicated on the dominance of the ethnic Turkish Sunni majority.

To reach a peaceful resolution to these three major political problems of "imperial legacy," the Turkish nation-state has to first and foremost officially recognize its historical failure to respect the equal political rights of all its citizens, a failure that I here contend not only lies at the roots of these problems, but the identification of which potentially makes peaceful resolutions possible. Hence, what the Turkish nation-state needs to undertake before all else is a reassessment of its priorities; it needs to respect its citizens' rights to acquire the political capacity to resolve its current domestic and international political problems and, in so doing, become more democratic.

Current Nation-State Narrative on Turkey's Major Political Problems

Even though the Armenian, Kurdish, and Cyprus problems have been present since the establishment of the Turkish Republic, the possibility of Turkey's European Union membership has made both their significance as well as their successful resolution more acute. Even though the EU has indeed become more influential in restructuring Turkish politics in line with this possibility, it has recently started to face increasing local resistance on the grounds that its perceived intent is the disintegration of the Turkish nation-state (Williams and Associates 2006).[1] Indeed, the only theme that connects these three problems in the current Turkish official narrative is that they were initially produced by the West to fragment the Turkish nation-state, just as the West had once attempted to break up the Ottoman Empire. This interpretation is referred to in literature (Kirişçi and Çarkoğlu 2003) as the "the Sèvres syndrome," named after the international treaty that provided for the partition of the territories of the Ottoman Empire among the European Powers after the First World War. The fear of loss of territory and the fear of abandonment not only became prominent themes in the

Ottoman Empire but also persisted into the Turkish nation-state and still influence the premise of its official narrative. As the Sèvres syndrome further
envelops the three major problems in the paralyzing emotion of fear, it renders
their possible resolution even more difficult.

Among the three issues, the Kurdish problem dominates the other two in
duration and significance: unlike the Armenians and the Greeks, the Kurds still
live in Turkey and comprise a significant portion—approximated at 20 percent—
of its population (McDowall 1997, 3).[2] In addition, the U.S. engagement in Iraq,
which has destabilized the region and led to the formulation of a more independent Kurdistan in northern Iraq, has made the problem more challenging by
generating the possibility of Turkey's incursion into Iraq. So I shall start the discussion with the Kurdish issue.

The Kurdish Problem

Turkey's Kurdish problem is currently defined outside of Turkey as the
oppression and denial of rights by a majority group (the Turks) of an ethnic
minority (the Kurds), leading to the interpretation of the civil war in southeastern Turkey that raged between 1984 and 1999 as a national liberation movement
(Cornell 2001). In official Turkish discourse, however, there is no mention of the
Kurdish problem or the civil war, but rather a socioeconomic issue in the southeastern region of the country and a problem of induced terrorism and violence
dependent on external support from foreign states that aim to weaken Turkey.
Hence, the Turkish nation-state insists on identifying the region through its geographical parameters as it interprets the employment of the term "Kurdistan" as
an endorsement of secession. The Kurdish organization that spearheads the
movement, namely, the Kurdish Workers' Party, better known as PKK (Parti
Karkaren Kurdistan), is referred to by the Turkish nation-state as a "terrorist
organization" and its members as "terrorists," terminology that acts as a litmus
test to identify those who are Turkish patriots and their supporters. Turkey has
also successfully campaigned for decades to have the PKK internationally
declared a terrorist organization. Still, the international media are careful to refer
to them as "Kurdish rebels." These alternate attributions do not change the fact
that what erupted during 1984 and 1999 in southeastern Turkey between the
Kurds and the Turkish state left at its wake at least seventy thousand casualties,
with Turkey officially declaring thirty-seven thousand people killed and the PKK
leader Abdullah Öcalan attesting that at least twenty-five thousand Kurds were
killed (Daloğlu 2007).

The term "Kurdish" applies to speakers of one of four closely related Indo-
Iranian languages (Kurmanji, Sorani, Zaza, and Gurani) or descendants of people
so identified who speak other languages (McDowall 2000, 9-10). Even though
the exact number of people within Turkey who satisfy this criterion is unknown,
scholars have argued (Kirişçi and Winrow 1997) that in the early 1990s roughly

13 percent of the total population in Turkey was Kurdish (van Bruinessen 1992, 15). If the Turkish-speaking descendants of Kurds are also included, however, the total number of Kurds in Turkey would certainly be much higher, probably reaching a quarter of Turkey's present population. The Kurds are located mainly in contiguous territory within the borders of Turkey, Iraq, and Iran with smaller indigenous populations in Syria and Armenia; the Kurds' stateless existence across many nation-states further complicates their condition. Data from the 1993 Turkish Demographic and Health Survey (TDHS) demonstrate that the Kurdish population in Turkey is relatively much worse off in terms of economic and political capital invested by the state than the Turkish population as a whole (İçduygu and Sirkeci 1999). Within Turkey, over the past two decades, millions of Kurds who were forced by the state to evacuate their villages for posing a security threat have settled as migrants in the cities of western Turkey; large numbers have also left for Western Europe, primarily Germany.

[T]he Turkish nation-state insists on identifying [southeastern Turkey] through its geographical parameters as it interprets the employment of the term "Kurdistan" as an endorsement of secession.

This forced internal Kurdish migration of the past two decades has affected the nature of the political engagement between the Kurds and the Turkish state (Kocher 2002). The PKK, a militant organization established in 1978 with the aim of creating an independent, Marxist-Leninist, Kurdish state in the region, was initially successful because of the suitability of the southeast to guerrilla warfare. However, the organization lost its efficacy as the vast internal migration induced by the Turkish state fundamentally altered the Kurdish demography, making it impossible for the PKK to rekindle the insurgency warfare, which was a rural phenomenon, in the new urban spaces. The PKK splintered from urban Turkish Marxist-Leninist youth groups that engaged in political violence in the mid-1970s and as such initially largely crosscut the Turkish-Kurdish divide. Yet, it also incurred criticism from the Kurds by attacking landlords and rightists in the Siverek region in the late 1970s (Kocher 2002).

Political unrest in Turkey's Kurdish-dominated areas in the southeast was almost simultaneous with the establishment of the Turkish Republic; the Sheikh

Said Rebellion in 1925 was a reaction to the increasingly secular and Turkish character of the emerging Turkish state and attempted to bring back the Caliphate. This rebellion combining nationalist and religious elements was followed by others in Ağrı in 1930 and Dersim (Tunceli) in 1937. Yet, the harsh reaction of the Turkish state demonstrated its turn toward authoritarianism, especially in defining the nation as homogeneous predicated on ethnic unity. This violent suppression was accompanied by the disappearance of the word "Kurd" from the lexicon, the ban of the Kurdish language, the replacement of the names of Kurdish villages and towns with Turkish ones, and the denial of the right of parents to give Kurdish names to their children (Barkey 2000). While some Kurds did assimilate and became Turkish, many others refused or became silent. Following Atatürk's death in 1938, the regime further deteriorated during single-party rule in terms of sustaining democratic elements.

Even though the Kurdish rebellions before World War II had a strong tribal and religious character rather than a national one, this pattern underwent significant change after Turkey held its first multiparty election in 1946. Later, during the 1970s, the continuing migration to the urban areas in western Turkey as well as the increased enrollment in higher education had escalated public awareness of the economic and political disparities between the southeast and the rest of Turkey, subsequently radicalizing state-society relations. Even though the Kurds were initially absorbed into the leftist movements predominant among the students in Turkish universities, they gradually formed separate political movements. Ultimately the PKK emerged on one side and a more traditionally nationalistic wing identified closely with Mustafa Barzani's Kurdistan Democratic Party on the other. The right-wing Kurdish nationalists nevertheless failed to prevail as internal tribal divisions among them weakened their strength and appeal, and their leaders, who were forced into exile after the 1971 military intervention, were eventually assassinated in northern Iraq (Cornell 2001, 38).

The PKK had initially described traditional Kurdistan as being under colonial rule where tribal leaders and the local bourgeoisie colluded to help the Turkish state exploit the lower classes and, therefore, identified Kurdish tribal society as a main target of its revolutionary struggle. Yet, the PKK also could not stay out of tribal politics as it had to negotiate with tribal leaders. This inconsistency and the subsequent violence the PKK employed against those it aimed to liberate disillusioned many Kurds and sapped its support. For instance, in the PKK's heyday in 1992, a poll reported by the Turkish *Milliyet* newspaper on September 6, 1992, conducted in the southeast showed that only 29 percent of the population viewed the PKK as the best representative of the Kurdish people. The PKK subsequently attempted to bolster its support and the ranks of its members by toning down its Marxist rhetoric and instead emphasizing Kurdish nationalism (Cornell 2001, 39).

The 1980 military coup inflicted heavy damage on the PKK by causing a small number of activists, including the leader Abdullah Öcalan and others, to flee Turkey for Syria and the Beka'a Valley of northern Lebanon. Still, as the Turkish army violently repressed all other leftist and Kurdish movements within the

country, the PKK, which managed to survive by leaving Turkey, ended up emerging as the only credible Kurdish challenger to the state. The impact of the 1980
coup on Turkey has been so strong that some scholars (Jacoby 2005) argue that
two separate regimes came into being: autocratic militarism in the eastern
provinces and semiauthoritarian incorporation in the west of the country. Some
scholars have argued (Ataman 2002) that the 1980s also witnessed the transformation in the ethnic policy of the state from the early Republican policy, which
accepted every citizen of Turkey as "Turks" while denying the existence of all
Muslim ethnic groups, to one that accepted the existence of Muslim ethnic
groups such as Kurds as well as that of non-Muslims. However, this transformation was not enduring.

The origins of the 1984 to 1999 civil war can also be traced to the subsequent
expulsion of the PKK leadership from Turkey in the aftermath of this 1980 military coup. The civil war began as a series of cross-border raids staged from northern Iraq (İmset 1992, 38-41). After a few tactically disastrous attacks against the
Turkish army, the PKK adopted a strategy of targeting civilians perceived as an
actual or potential collaborator with the state (including mayors, schoolteachers,
and tribal chiefs), eventually managing to sustain its hold over rural areas,
although not towns or urban centers (Barkey and Fuller 1998, 28-29; İmset 1992,
34-35, 44, 100). The strategy the PKK employed seemed to conform closely to
the classic Maoist principles of an "insurgency" that does not target the state's
military forces, but rather focuses on creating a general climate of insecurity and
lack of public confidence by reducing contact between the population and its
government. Also, the PKK is known to have engaged in kidnapping as a tool of
recruitment, and Kurdish families have had to pay revolutionary surcharges to
the PKK of approximately $2,500 if they permitted their sons to be drafted to the
Turkish military for their mandatory service (İmset 1992, 84-86; Rosenberg 1994).

The Turkish state countered by adopting counterinsurgency tactics (İmset
1992, 100). One rural defense tactic entailed recruiting tribesmen into a local
militia known as "village guards" (korucu). The other tactic involved forcing civilians to "evacuate" their villages, thereby aiming to disrupt guerrilla logistics by
physically removing the population. As of 1999 when the civil war finally ended,
according to Turkish government estimates, 3,236 settlements had been cleared
in southeastern Turkey, forcibly displacing 362,915 persons (U.S. Department of
State 2000, 18). In the process, not only were the Kurdish villages often
destroyed by fire to deny their use as bases by guerrillas and to prevent the return
of residents, but the evacuations were also brutally executed with beatings, rapes,
and selective instances of extrajudicial killing (Ron 1995). In addition, in the early
to mid-1990s, several members of Kurdish parties were gunned down in "mys-
tery killings," presumably committed by government-supported contra-guerrillas
(Kocher 2002, 6).

With the commencement of the military operations in 1984, the Turkish state
and the PKK became identified as the two sides between which one had to
choose (Cornell 2001, 39). From then on, the Turkish nation-state insisted on
equating virtually all expressions of Kurdish identity with PKK terrorism, and the

Turkish military in particular was adamant about pursuing solely an armed solution to the Kurdish problem. Within this polarized environment, the PKK generated resources with the support of Kurds in exile, primarily in Western Europe, the narcotics trade in the region, and the indirect and direct support from states like Syria that had an interest in weakening Turkey. Even though Turkey's economic development program for southeastern Anatolia inaugurated in the 1980s planned to use water from the Euphrates and Tigris Rivers to irrigate large tracts of the arid region, the Turkish nation-state faltered as it failed to acknowledge and respect Kurdish identity; did not consider unarmed solutions, engaging instead in extralegal activities such as drug trafficking and terrorism to curb the reach of the PKK; and, in the process, became further alienated from the local populace through its indiscriminate repression and violence (Radu 2001).

The Gulf War initially proved beneficial to the Kurds of Turkey as the coalition against Iraq and Operation Provide Comfort removed northern Iraq from the control of the Iraqi state and also created a U.S.-backed Kurdish Federated State. In an attempt to keep the PKK out of the area, the Turkish state undertook an active role in working out the power-sharing agreement in this federated state between Barzani's Kurdistan Democratic Party (KDP) and Celal Talabani's Patriotic Union of Kurdistan (PUK). Yet, the conflicts between the KDP and PUK instead fostered the growth of the PKK, which based its operations there, wresting by 1994 large chunks of territory away from the control of the Turkish military. The subsequent change in the tactics of the Turkish state by the middle of the 1990s, with the introduction of better health care and education for the local population, adaptation to guerrilla warfare, and the large population deportation of the Kurds from the region to urban centers elsewhere in the country, sapped the PKK's control, with the result that by 1998 Syria remained the PKK's only remaining supporter. The Turkish state then exploited its alliance with Israel to threaten Syria with war unless it expelled Öcalan and the PKK bases in the Beka'a Valley. Damascus complied by expelling Öcalan in October 1998, and he was later captured and delivered to the Turks; the PKK forces that were relocated from Syria to northern Iraq were likewise delivered a severe blow by the Turkish military in 1999, effectively ending the civil war (Radu 2001; Cornell 2001).

Even though many scholars conjecture that the joint activities of the Turkish state and the PKK radicalized and polarized the local population (McDowall 2000), ethnic mobilization and assimilation often occurred simultaneously. The institutions of nation building, principally conscription and universal education, are still in place; most Kurds state that if teaching Kurdish culture became a realistic option, they would teach their children Turkish culture for opportunity and Kurdish culture for identity (Kocher 2002, 11). Since the capture of Abdullah Öcalan in February 1999, a new political movement has begun to emerge in Turkey, favoring electoral competition and noninstitutional pressure tactics over violence. The recent July 2007 election to the Turkish parliament of Kurdish deputies as independents as well as the presence among the ranks of the reigning Justice and Development Party of other deputies of Kurdish origin have further bolstered this movement. That most Kurds never favored secession and most still do not favor it, opting instead for a stable multiethnic solution, renders any political solution based on autonomy or federalism obsolete and impractical (Göktaş 2007).

That most Kurds never favored secession and most still do not favor it, opting instead for a stable multiethnic solution, renders any political solution based on autonomy or federalism obsolete and impractical.

Two observed patterns therefore become significant in determining the future course of Kurdish-Turkish relations, one entailing the divergence in perception between the Turkish state and society and the other the altered political contours of the region. First, interestingly enough, despite almost two decades of armed conflict instigated by the Turkish nation-state and the subsequent casualties, the boundaries between the Kurds and the Turks within society have historically been porous and crosscut by key religious cleavages, with about 30 percent of the Anatolian Muslims being historically and doctrinally related to Shi'ism, with Alevis as the largest group. A significant portion of Turkey's current political and business elite is also of Kurdish origin (Cornell 2001). In addition, not only has the strong tendency to marry within one's own ethnic group decreased significantly between the early 1960s and the late 1990s, but the intermarriage rate between Kurds and Turks has also increased significantly (Gündüz-Hoşgör and Smits 2002). As the two communities remain accommodating to each other and societal-level tensions remain manageable, the Kurds in Turkey would in the future probably remain bilingual and integrate into mainstream political life where the majority of the Kurds would vote for rightist and Islamist parties (Kocher 2002). The participation in national and local politics has also provided the movement with a new institutional basis for public gathering, legal protection from prosecution, new access to domestic and international audiences, and new symbolic resources (Watts 2006).

There are also no political grounds for a return in the future to generalized violence between the Turks and the Kurds unless it was purposefully instigated by the Turkish military to maintain the status quo. In addition, Kurds in Turkey still face discrimination, as there is no overt public acknowledgement, recognition, or respect of their ethnicity. Even though compulsory education, mandatory military service, and state-controlled radio and press have enabled the Turkish Republic to create a unified monolithic national culture as well as economic opportunity structures that in general increased the participation of all social groups in and commitment to the system, the participants would only have access to the resources generated by the state by foregoing their ethnic non-Turkish identity (Cornell 2001). The institution that is most significant in maintaining and reproducing this public discrimination is the Turkish military, which very fastidiously upholds the official stand of ethnic homogeneity to ensure there is not a single high-ranking Kurdish—or Armenian or any member of a minority group—officer who is officially recognized as such. On the contrary, it is rumored that the military strictly investigates the files of all future officers with the intent to weed out such "impure" individuals. The same uncompromising stand also translates into practice as the current chairman of the Joint Chiefs of Staff of the Turkish military, General Yaşar Büyükanıt, declares that there is no difference between the "Kurdish terrorists" and those who provide them with shelter. The Turkish army has also long opposed any easing of its strict legislation governing terrorism, freedom of expression, and cultural rights, and has done so by justifying its position with the argument that reform would imply concessions to terrorists (Zengin 2007). The Turkish state thus still refuses to recognize the cultural identity of its Kurdish citizens by prohibiting the teaching of Kurdish in schools and the full unlimited broadcasting of Kurdish radio and television programs, especially in their ancestral region in the southeast where they predominate (Ergil 2000). The Turkish nation-state's ensuing single-minded focus on a military response to the PKK continually polarizes identity and opinion, turning peaceful civilians into militants (Kocher 2002).

The impact of the Iraq war on Turkey points to the struggle between the EU pressures to improve the rights of Kurds and the state's reluctance to implement such democratic reforms because of increased insecurity as well as the imagined threat of greater Kurdish autonomy. Still, the recent attitude of the ruling Justice and Development Party toward Iraq signals the future possibility of a more pragmatic approach leading to either the de-securitization of the Kurdish issue by the civil authorities or its resecuritization by the military (Tarık 2005). The crucial underlying issue is nevertheless putting into practice the existing legislation. Previously, Turkey's main problem stemmed not from the legislation itself, but from a state bureaucracy that was either unable or unwilling to implement reforms. Even though the growth of the public sphere and civil associations in Turkey are positive indicators of democratization and economic development, the current engagement of the Turkish state and especially the military in northern Iraq very conveniently curbs these positive transformations. It is particularly the "national security" or "Sèvres" syndrome in Turkey that modulates the pendulum swing between security and liberalization to reveal that in relation to the PKK, the Turkish nation-state has difficulties designing postterror policies, while the PKK appears unprepared to fully disarm and give up, which leaves political struggle as the only option (Aydınlı 2002).

The Cyprus Problem

The most significant historical event in creating the Cyprus problem in Republican history was the 1974 invasion of the northern tip of the island of Cyprus by the Turkish military. Cyprus had initially become politically independent in 1960 when the negotiations among the Greek-Cypriot and Turkish-Cypriot communities with Great Britain, Greece, and Turkey as "guarantor powers" led to the formulation of a constitution. The ensuing single, ethnically mixed, bicommunal Republic of Cyprus had equal representation between the minority Turkish-speaking Muslim community (20 percent) and the Greek-speaking Orthodox Christian one (80 percent) (Bahcheli 2000, 205). Yet by the end of 1963, interethnic violence led to the collapse of this bicommunal political construct; the Turkish-Cypriot community subsequently withdrew from the government to set up its own political structure. Even though the United Nations Security Council intervened the following year to stop the continuing violence, the coup by the Greek government a decade later in 1974, which effectively removed the president of the Republic of Cyprus, led to the Turkish invasion of the northern part of the island. The Turkish nation-state justified the invasion by stating that it was acting in its capacity as one of the guarantor powers of the 1960 arrangement (Moulakis 2007, 538). From then, relations with Greece remained tense as the 1976 and 1987 crises over the Aegean continental shelf and the 1996 crisis over the Imia islets in the Aegean Sea occurred, highlighting the contested boundaries of the two nation-states.

Meanwhile, while Greece signed the EU Association Agreement in 1961 and Turkey in 1963, Greece became an EU member in 1981 while Turkey could only become a candidate in 1999. The lack of further progress after 1970 for Turkey's accession into the EU was partly a result of the economic and political crises that led to disruptions in the democratic system by the military in 1960, 1971, and 1980. The import-substitution strategy of the 1960s and the 1970s caused overdependence on imports and foreign borrowing. After the oil crises of 1974 and 1979, Turkish governments also faced severe foreign exchange shortages, leading to precautionary rationing of some essentials (Öniş and Webb 1992). Such economic pressure had transformed ideological radicalism into day-to-day violence. With the collapse of the Soviet Union and the end of the cold war, the EU once again put possible negotiations with Turkey on the back burner. The prospects for Turkish membership were so weak that the 2000 summit held in Nice did not even hypothetically provide for the number of future Turkish votes or members of the European Parliament (Pahre and Uçaray 2005).

The Greek-Cypriot-led Republic of Cyprus applied for EU membership in 1990, and even though Cyprus was located on divided territory, the European

Council did not treat Cyprus any differently from the other candidates such as the Czech Republic, Estonia, Hungary, Poland, or Slovenia. The EU instead adopted in 1994 a "first solution then membership" approach by announcing that the subsequent phase of enlargement would include Cyprus and Malta, without specifying what would happen if the Cypriot problem had not been resolved by the time negotiations had concluded. In retaliation to this stand of the EU, the Turkish Republic of Northern Cyprus (TRNC) started instead the process of partial integration with Turkey. Clashes occurred between Greek- and Turkish-Cypriots throughout the summer of 1996. When full accession negotiations with Cyprus and the other candidates of the Czech Republic, Estonia, Hungary, Poland, and Slovenia commenced in 1998, the EU's inability to deal with the bifurcated political structure of the island of Cyprus led to its total avoidance of a discussion of the future participation of the Turkish-Cypriot community. Right after the ensuing accession of the Greek-Cypriot-led Cyprus in 2003, the United Nations peace plan referred to as the "Annan plan" failed and was voted down by the Greek side in a referendum. Currently, with the intent to end the isolation of the Turkish-Cypriot community, the EU has recently proposed a comprehensive package of aid and trade to the TRNC, which it has also included in its new Neighborhood Policy (Moulakis 2007).

In explaining the causes of conflict in Greek-Turkish relations in general and the Cyprus problem in particular, all studies emphasize the role of negative perceptions and representations of the other that are reproduced and maintained through education, media, and literature and thereby naturalized as fact. For instance, the perception of threat from Greece in Turkey is sustained by the association of Greeks with Byzantine intrigue and diplomatic tricks as well as by memories of the Greek invasion of Turkish territories after the First World War, even though since the mid-1990s historians in Greece and in Turkey have made collaborative efforts to purge the schoolbooks of chauvinistic content and demonizing references (Milas 2000).

Still, the prevailing Turkish foreign policy of deterrence toward Greece is based on a suspicion that since its inception, Greece, inspired by the "Megali Idea" of a Greater Greece including the former lands of the Byzantine Empire, has been pursuing a policy of constant territorial expansion against Turkey. Greece's gaining EU membership ahead of Turkey has led Turkey to also perceive the European Union as yet another venue for the revisionist agenda of Greece against Turkey. Within this policy framework of the Turkish nation-state, any international attempt to legitimate policies by alluding to the EU is immediately interpreted by the Turks as concessions made to Greece. The attitude of the Turkish nation-state toward the Cyprus problem mimics its stand toward Greece. Turkish public opinion, shaped by the military bureaucratic authority to "not abandon national causes," has severely hindered the possibility of conflict resolution (Adamson 2001; Kirişçi and Çarkoğlu 2003). Yet, the course of Greek-Turkish relations started to shift with the devastating earthquakes suffered by Turkey and Greece in August and September 1999 as the positive influence of civil society started to prevail in both contexts over that of the state.

The Armenian Problem

Among the three current problems faced by Turkish state and society, only the Armenian problem was jump-started in the Republican period by forces outside of the control of the Turkish nation-state. Commencing in 1975—and lasting until 1986—two secret Armenian organizations named the Justice Commandos against the Armenian Genocide (JCOAG) and the Armenian Secret Army for the Liberation of Armenia (ASALA) decided to draw attention to the 1915 ethnic cleansing of the Armenians the Ottoman state had committed without subsequent accountability through a series of assassinations of Turkish diplomats and the bombings of Turkish sites (Şimşir 2000).

When these attacks first started, the Turkish state and society for a long time searched for world powers that might have instigated them, as they could not comprehend that it was actually Armenians executing these actions on their own. The mythified version of the Turkish past, devoid of any account of state violence, had been widely ingrained through mass education for a couple of generations; the Turkish nation-state had also considered the Armenian issue "closed" at the Lausanne Peace negotiations in 1922 and 1923. There did not exist at the Turkish Foreign Ministry a single English-language text depicting the Turkish state's version of 1915 to be sent to Western courts to inform public prosecutors of the perpetrators of the attacks and assassinations who were being tried (Şimşir 2000, vol. I, 108).

The attacks caused both the state and military to intervene by fostering, organizing, and institutionalizing the propensity to symbolic violence against the Armenians, particularly in two ways. First, through the 1980s a nationalized historiography of the Armenian issue was developed, penned mostly by retired diplomats, along the lines of the mythified history taught in schools since the inception of the republic. Second, the state established a series of organizations with the overt purpose of studying and researching the Armenian issue. Then in 1980 the military launched a covert paramilitary organization to go after and murder the assassins of the Turkish diplomats that the Western powers either could not arrest or released after short prison sentences (Özdemir 1997). The speeches of state officials and military officers at the diplomats' funerals gradually transformed from mourning to seeking vengeance, to promising the Turkish populace that "their blood would not remain on the ground" (Şimşir 2000, vol. 1, 449). Indeed, it was after the 1980 military coup, during the former general Kenan Evren's presidency, that a clandestine paramilitary organization was established to pursue the assassins (Özdemir 1997). These attempts alongside the nationalized mythified historiography indicated that the Turkish state and military were intent on institutionalizing the propensity for symbolic violence rather than alleviating it. And this propensity went hand in hand with the reaction of the populace.

The emotional upsurge in the newspapers (Şimşir 2000, vol. I, 358-59) immediately singled out the Armenians in Turkey, stating "our Armenian citizens" were living in peace, that is, without being murdered, and that they were also wealthy to boot. Of course, this depiction revealed in and of itself the prejudice inherent in Turkish society by singling them out as "Armenians"; by patronizing them as "our"; and, once again, by drawing attention to their wealth, which had not only previously incurred the wrath of the Muslims multiple times, but which had by this point become insignificant in relation to the immense wealth of the new "Turkish" bourgeoisie. Then, as the assassinations and attacks continued, the Armenian community was asked by various newspaper editors to write to their brethren in Western countries "to tell them to stop the attacks," and the Armenian patriarch in Turkey had to issue press releases condemning the attacks and to hold mass in honor of the assassinated Turks (Şimşir 2000, vol. I). The implied connection the Turkish newspapers took for granted as existing between the Armenians in Turkey and the radical Armenian organizations revealed yet another source of prejudice. That the Armenian community was brought under pressure by the state to constantly issue statements that they lived in peace in Turkey, that they condemned the attacks, and that they professed their undying allegiance to the Turkish Republic is only recently being publicly acknowledged by the community (Şimşir 2000, vol. I).

That the Armenian community was brought under pressure by the state to constantly issue statements that they lived in peace in Turkey, that they condemned the attacks, and that they professed their undying allegiance to the Turkish Republic is only recently being publicly acknowledged by the community.

Likewise during this period, the Turkish state mobilized the Jewish community, especially in relation to their connection to the Jewish lobby in the United States, to counter and oppose the weight of the Armenian Diaspora, which actively began the attempt to get the Armenian ethnic cleansing in 1915 politically recognized as genocide in the United States and elsewhere. This was especially difficult for the Jewish community that had, after all, suffered the Holocaust; indeed, the developments in social sciences and ethics to cope with the occurrence and impact of the Holocaust had produced the entirely new critical historical scholarship that had enabled philosophers, social scientists, and humanists to study so well the social acts of racism, violence, and discrimination.

The Jewish community at large might have been expected to be the primary supporters of Armenian genocide recognition, yet two factors initially inhibited them; one was the argument of the uniqueness of the Holocaust, and the other the support the Turkish state promised and gave Israel in the Middle East as well as the Jewish community in Turkey. Only very recently has the Jewish lobby in the United States decided to reverse its policy based on the argument that ethical principles ought to precede political concerns (Banerjee 2007).

Toward the end of the 1980s, however, Turkey started to undergo a series of transformations that began to diminish the hold of the state and the military over society. The emerging Anatolian bourgeoisie in the provinces brought to power the Justice and Development Party in spite of the opposition of the state establishment and the military. Because the Justice and Development Party was rooted in Anatolia, it had access to and awareness of the local histories that were cognizant of what had actually happened to the Armenians in 1915; in addition, many of the members were devout Muslims whose ancestors had once presumably opposed the Armenian deportations on religious principles alone. As a consequence, the possibility emerged of their considering an alternate discourse on the Armenian issue to that of the Turkish state, one that could be especially formulated in cooperation with the liberal public intellectuals who, equipped with the forces of civil society and the tools of new critical scholarship, had also started to take a critical look at their own past and produce research along these lines.

The location of the minorities within the social structure initially continued unchanged as the rhetoric sustained that they were citizens with equal rights, while in practice they continued to face legal, social, and political discrimination. Yet, the increased significance of identity politics and the possibility of European Union membership resulted in liberalization in Turkey, which enabled many minorities, including (in addition to Greeks, Armenians, and Jews) Kurds, Alevis, Assyrians, and Lazis to assert their rights. The more liberalized environment enabled all these groups as well as the public intellectuals and the flourishing civil society and nonprofit organizations to voice their concerns. Even though the location of such minority groups within the Turkish social structure and the prejudice and discrimination they faced could be more publicly articulated, however, it still could not prevent lawsuits from being brought against books and articles on these issues for "insulting Turkishnsess," and for a journalist like Hrant Dink from being assassinated on January 19, 2007, by an ultra-nationalist Turk (Arsu 2007).

In summary, then, the Turkish nation-state, rather than confronting its past and the violence contained therein against minorities in general and the Armenians in particular, chose to deny it by constructing an official counternarrative. It also took issue with the international employment of the term "genocide" to refer to what had occurred in 1915—even though what occurred certainly fit the 1948 United Nations definition—and instead spent and continues to spend millions of dollars to prevent all the countries of the world from recognizing what happened to the Armenians in 1915 as genocide.

An Alternate Conceptualization

The official narratives of the Kurdish, Cyprus, and Armenian problems discussed above all reveal the staunch, defensive stand of the Turkish nation-state in constantly seeking behind every action ploys that might be inspired by the West to decimate and destroy its existence. Given this initial stand of distrust, it is no accident that the Turkish nation-state is incapable of reaching peaceful resolutions in any one, let alone all three, of these problems. Yet, I would argue here that such peaceful solutions to these problems could become possible only and primarily upon challenging the temporal boundaries of the official Turkish narrative. Such a challenge would reveal the common origins and cause of these problems and, in so doing, render possible peaceful solutions to all three.

I argue specifically that the origins of the Kurdish, Cyprus, and Armenian problems can all be traced to one particular historical event: a treaty in 1878. During March 1878, at the end of the 1876 to 1878 Russo-Turkish war that proceeded disastrously for the latter, the Russian army swept through the Ottoman defenses in the Balkans to literally end up on the outskirts of Constantinople. The Ottoman state had to sign a treaty on very unfavorable terms at San Stefano, very close to the imperial capital. This treaty was regarded by the Ottoman state as the historical juncture when the "Armenian issue" became internationalized, for the Ottoman Armenian subjects of the empire had sent a delegation to the Russian tsar, asking him to include among the peace articles a guarantee for the protection of Armenians in the Ottoman Empire. This move by the Ottoman Armenian community actually represented the end of their frustrated long wait since the beginning of the nineteenth century for the actualization of the promised—but never delivered—reforms of equality and protection for all Ottoman minorities (Göçek 2008).

As the Ottoman land tenure system was transformed due to the increased need of the Ottoman treasury for cash, landholding patterns were also altered. Both the exploitation of the lands and the peasants on them to attain better yields, as well as the 1858 declaration of private property in the empire, had benefited the dominant Muslim majority at the expense of the minorities. The non-Muslim minorities lived in self-contained communities within a social structure based on the Islamic legal system of the *sharia*; they were obliged to pay a special tax in return for the protection offered to them by the Ottoman state, and they were prevented by law from bearing arms themselves. This limitation was especially problematic in the eastern and southeastern provinces of the empire, where the Kurds often aggressed upon, plundered, and even seized the lands of the Armenian Greek and Assyrian peasants who could not protect themselves (Klein 2007). The Kurds would then flee into the Russian Empire to escape punishment and seek the tsar's protection, and the Ottoman state often restrained from punishing such Kurds lest they switch their loyalties to the Russian state. Therefore, the complaints of the Armenians and others would often go unaddressed. The long-awaited reforms became destined for failure. Hence, it was in this context that the Armenians and the Kurds first became social actors in Ottoman and later Turkish history.

Concerned with these events occurring in the eastern provinces of the empire and wary of the hold the Russian Empire was about to acquire over the Ottoman state at their expense, the French and the British insisted upon convening in Berlin and signing another treaty, one whose paragraph 61 guaranteed the life and property of the Armenians in the Anatolian provinces and promised reforms (Göçek forthcoming). In addition, faced with the loss of vast territories in the Balkans, the Ottoman state requested the intervention of the British. Yet, the British refused to intervene unless they were given the island of Cyprus by the Ottoman sultan. Hence, after the occasion of the Berlin Congress, the island of Cyprus, which had been under Ottoman rule since its conquest in the late sixteenth century, passed onto the hands of the British and subsequently became a much contested territory. Therefore, the three subsequent problems of contemporary Turkey were all located in this particular historical juncture of 1878 within the larger framework of the Ottoman negotiation with political modernity.

More significant, however, was the main cause that bestowed all three problems with social agency, namely, the inability of the Ottoman state to carry out the reforms that would guarantee the equality of the rights of all its subjects regardless of ethnicity. The Ottoman state was unable to deliver this equality before the demise of its empire, and it left this problem as a legacy to the emerging Turkish nation-state. Just as the Ottoman Empire had always put the preservation of the state and the dynasty before all else, including the well-being of its subjects, the burgeoning Turkish nation-state, too, made this primacy of the state its founding principle. Consequently, it frequently infringed upon the rights of its citizens. As the Turkish state was unable and unwilling to confront, acknowledge, and transform this priority and the powerful relations it entailed, it positioned instead this internal failure of the sharing of power with its citizens on the imagined designs the West had made toward its destruction (Göçek forthcoming).

Turkey's desire to become a part of Europe had its roots in the nineteenth century and in the negotiation of the Ottoman Empire with Western political modernity, starting with a series of reforms endorsed by many legal declarations such as the 1839 Declaration to "Reorder" the empire, also known as the Tanzimat. Turkey has thus been self-consciously converging with European practices and preferences for a long time. Still, its inability to face the challenges brought upon by this transformation to a Western democratic system leads the Turkish state to instead promulgate, carefully maintain, and practice a legal system that contains articles making the freedom of thought in the country a crime.

Even though the Turkish state, including the military, constantly blames the expansionist tendencies of European powers, the West does nevertheless continue to occupy a privileged place in the mind's eye of Turkish state and society, thereby contributing to the democratization process. Significant developments in this regard have been Turkey's transition to a multiparty regime in 1946; its alignment with NATO in 1952; and its opening up in the 1980s to the world economy and undertaking significant efforts to alter its state-controlled, protectionist economic and political structure. Still, the military continues to consider itself the guardian of the state, established and maintained according to Republican and secularist principles to be protected not only against external threats but also against its internal enemies.

In summary, then, what enables the discovery of the common roots of these three issues is the ability to confront, analyze, and challenge them within their own historical context. Hence, the first step the Turkish nation-state ought to take toward the resolution of its Kurdish, Cyprus, and Armenian issues is to confront its history in its entirety rather than through fragments. Once this is done, the observation emerges that all three cases contain the consequences—often unintended—of the dissolution of an empire, the violence of which was directed against the minorities who were too weak to defend themselves. The manner with which all three cases were dealt points out the fundamental priority of the Turkish state, namely, state preservation at all costs, including, especially, the lives of its citizens. I would argue that this prioritization needs to change for the Turkish nation-state to stop seeing the past "through a glass darkly," and to become one with its society and citizens, instead of surviving and sustaining itself at their expense.

Notes

1. The two questions asked to capture the Turkish attitude toward the European Union were as follows: (1) "The current EU requirements are similar to those required by the Treaty of Sèvres (with which the Ottoman Empire was dismembered after World War I and the National Independence Struggle fought)." The responses were *totally disagree*, 10 percent; *disagree*, 8 percent; *agree*, 40 percent; *totally agree*, 17 percent; and *don't know/no answer*, 25 percent. (2) "The West wants to divide and break Turkey like they broke the Ottoman Empire." The responses were even stronger at 13 percent, 10 percent, 16 percent, 52 percent, and 10 percent, respectively. The nationally representative sample was composed of 1,215 plus an additional 300 youth.

2. It is extremely difficult to estimate the size of the Kurdish population in Turkey because official population surveys do not collect—or at least do not officially dispense—such information; "Turkish" citizenship is regarded by the state as an all-inclusive category. As the earliest Republican population survey had included a question on the main language spoken in the household, this question has often been employed to estimate the size of the Kurdish population. Yet, this question was then omitted in the more recent surveys, leading different scholars to employ diverse multipliers in estimating the current Kurdish population. This explains the many disparate figures on the Kurdish population proportion.

References

Adamson, Fiona B. 2001. Democratisation and the domestic sources of foreign policy: Turkey in the 1974 Cyprus crisis. *Political Science Quarterly* 116 (2): 277-303.

Arsu, Ebnem. 2007. Armenian editor is slain in Turkey. *New York Times* (Europe section), January 20.

Ataman, M. 2002. Özal leadership and restructuring of Turkish ethnic policy in the 1980s. *Middle Eastern Studies* 38 (4): 123-42.

Aydınlı, Ersel. 2002. Between security and liberalization: Decoding Turkey's struggle with the PKK. *Security Dialogue* 33 (2): 209-25.

Bahcheli, Tozun. 2000. Searching for a Cyprus settlement: Considering options for creating a federation, a confederation, or two independent states. *Publius* 30 (1): 203-16.

Banerjee, Neela. 2007. Armenian issue presents a dilemma for U.S. Jews. *New York Times* (U.S. section), October 19.

Barkey, Henri. 2000. The struggles of a strong state. *Journal of International Affairs* 54 (1): 87-105.
Barkey, Henri J., and Graham E. Fuller. 1998. *Turkey's Kurdish question*. Lanham, MD: Rowman & Littlefield.
Cornell, Svante E. 2001. The Kurdish question in Turkish politics. *Orbis* 45 (1): 31-47.
Daloğlu, Tülin. 2007. Kurdish terror and the West. *Washington Times*, October 30.
Ergil, Doğu. 2000. The Kurdish question in Turkey. *Journal of Democracy* 11 (3): 122-35.
Göçek, Fatma Müge. 2008. Deciphering denial: Turkish state and the Armenian ethnic cleansing of 1915. Manuscript.
Göktaş, Hıdır. 2007. Interview: Turkish Kurds want democracy not state says MP. Reuters, August 3.
Gündüz-Hoşgör, A., and J. Smits. 2002. Intermarriage between Turks and Kurds in contemporary Turkey: Inter-ethnic relations in an urbanizing environment. *European Sociological Review* 18 (4): 417-32.
İçduygu, A., D. Romano, and İ. Sirkeci. 1999. The ethnic question in an environment of insecurity: The Kurds in Turkey. *Ethnic and Racial Studies* 22 (6): 991-1010.
İdiz, Semih. 2006. Article 301 and its European cousins. *Turkish Daily News*, October 19.
İmset, İsmet G. 1992. *The PKK: A report on separatist violence in Turkey*. Ankara: Turkish Daily News Publications.
Jacoby, Tim. 2005. Semi-authoritarian incorporation and autocratic militarism in Turkey. *Development and Change* 36 (4): 641-65.
Kirişçi, Kemal, and Ali Çarkoğlu. 2003. Perceptions of Greeks and Greek-Turkish rapprochement by the Turkish public. In Barry Rubin and Ali Çarkoğlu (Eds.), *Greek-Turkish relations in an era of détente*, pp. 117-153. London: Frank Cass.
Kirişçi, Kemal, and Gareth M. Winrow. 1997. The Kurdish question and Turkey: An example of a trans–state ethnic conflict. Portland, OR: Frank Cass.
Klein, Janet. 2007. Kurdish nationalists and non-nationalist Kurdists: Rethinking minority nationalism and the dissolution of the Ottoman Empire, 1908-1909. *Nations and Nationalism* 13 (1): 135-53.
Kocher, Matthew. 2002. The decline of PKK and the viability of a one-state solution in Turkey. *Journal on Multicultural Societies* 4 (1): 1-20.
McDowall, David. 1997. *A modern history of the Kurds*. London: I.B. Tauris.
McDowall, David. 2000. *A modern history of the Kurds*. 3rd ed. New York: I. B. Tauris.
Milas, Herkül. 2000. *Türk Roman? ve Öteki: Ulusal Kimlikte Yunan Imaji* [The Turkish novel and the other: The Greek image in national identity]. Istanbul, Turkey: Sabancı Universitesi.
Moulakis, Athanasios. 2007. Power-sharing and its discontents: Dysfunctional constitutional arrangements and the failure of the Annan plan for a reunified Cyprus. *Middle Eastern Studies* 43 (4): 531-56.
Öniş, Ziya, and Steven B. Webb. 1992. Political economy of policy reform in Turkey in the 1980s. World Bank Policy Research Working Paper Series no. 1059, World Bank, Washington, DC.
Özdemir, Veli, ed. 1997. *Susurluk Belgeleri* [Susurluk documents]. Istanbul, Turkey: Scala Yayıncılık.
Pahre, Robert, and Burcu Uçaray. 2005. The myths of Turkish influence in the European Union. paper presented at the Annual Meeting of the Midwest Political Science Association, Chicago, Illinois, April 7, 2005.
Radu, Michael. 2001. The rise and fall of PKK. *Orbis* 45 (1): 47-63.
Ron, James. 1995. Weapons transfers and violations of the laws of war in Turkey. New York: Human Rights Watch.
Rosenberg, Michael. 1994. On the road: Archeological adventures in Anatolia. *Middle East Quarterly* 1 (1), 1-4.
Şimşir, Bilal. 2000. *Şehit Diplomatlarımız* [Our martyred diplomats]. 2 vols. Ankara, Turkey: Bilgi.
Tarık, Pınar. 2005. The effects of the Iraq war on the Kurdish issue in Turkey. *Conflict, Security and Development* 5 (1): 69-86.
U.S. Department of State (DOS), Bureau of Democracy, Human Rights and Labor. 2000. *Country reports on human rights*. Washington, DC: U.S. Department of State.
van Bruinessen, Martin. 1992. *Agha, Sheikh and the State*. London: Zed.
Watts, Nicole F. 2006. Activists in office: Pro-Kurdish contentious politics in Turkey. *Ethnopolitics* 5 (2): 125-44.
Williams and Associates. 2006. Survey of Turkish Public Opinion, conducted between November 18 and December 5. Salem, MA: International Republican Institute.
Zengin, Nilüfer. 2007. Büyükanit calls human rights "psychological operation." BIANet News in English, December 12.

The Japanese History Textbook Controversy in East Asian Perspective

By
CLAUDIA SCHNEIDER

Controversy over the inadequate presentation of Japan's colonial and wartime past in the country's history textbooks is one of the most protracted, notorious, and politically relevant "history problems" currently troubling East Asia. This article provides an overview of the controversy's evolution since 1982, situating it in changing domestic and regional contexts, analyzing its particularities and interrelations with other controversial issues, and evaluating its impacts on textbooks and societies at large. It shows how increased domestic and foreign scrutiny and contestation have triggered cycles of greater openness, conservative counterreactions, subsequent backlashes, and renewed debate in the field of textbooks and have overall contributed both to reinforcements and to reconsiderations of foreign relations in the region.

Keywords: East Asia; history education; textbook controversies/debates

A fter decades of relative respite, criticism of Japan's colonial and wartime actions has ricocheted with a vengeance. The country is criticized in most of the history debates taking place in the region for failing to come to terms appropriately with its past. Issues like the visits of its prime ministers to the controversial Yasukuni Shrine, repeated denials of state-involvement in the system of forced wartime prostitution,[1] repeated attempts to justify the Asia-Pacific War, rulings denying state compensation for forced labor, and positive evaluations of the Japanese colonial period[2] have periodically put serious strains on Japan's relations

Claudia Schneider is a PhD candidate at the Institute of East Asian Studies at the University of Leipzig, Germany. Her thesis carries the working title "Reconfiguring National Stories in a Globalizing World: History Textbooks in Contemporary China, Taiwan, and Japan." She has edited an issue of the journal International Textbook Research *and contributed chapters to edited volumes, most recently* Contested Views of a Common Past: Historical Revisionism in Contemporary East Asia *(ed. Steffi Richter; Frankfurt, Germany: Campus).*

DOI: 10.1177/0002716208314359

with its most important neighbors, the People's Republic of China and the Republic of Korea,[3] and have reinforced Japan's international image as a non-apologist.[4]

The cold war alliance made it possible to leave many war-related questions unresolved, providing a lingering source of debate between Japan and neighbors that see themselves as its victims. It was not until the 1980s, and particularly the 1990s, that many of these issues became contested. This article provides an overview of one of the most prolonged and notorious issues: the so-called "textbook controversy," the debates surrounding the treatment—essentially the non-coverage—of Japanese wartime behavior in the country's history textbooks.

The controversy is worth studying for various reasons. It is a prism of the changes in East Asia over the past two decades, attesting to altered distribution of power in the region, changed state–society relations and prevailing national self-images, as well as the heightened significance of the past for the present—the global "memory boom." It also holds a particular place among the region's numerous history debates: textbooks serve as one of the important arenas where the past, as well as a country's image of itself and others, is contested. The perceived characteristics of school textbooks make the controversy particularly complex and difficult to solve. The controversy has had far-reaching implications that go beyond the realms of textbook content—the issue has been both a part of and a cause for conflicts on both the diplomatic and popular levels.

Recognizing that a short article cannot provide a comprehensive, in-depth analysis, I seek to achieve three objectives: First, I show the issue's appearance and periodic recurrence to be the result of specific conditions and shifts in the domestic and international contexts of Japanese, Chinese, and South Korean politics, focusing on the media, governments, and citizen movements as influential actors. I then examine the textbook issue's connections with, and particularities vis-à-vis, other controversial history issues and explore why textbooks per se have generated such heated debates. Finally, I seek to provide insights into the ambiguous impacts that the controversies have had on textbook content and on the handling of the region's connected but divided history in broader terms. In East Asia, history textbooks have been important in shaping mutual perceptions and images of the twentieth century—perhaps more outside than inside the classroom.

Emergence and Evolution

The textbook controversy has a long narrative in Japan's domestic politics of history. In 1955, conservative politicians called then-existing history textbooks "deplorable," arguing that they reflected anti-Japanese and pro-Chinese leftist thought, and since then textbooks have (at various points) been the object of heated debates between the conservative establishment (the governing Liberal Democratic Party [LDP] and its predecessors) and "progressive" forces, composed mainly of left-leaning intellectuals, academics, and schoolteachers supported by the formerly influential Japan Teachers' Union. While bureaucrats at the Ministry of Education (MOE)[5] consider themselves neutral in these debates (Dierkes 2005), they have been arguably partial arbiters. Textbook accounts of Japan's history have long been predominantly conservative. The MOE generally sides with the conservative camp, as evidenced in the long-lasting trials that the progressive historian Ienaga Saburô fought against the MOE and the Japanese government over the censorship he encountered as a textbook author.[6]

The transformation of history textbooks into objects of international debate dates from the summer of 1982. It was triggered by news reports that the Japanese MOE had ordered history textbook authors to make various revisions, most notoriously changing the term "aggression/invasion" into "advancement" to describe Japanese military action in northeast China in the 1930s. This particular news item was a *canard*: apparently there had been no such request during that round of state textbook approvals. A general disposition of this sort did exist, and it was closely watched and duly reported by Japanese newspapers; but the story had not, until 1982, spilled across the country's borders. Japan's neighbors, up until then refraining from complaint, now had reason to become vocal: not only was textbook coverage of Japanese military action rather evasive, the dominant consciousness in Japan was not primarily that of having been an aggressor toward Asian countries, but rather of having been a victim—principally of American (atomic) bombing.

This first affair displayed various characteristics that would mark those that followed.[7] First, it was triggered and shaped by the mass media, mainly newspaper reports often reflecting cross-national interaction.[8] It also included a certain amount of bona fide but unexamined mutual copying of portions of text, conducive to producing inaccuracies that further enlarged the debates. Second, it was furthered by specific domestic conditions and was, or became, part of discussions on larger domestic issues. Earlier in Japan, a conservative "patriotic education" campaign had begun to gather momentum. Discussions in South Korea stimulated sensitive issues of democratization and decreased dependency on Japan, leading the authoritarian government of Chun Doo-hwan to initiate tighter press control. In China, Deng Xiaoping was facing power struggles with "old guards" in the army and felt obliged to mend his crumbling ideological front with a campaign for "socialist spiritual civilization" (Rose 1998, 72-77). Third, the issue became both a source of and a potential challenge to government legitimacy. In Japan, where the issue had already taken root, the hapless way the government handled it left such major domestic actors as the Ministry of Foreign Affairs (MOFA) and the MOE dissatisfied and contributed indirectly to Prime Minister Suzuki Zenkô's resignation. For the Chinese and South Korean governments, it became part of the "history card" (Yang 2002)—a tool available for shaming, pressuring, and gaining leverage on the Japanese government.

An immediate result of the affair was the Japanese MOE's addition to the criteria for textbook authorization of what came to be called the "Neighboring Countries Clause." It stipulated that consideration should be given to neighboring countries' perspectives, somewhat facilitating the inclusion of more critical passages into textbooks. The clause has been a source of discontent for conservative/right-wing forces who believe it is a sign that the Japanese are succumbing to diplomatic pressure on genuinely internal affairs. They lobby for the deletion of the clause (Rose 2005, 59).

One such conservative counterreaction led to the second major textbook debate. In March 1986, a high school history textbook for seniors, created by the National Committee for the Protection of Japan and titled *New History of Japan*, received official approval. As in the first debate, reactions from Seoul were stronger than those from Beijing, which, for internal reasons, instructed its mass media once more to refrain from a campaign (Whiting 1989, 57-64). While the debate again put the Japanese prime minister in a difficult position between diplomatic imperatives on one side and domestic loyalties and bureaucratic procedures on the other, it also provided insight into the conservative outlook of the Japanese political establishment. When asked about the textbook problem, then–Minister of Education Fujio Masayuki made insensitive comments about the Nanjing Massacre, the Yasukuni Shrine, and Japanese actions in Korea (Rose 1998, 185). While he had to resign, like many of his peers who were guilty of similar slips of the tongue, the incident nonetheless confirmed the impression of Japan as unrepentant toward its neighbors.

The 1990s saw a number of significant changes. In Japan, general awareness of unresolved issues and Japanese responsibility in the war increased,[9] and the role of Japan as victimizer penetrated public consciousness more deeply (Seraphim 2006, 34). A short period of non-LDP rule also brought a more forthright official attitude. In 1993, Prime Minister Hosokawa acknowledged that Japan had conducted a war of aggression. And in 1995, a resolution in the Diet and a statement on August 15 by Hosokawa's successor, Prime Minister Murayama, contained formal expressions of apology and regret (Rose 2005, 19, 60; for excerpts of the statement by Murayama, see pp. 135-36). Although highly contested at the time, they have established a baseline from which Japanese governments have not officially retreated.

In the eyes of conservatives and right-wingers, these tectonic shifts in Japanese politics of history were a cause for concern. Various revisionist groups were organized to counter this trend.[10] They both contributed to and profited from a turn toward a defensive and defiant nationalism among parts of the Japanese population. As the long period of strong economic growth ended in the early 1990s, the new defiant nationalism was fed by feelings of insecurity and frustration, in particular vis-à-vis a rising China. The conservatives' activities spanned a wide range, from more academic endeavors to crudely nationalist *mangas* appealing to the broader public; some directly targeted history education, charging that it transmitted a "masochistic" view of Japanese history.[11]

One such group, established in late 1996 and tellingly named Japanese Society for History Textbook Reform, or Tsukuru-kai,[12] produced a junior high textbook titled *New History Textbook*. It presents a peculiar version of Japan's history, marked by a statist, at times even militaristic nationalism, buttressed by an insular and self-affirming perspective on Japan, an underlying West-centrism, and an often condescending view of Japan's East Asian neighbors.[13] In some instances, its authors had tried to whitewash or justify the country's colonial and wartime actions to such a degree that even the conservative textbook examiners at the Ministry of Education, Culture, Sports, Science and Technology (MEXT) had been compelled to demand more consideration for neighboring countries (Schneider 2008). It was approved in spring 2001 after an unusually high number of officially demanded revisions.[14]

In the eyes of conservatives and right-wingers . . . tectonic shifts in Japanese politics of history were a cause for concern.

The third major international textbook controversy was a continuation of old troubles with some new parameters. The academic paradigm had shifted, and the Tsukuru-kai's employment of constructivist/relativist arguments—that histories naturally differed from nation to nation—made criticism of treating events as factually "right or wrong" more difficult. A battle in the media again contributed to the prominence of debates on the issue, this time on the domestic front—that is, between the progressive *Asahi* and the conservative *Sankei* newspapers (Ducke 2002, 12).

The greatest change in the course of the textbook controversies, however, can be attributed to the appropriation of history by "civil society" actors. In the 1990s, these groups experienced an explosion of numbers in South Korea, considerable growth in Japan, and an emergence in China. Among these, the Tsukuru-kai, while doubtlessly well connected to conservative political, economic, and media circles, should be seen as a conservative citizen group rather than a scheme inflicted by the state on its pacifist people (Oguma and Ueno 2003). Progressive Japanese citizens' groups, using networks such as Children and Textbooks Japan Network 21, and in some cases linking up with Korean counterparts (Ducke 2002), lobbied local school boards against the selection of the *New History Textbook* and contributed to its extremely low rate of adoption (0.04 percent of all schools).[15]

Korea and China, where such history-related issues as reconciliation and compensation had long been managed in a top-down way by governments, developed their own agendas through bottom-up civil society–based efforts made possible by democratization in Korea and limited liberalization in China. The two governments, which had previously shifted toward a more cautious and/or conciliatory policy, were thus put on the defensive by the textbook controversy. South

Korean president Roh Moo-hyun launched diplomatic protests only after pressure from the political arena and the public (Soh 2005). The official Chinese reactions included the usual accusatory rhetoric and some cancelled visits, but no measures were taken with potentially negative long-term effects on other, particularly economic, aspects of its bilateral relationship with Japan (Rose 2005, 63-65).

The controversies were fuelled by popular nationalisms that have been rising vis-à-vis these and other Japanese "attacks." They could now be articulated more openly. Soh (2005, 149) has identified an "intensely ethnonationalistic complex of Korean self-image as both victim and victor vis-à-vis Japan" in history-related protests. In Sino-Japanese relations, reactive nationalisms—perceived by the other side as assertive—have been mutually stimulating each other (Chan and Bridges 2006). For citizens of both countries, activities against Japan's perceived whitewashing of its history may be seen and justified as a "patriotic duty," grounded in anticolonial/anti-imperialist traditions (Soh 2005; Klein 2005). Consequently, when popular outrage is riding high, the respective governments have to be cautious to not appear weak—at least rhetorically.

This even concerns authoritarian China, where the state no longer holds a complete definitional monopoly on many historical narratives. Apart from relying on anti-Japanese sentiments for its own legitimization, it cannot entirely ignore—or suppress—"popular will" in history-related affairs, and populist "history activism" has turned into a force that can mobilize popular resentments and potentially exacerbate bilateral relations (Reilly 2006). Moreover, in an untimely coincidence, in the inner-Chinese discourse, the Chinese Communist Party's former "victor narrative" focusing on heroic anti-Japanese resistance has been superseded by a "victim narrative" emphasizing Chinese suffering and Japanese atrocities (Gries 2004). Thus, when news of Japanese government approval for the revised version of the *New History Textbook* was transmitted in the spring of 2005, it prompted partially violent popular anti-Japanese demonstrations in a number of Chinese cities— which ended up considerably embarrassing Beijing's pre-Olympics posturing.

Again, the furor over textbooks did not stand in isolation—Chinese discontent had been building up on a number of other issues, such as Japanese efforts to gain a permanent seat on the United Nations Security Council. The recent controversies also illustrate how new tools of communication have come to play an important role for all sides involved. Both protesters and Chinese authorities resorted to text messaging to organize their activities—and subsequently to subdue them. Online petitions, for instance against the *New History Textbook*, have become a widespread phenomenon; there have been blogs voicing anti-Japanese outrage (and hate) and reports of Korean and Chinese "cyber attacks" paralyzing Web sites of Japanese institutions (cf., for instance, Fiola 2005).

In the meantime, some already see the Tsukuru-kai as having arrived at a dead end (Saaler 2006). If the *New History Textbook* continues to exist, it will most likely—like its 1986 "predecessor in spirit"—remain a marginal presence on the textbook market. But given the currently rather conservative atmosphere in Japan, it could soon be replaced by a similar undertaking even if it disappeared completely.[16]

Particularities

Textbooks are inherently political. They represent temporary outcomes of negotiations between various social actors over what counts as legitimate knowledge. The state remains involved through various restraining and control mechanisms,[17] even in countries with a pluralistic textbook system. History and civics textbooks, after all, are also charged with transmitting collective self-concepts and values.

Apart from these structural properties, the perceptions (and subsequent actions) of the involved actors and of the general public contribute largely to the tendency of textbooks to become objects of contention. First, because they are authorized or approved by the state, Japanese textbooks are imbued with a quasi-official character. This problem is perhaps even more pronounced because China and South Korea have until recently kept to a system of state-issued textbooks.[18] This has partially led to misunderstandings regarding the workings of the Japanese textbook approval system and the possibilities for, and limits on, the influence of the Japanese government in the process. From a strictly legal point of view, in the beginning the government was much less powerful vis-à-vis the MOE/MEXT than its counterparts in neighboring countries considered it to be. Second, and closely related to the first point, in many parts of the world, history textbooks are often invoked as powerful symbols of a country's sincerity to deal with a negative past. In this respect, the Japanese case tends to be viewed negatively in comparison with the often-cited positive counterexample, Germany, and the latter's postwar cooperation with its major adversaries in World War II—France and Poland. Third, their very broad and peculiar target audience—young children, understood as the impressionable, and thus fragile and volatile, future of the nation—causes them to be considered very influential in a double sense—both for the individual child's historical consciousness and for the nation's future.

In the Japanese case, the latter concerns have also become highly institutionalized. Conservative politicians have often made educational issues a field of their political activity; there are several parliamentary study groups on the subject, and some LDP politicians are members of the Tsukuru-kai (Saaler 2005, 81). Progressive associations like Children and Textbooks Japan Network 21 have also been organized and dedicated to the other side of these issues. The attitudes of these groups toward history education mainly reflect their divergent views on the war and colonialism and, correspondingly, on Japan's role in Asia. Conservative groups expect history textbooks to create a positive Japanese self-image, national pride, and dedication—elements said to be undermined by external pressures and domestic "historical masochism." Progressive groups aim to promote a self-critical Japanese self-image, national introspection, and responsibility toward significant East Asian "others"—a stance the dominant conservative agenda of Japan's politics of history appears to block.

The international debates have mainly focused on the exact phrasing and specifics—terms, numbers, actors—of particular events. Two of the topics that currently matter most to the Chinese and Korean sides—but are actually the most difficult to implement in the Japanese context—are, respectively, the Nanjing Massacre and comfort women.[19] The textbook-related controversies about these issues are fueled by somewhat different considerations. When history textbooks are used as battlegrounds, discussions can take place on two levels: First, did this particular event "happen"?[20] This is an academic question, in the domain of history and historiography. Second, assuming that it happened, should it be included in textbooks? This is a moral/educational question, pertaining to the politics of history education.

The problem of the Nanjing Massacre exemplifies the former category. There are three major schools of thought reflected in the heated Japanese debate: (1) the "Illusion," (2) "Middle-of-the-Road," and (3) "Great Massacre" schools. Their understanding diverges strongly on the event's spatial and temporal extent, the number of casualties, and the appropriate terminology for discussing it (Askew 2004).[21] In that vein, Fujioka Nobukatsu, cofounder of the Tsukuru-kai, argued that the high number of victims included in mid-1990s textbooks was greatly exaggerated (Yoshida 2000, 98). The so-called "comfort women" issue, though also generally contested,[22] raises the moral/educational question. Conservative voices for excluding the issue do not necessarily argue for doing so on factual grounds but, rather, on moral(izing) grounds, since the issue raises uncomfortable questions about gender relations and sexuality that junior high students are supposedly too young to handle. Moreover, they are dismissed as irrelevant to the orthodox narrative of national history that school education is supposed to teach (Sakamoto 2003, 152ff.).

The issue is further complicated by the fact that, globalization notwithstanding, regular textbooks have so far been largely restricted to national territory, for institutional as well as political reasons.[23] For both the Chinese and Korean sides, the textbook controversy is mainly one of the numerous fields where self-affirmation in the face of general Japanese denial of important elements of their self-image as "victims" is deemed necessary. While this is completely in tune with progressive Japanese groups, who accept Japan's image of "victimizer" with all the moral obligations that follow from it, the Tsukuru-kai and other conservative groups see it as an attack on the "protected zone" that history education should be. In practice, Chinese and Korean demands to present the historical truth (if such a thing were assumed to exist) may not be effective against the counter-arguments of Japanese conservatives, since the latter might frame demands for changes as unjustified foreign pressure and interference into Japan's internal affairs. An indifferent Japanese public might accept such counterarguments.[24] This is especially the case when demands to teach "correct history" are advanced by an authoritarian regime like that of the People's Republic of China, itself notorious for engaging in the manipulation of history.

Furthermore, one needs to bear in mind that the promotion of patriotism remains a central goal of history education not only in the eyes of Japanese conservatives and revisionists but also in Korean and Chinese curricula. There, the central objectives of fostering national self-respect and unity are especially pertinent with regard to descriptions of the Japanese colonial period (Korea) and the Anti-Japanese War of Resistance (China). Moral lessons on the importance of "righteous resistance" and upholding a positive image of the nation appear more important than historical lessons on the actual complexities of such periods (Schneider 2008).[25] Thus, unless efforts become evident from all sides involved (with Japan having to take the first step), history textbooks will remain trapped in a mutual siege of structurally similar but content-wise mutually excluding nationalisms for domestic consumption.[26]

Chinese and Korean demands to present the historical truth (if such a thing were assumed to exist) may not be effective against the counterarguments of Japanese conservatives, since the latter might frame demands for changes as unjustified foreign pressure and interference into Japan's internal affairs.

Repercussions

Textbooks are a conservative medium. Often there are gaps between academic trends and the content of textbooks, and textbooks have been noted for their tendency to legitimize the existing (political) order and state of power relations. Moreover, they present highly controlled and institutionalized knowledge in a manner made didactic, so changes and continuities in their content may be hindered or fostered by political as well as educational considerations and institutional factors. I suggest in this section that the controversies have not only been relevant for textbooks but also—perhaps even more important—have had broader implications for the handling of the entangled, but not shared, past in society at large.

In Japan, the politicized controversies have indeed stimulated changes in textbook content.[27] On particularly contested and scrutinized issues, textbooks have displayed pendular movement, rather than a unidirectional trend. The outbreak of textbook-related controversies fostered openings in the debates and practices, culminating in the mid-1990s, while the main effect of the ensuing Tsukuru-kai backlash was a general shift back to more subdued and cautious positions.

The Nanjing Massacre may serve as a telling example here. While all junior high school textbooks approved in 1997 cited relatively high figures for the number of victims (Yoshida 2000, 98), books published in 2005 generally refrain from giving *any* numbers. Likewise, the term "massacre" almost completely disappeared, replaced by the previously used term "incident." On the other hand, added scrutiny also shifted the baselines and raised the bar for the conservative camp. Even the *New History Textbook* makes scant reference to the massacre (although the 2005 version tries to hide it by literally relegating it to a footnote). The victims of sexual slavery have seen a similar fate. Mentioning them in all junior high textbooks in the mid-1990s especially angered conservatives, and by 2005 the term "comfort women" was again erased from the pages of the history text.[28]

Current developments, setbacks in themselves, also hide a host of other problems. Any insertions made in textbooks so far appear as signs of concessions in the political push and pull, not as reflections of revisions in the general agenda of the politics of Japanese history education. As Barnard (2003) has shown in his linguistic analysis of coverage of this and other war-related events, the bare mention of war crimes alone does not guarantee that they are adequately portrayed with their causes; main actors; and historical, moral, and other implications. The debates have also led to negative amplifications in Chinese textbooks, where coverage of the Nanjing Massacre is not only obligatory but is covered in an apodictical (e.g., on the number of victims) and graphical fashion. Some versions even include explicit references to Japanese attempts at denial and to the *New History Textbook*—bringing the controversy full circle. Nevertheless, it should be noted that the workings of cross-national influence are more complex than knee-jerk reactions in the face of denial. For instance, the recent appearance of the comfort women issue in a few junior high Chinese History textbooks is rather linked to some authors' specific field of research.

Another tendency to note is the fragmentation, in two senses, of the textbook problem. First, while the highly scrutinized topics noted earlier are subject to an "in/out" circle or cycle, textbooks *could* become somewhat more open in the treatment of other, related issues, such as cases of exploitation, forced assimilation, and resistance under Japanese colonial rule. Second, the diverging images of postwar Japan underlying the debates between progressives and conservatives are, within the strict limits set by textbook screening, reflected in history textbooks. Left-leaning textbooks can be shown to try to convey a self-image of a "responsible," self-reflective nation within East Asia and generally to pay more attention to significant (weak, victimized) others in an attempt to provide historical and social justice and to empower the periphery. Some go so far as to insert excerpts from the textbooks of other Asian countries, to make students aware of possible differences in perspectives. On the other hand, the *New History Textbook*, in its attempt to create a "bright" image of Japan, portrays it as a misunderstood and unjustly criticized country with unique traditions (Schneider 2008).

The controversy has not only affected the Japanese defendant but also the Korean and Chinese plaintiffs, where it has fostered both counterreactions and introspection as well as established history textbooks as items worthy of reporting on, examining, and debating. In Korea, it has provided ammunition for arguments going in opposite directions—in favor of a more democratic, pluralistic textbook system, as well as providing stronger national history education in view of Japanese (as well as Chinese) attacks.[29] A number of institutions have also been established, in part with government support, to act both as self-avowed watchdogs on distortions of history (and history textbooks) by other countries and as promoters of regional understanding.[30]

In China's first major textbook affair in early 2006, textbooks on modern Chinese history were not only openly criticized for being ethnocentric and even xenophobic but also equated with their Japanese counterparts as "lacking deep reflection on their contemporary history" (Yuan 2006).[31] East Asia's familiarity with textbook issues might have also been one of the reasons for the dedication in the summer of 2006 of an entire *New York Times* article to revised Shanghai high school history textbooks, which caused a second public debate.[32] This, in turn, will in the future most likely cause Chinese textbook authors to write with an eye on possible public reactions.

The effects of the controversies on societies at large may be described as two-sided. It has been noted that public debates on this and other history-related issues initially had the positive side effect of making large parts of the Japanese population aware of the problems stemming from the country's wartime actions and of the international implications of a myopic self-concept as victimhood. In the past few years, however, they can be seen to have contributed to the deterioration of mutual public perceptions (Yang 2002, 13). Consequently, fallout from the controversies has led to a search for solutions. Acknowledging the need for constructive, depoliticized dialogue, the region's governments have finally agreed on the establishment of bilateral joint history committees, in 2002 between Korea and Japan, and in 2006 between China and Japan. Although the discussions are difficult, and currently mainly focus on the academic side of the existing problems, their findings may in the future become new points of reference for textbook authors.[33]

Additionally, the controversies have prompted a number of initiatives by scholars and educators aiming at cross-national dialogue and mutual understanding, often through working on joint history texts.[34] For political reasons, the longest-standing and most active among them have been bilateral Japanese–Korean working groups, while the Japanese–Chinese efforts might be said to lag. One of them, which had taken up its work in 1991, experimented with different forms of cooperation and saw some of their detailed analyses and recommendations taken up by Japanese textbook authors; it has recently published a supplementary textbook titled *The History of Japanese-Korean Relations*.[35]

The post-Tsukuru-kai era ushered in a new wave of activities. For example, a Korean–Japanese feminist group tried to break away from the predominantly national framework within which its predecessors had been operating and published a reader in the modern and contemporary history of the two countries from a gender perspective (Committee I 2005). Additionally, a three-nation intellectual collaboration, first attempted but not systematically sustained after the 1982 textbook controversy, achieved a major breakthrough in 2005 with the simultaneous publication of a supplementary history textbook in China, Japan, and Korea (Committee II 2005). It is difficult to determine how much this book is used in classrooms, but it has sold relatively well in all three countries, attesting to the general interest in such efforts. While it has received much praise as a well-intended project, the actual result has also drawn a number of criticisms.[36] By demanding self-introspection mainly on the Japanese side and leaving Korean and Chinese nationalist self-images largely untouched, it represents a reflection of existing perspectives and necessary compromise more than a real conceptual breakthrough. Yet it could be argued that this path and similar forms of cooperation may be worthwhile goals in themselves.

Conclusion

Textbook-related controversies will probably continue to flare up in the region for some time. Eliminating the underlying sources of friction by ensuring textbook content that gives no ground for dissatisfaction on the part of the victim states would necessitate an overall change in the politics of Japanese history education—a change in the direction of the German model of teaching national introspection and learning from past mistakes. For a number of reasons, this is currently rather unlikely to happen.

Eliminating the underlying sources of friction by ensuring textbook content that gives no ground for dissatisfaction on the part of the victim states would necessitate an overall change in the politics of Japanese history education.

Overall, Japan's strategy toward its neighbors is motivated by pragmatic concerns rather than by a moral conviction of the need to "settle the past." The country will thus continue to make indispensable concessions to accommodate criticism from other Asian countries, but no more. As there is still no domestic consensus on the evaluation of the country's modern history, it would need a strong "enlightened leader"[37] who could gather public support for, and carry out, even potentially unpopular measures targeted at reconciliation. Even Prime Minister Fukuda Yasuo, himself considered China-oriented, is probably not in the position to do so. The ugly past does not go well with currently very vocal conservative calls for a more "patriotic education." The mass media remains divided, with subtle but significant shifts toward a more conservatively dominated discourse.[38] For few Japanese is the country's relationship with its Asian neighbors a high priority at this time, but a large majority do acknowledge the need to reflect on Japan's past attacks and colonial rule over Asian nations.[39]

In sum, I have sought to show that textbooks—and textbook controversies— are above all reflections of broader sociopolitical constellations and changes, more than just historically influential factors in their own right. Finally, European experiences remind us that textbook cooperation should not be expected to be the spearhead of historical reconciliation, although it can, under favorable circumstances, help to shape a discourse directed toward mutual understanding and reconciliation.

Notes

1. See the article by Hayashi Hirofumi (2008) in this volume.

2. The "Asia-Pacific War" is considered to have started in 1931 with Japan's occupation of Manchuria. While it is considered a war of aggression by the victim countries and the majority of the Japanese population, some conservatives and right-wingers argue that it was a war of Asian liberation from white colonial rule and/or a legitimate effort to defend its national interests. Evaluations of the colonial period in Korea and Taiwan became particularly disputed with the introduction of the concept of "colonial modernity" that shifted the attention from the binary of aggression and exploitation versus resistance toward the modernizing effects it has had on the respective societies.

3. For reasons of space, this article will hereafter use the terms "Korea" and "Korean," but it is understood that all references are made to the Republic of Korea.

4. In his study of the 2001 Japanese textbook controversy in the British media, Seaton (2005) found that it presented a stereotypical and biased version of Japanese war memory, with the complexity of the inner Japanese debate largely underrepresented.

5. Hereafter the Ministry of Education is abbreviated as MOE, respectively MEXT, as it was renamed "Ministry of Education, Culture, Sports, Science and Technology" in 2001.

6. Nozaki and Inokuchi (2000) presented an excellent overview of the three lawsuits that Ienaga fought from 1965 to 1997.

7. For an in-depth analysis of the 1982 controversy, including its different stages, see Rose (1998).

8. It evolved from a bilateral, Sino-Japanese, into a regional (including South Korea) issue through the latter being inspired by the former.

9. Conrad (2003, 98) provided a thorough discussion of the factors leading to what he calls the "return of 'Asia' into Japanese discourse" in the 1990s.

10. On the rise of "historical revisionism" (understood as a social movement with an explicit political agenda) in 1990s Japan, and the various leagues and committees formed at the time, see Yang (2008).

11. For instance, the Diet Members' League to Consider Japan's Future and History Education. The largest umbrella organization is the Japan Conference, founded in 1997, which counts many Liberal Democratic Party (LDP) Diet members among its members.

12. The Japanese original *Atarashii rekishi kyôkasho wo tsukuru-kai* (Society for the Creation of New History Textbooks) is even more telling. Hereafter, the abbreviation Tsukuru-kai will be used.

13. For an in-depth analysis of the contents of the *New History Textbook*, see Nelson (2002).

14. Saaler (2005) provided an accessible English-language overview of the Japanese sociopolitical background in the 1990s, the Tsukuru-kai's aims and agenda, and the domestic debate in 2001.

15. It can be argued that the *New History Textbook* stimulated so many activities because middle school textbooks are selected by local school boards (unlike high school textbooks, which are selected by each school), thus opening more possibilities for direct influence for both camps. In the 2005 selection round, the *New History Textbook*'s selection rate had "risen" to 0.4 percent.

16. Taiwan makes for an intriguing counterexample for its recent relative absence of protests—even though it is in many respects comparable to South Korea. It was a Japanese colony from 1895 to 1945, followed by an authoritarian (Nationalist Chinese) period, whose history education included much "anti-Japanese" content, and has—since the late 1980s—undergone democratic transition. However, both in 2001 and in 2005, protests were mainly limited to academics (Zhu 2006). This is because the island's already precarious international standing makes it unwise for the government to upset a traditionally close ally; while the public is caught up in other, domestic and cross-Strait issues—in particular the thorny "national identity" question.

17. Such as issuing teaching guidelines, setting up screening procedures, and the like.

18. Interestingly, (authoritarian) China introduced textbook pluralization in the late 1980s—about a decade earlier than (democratic) South Korea.

19. The reasons why these two issues have taken on such great symbolical significance are manifold and cannot be explored here.

20. This division is made for analytical purposes only. It is not to imply that there are preexisting entities "uncovered" by impassionate research. Instead, their "re-creation" also involves ethical and political aspects.

21. Askew (2004) himself prefers a division into "serious historians" and "myth-makers." Yoshida (2000) discussed the evolution of the debates in postwar Japan.

22. Faced with overwhelming research evidence and testimonies of former victims, then–Chief Cabinet Secretary Kono Yôhei issued an official apology to the victims in 1993. Conservatives have worked since then toward a revision of this statement. See also the article by professor Hayashi Hirofumi (2008) in this volume.

23. An exception is the regular high school textbook *Europe and the World since 1945* published—with considerable political support—in identical versions (in their own languages) in France and Germany in summer 2006.

24. Soh (2005, 172) cited the results of opinion polls supporting this argument.

25. In Chinese textbooks, for instance, Chinese actors during that war are portrayed as either models of heroic resistance (embodying the "national spirit"), victims (symbolizing the violated "national body"), or traitors (expunged from "the nation"). For Korea, see Soh (2005).

26. The term is borrowed from Lim (2008).

27. This is not to say that academic trends have gone completely unnoticed, but textbooks on the junior high level have kept to the "empiricist historiography" identified by Dierkes (2005) and others. The central curriculum guidelines have also remained relatively stable, with the addition in 1998 of the goal of "deepening student's understanding and love of our country's history," giving somewhat more leeway to conservative efforts.

28. Moreover, the only junior high textbook to have retained any mention of the comfort women's plight (published by Nihon Shoseki Shinsha) gives graphic proof of the necessary compromises: the 2001 photo of a crying victim was replaced by a newspaper cutting announcing the establishment of a Japanese compensation fund for the victims in 1995, implying Japan's well-intended efforts to come to terms with its past.

29. Interview with a Korean education official in Seoul, December 2006. See also the article "Changing History Education," in the *Asahi Shimbun* (electronic English version), http://www.asahi.com/english/Herald-asahi/TKY200706150138.html (accessed June 18, 2007).

30. The biggest is the Northeast Asian History Foundation, established by the government in 2006.

31. The official wrath that the article had incited led to the temporary closing of the weekly magazine *Freezing Point* in which the article had been published.

32. This well-intended report (Kahn 2006) did the reforms a bad turn, as many of its implications—in particular the title itself, which implied Mao Zedong had been eliminated from the accounts—rang alarm bells in (otherwise noninvolved) Beijing. The textbooks were submitted to drastic revisions.

33. The first phase of the Korean–Japanese research finished in 2005; the reports of the Sino-Japanese commission are due in 2008.

34. Recent examples on the academic level include Liu, Mitani, and Yang (2006).

35. For an English introduction to the group's work by one of its members, see Kimijima (2000).

36. Not only have political sensitivities necessitated many twists and omissions in the portrayal of postwar East Asia, but the book also presents the three nations as the historical subjects in a self-evident manner and lacks adequate treatment of the complexities of colonialism (Narita and Iwasaki 2008).

37. The concept of "enlightened leadership" is brought forward by Yang (2002, 22).

38. A comparative analysis of the 2001 and 2005 coverage of the *New History Textbook* shows the traditionally critical nationwide *Asahi* newspaper to have become more cautious, the supporting conservative counterparts more outspoken. Nevertheless, articles criticizing the *New History Textbook* continued to outnumber sympathetic accounts (Fujinaga 2006).

39. Opinion poll by Yomiuri Shimbun at the end of 2006 and in January 2007; http://www.mansfieldfdn.org/polls/poll-07-2.htm.

References

Askew, D. 2004. New research on the Nanjing incident. *Japan Focus* 126. http://japanfocus.org/products/details/1729.

Barnard, C. 2003. *Language, ideology, and Japanese history textbooks*. London: RoutledgeCurzon.

Chan, C., and B. Bridges. 2006. China, Japan, and the clash of nationalisms. *Asian Perspectives* 30 (1): 127-56.

Committee I: Japanese-Korean Women's Committee for the Writing of a Common History Teaching Material. 2005. *Japanese-Korean modern and contemporary history from a gender perspective* [in Japanese]. Tokyo: Nashinokisha.

Committee II: Japanese-Chinese-Korean Committee for Common History Teaching Materials of the Three Countries. 2005. *History that opens the future: Modern and contemporary history of three East Asian countries* [in Japanese]. Tokyo: Kôbunken.

Conrad, S. 2003. Entangled memories: Versions of the past in Germany and Japan, 1945-2001. *Journal of Contemporary History* 38 (1): 85-99.

Dierkes, J. 2005. The stability of postwar Japanese history education amid global changes. In *History education and national identity in East Asia*, ed. E. Vickers and A. Jones, 255-74. New York: Routledge.

Ducke, I. 2002. The history textbook issue 2001. A successful citizens' movement or foreign intervention? DIJ Working Paper 02/6, Deutsches Institut fuer Japanstudien [German Institute for Japanese Studes], Tokyo.

Fiola, A. 2005. Anti-Japanese hostilities move to the Internet. *Washington Post*, May 20. http://www.washingtonpost.com/wp-dyn/content/article/2005/05/09/AR2005050901119_pf.html.

Fujinaga, T. 2006. The 2005 history textbook issue and Japanese society: The discussion on the Tsukuru-kai textbook [in Japanese]. Paper presented at the fourth international symposium for a common historical perspective in East Asia, Seoul, Republic of Korea, December.

Gries, P. 2004. *China's new nationalism: Pride, politics and diplomacy*. Berkeley: University of California Press.

Hayashi, Hirofumi. 2008. Disputes in Japan over the Japanese military "comfort women" system and its perception in history. *The Annals of the American Academy of Political and Social Science* 617:123-132.

Kahn, J. 2006. Where's Mao? Chinese revise history textbooks. *New York Times*, September 1. http://www.nytimes.com/2006/09/01/world/asia/01china.html?partner=rssnyt&emc=rss.

Kimijima, K. 2000. The continuing legacy of Japanese colonialism: The Japan-South Korea Joint Study Group on History Textbooks. In *Censoring history: Citizenship and memory in Japan, Germany, and the United States*, ed. L. Hein and M. Selden, 203-25. Armonk, NY: M.E. Sharpe.

Klein, T. 2005. Staging a tradition? The 2005-anti-Japanese protests in the People's Republic of China in historical perspective [in German]. *Historische Anthropologie* 13 (3): 403-13.

Lim, J. 2008. The antagonistic complicity of nationalisms—On nationalist phenomenology in East Asian history textbooks. In *Contested views of a common past: Historical revisionism in contemporary East Asia*, ed. S. Richter, 197-214. Frankfurt, Germany: Campus.

Liu, Jie, Mitani, Hiroshi, and Yang, Daqing, eds. 2006. Historical views that transcend national boundaries: An effort toward Sino-Japanese dialogue [in Chinese and in Japanese]. Tokyo: Tokyo University Press/Beijing: Social Sciences Academic Press.

Narita, R., and M. Iwasaki. 2008. Writing a history textbook in East Asia—The possibilities and pitfalls of "history that opens the future." In *Contested views of a common past: Historical revisionism in contemporary East Asia*, ed. S. Richter, 263-75. Frankfurt, Germany: Campus.

Nelson, J. 2002. Tempest in a textbook: A report on the new middle-school history textbook in Japan. *Critical Asian Studies* 34 (1): 129-48.

Nozaki, Y., and H. Inokuchi. 2000. Japanese education, nationalism, and Ienaga Saburo's textbook lawsuits. In *Censoring history: Citizenship and memory in Japan, Germany, and the United States*, ed. L. Hein and M. Selden, 96-126. Armonk, NY: M.E. Sharpe.

Oguma, E., and Y. Ueno. 2003. *Pain-relieving nationalism* [in Japanese]. Tokyo: Kei gijuku daigaku shup-pankai.

Reilly, J. 2006. China's history activism and Sino-Japanese relations. *China: An International Journal* 4 (2): 189-216.

Rose, C. 1998. *Interpreting history in Sino-Japanese relations*. London: Routledge.

———. 2005. *Sino-Japanese relations: Facing the past, looking to the future?* London: Routledge.

Saaler, S. 2005. *Politics, memory and public opinion: The history textbook controversy Japanese society*. Munich, Germany: Iudicium.

———. 2006. Historical revisionism in crisis. The end of the history textbook controversy in Japan? [in German]. *Internationale Schulbuchforschung* 28 (1): 85-93.

Sakamoto, T. 2003. How should textbooks be written? In *The contested past: A historians' debate in Japan* [in German], ed. S. Richter and W. Hoepken, 151-66. Weimar, Germany: Boehlau.

Schneider, C. 2008. National fortresses besieged: History textbooks in contemporary China, Taiwan, and Japan. In *Contested views of a common past: Historical revisionism in contemporary East Asia*, ed. S. Richter, 237-62. Frankfurt, Germany: Campus.

Seaton, P. 2005. Reporting the 2001 textbook and Yasukuni Shrine controversies: Japanese war memory and commemoration in the British media. *Japan Forum* 17 (3): 287, 309.

Seraphim, F. 2006. Relocating war memory at century's end: Japan's postwar responsibility and global public culture. In *Ruptured histories: War, memory, and the post-cold war in Asia*, ed. S.M. Jager and R. Mitter, 15-46. Cambridge, MA: Harvard University Press.

Soh, C. 2005. Politics of the victim/victor complex: Interpreting South Korea's national furor over Japanese history textbooks. *American Asian Review* 21 (4): 145-78.

Whiting, A. 1989. *China eyes Japan*. Berkeley: University of California Press.

Yang, D. 2002. Mirror for the future or the history card? Understanding the history problem. In *Chinese-Japanese relations in the twenty-first century: Complementarity and conflict*, ed. M. Söderberg, 10-31. London: Routledge.

———. 2008. Historical revisionism in East Asia: What does politics have to do with it? In *Contested views of a common past: Historical revisionism in contemporary East Asia*, ed. S. Richter. Frankfurt, Germany: Campus.

Yoshida, T. 2000. A battle over history: The Nanjing Massacre in Japan. In *The Nanjing Massacre in history and historiography*, ed. J. Fogel, 70-132. Berkeley: University of California Press.

Yuan, W. 2006. Modernisation and history textbooks [in Chinese]. *Freezing Point* 574, January 11. http://zqb.cyol.com/gb/zqb/2006-01/11/content_118530.htm.

Zhu, D. 2006. Perspectives on the 2005 Japanese history textbook issue: The perspective of Taiwanese society. Paper presented at the Fourth International Symposium for a Common Historical Perspective in East Asia, Seoul, Republic of Korea, December.

Disputes in Japan over the Japanese Military "Comfort Women" System and Its Perception in History

By
HIROFUMI HAYASHI

In 2007, then–Japanese Prime Minister Abe stirred up controversy by denying that "comfort women" were coerced by the Japanese military. He was supported by more than a few politicians, and his opinion may be viewed as a reflection of the nationalistic atmosphere of Japanese society. Since the early 1990s, research has been establishing proof that the Japanese government and military were fully and systematically involved in the comfort women system and that the system violated numerous international and domestic laws. Ultrarightist groups have been trying to erase the fruits of such research. The U.S. House of Representatives' resolution in July 2007 (H. Res. 121) and Abe's sudden resignation seem to mean that the ultrarightist movement toward historical revision has come to a deadlock. The comfort women issue and other questions about Japan's war responsibilities may have an important impact on Japan's future.

Keywords: comfort women; sexual slavery; perception of history; war responsibility

Prime Minister Abe in Defense of the Japanese Imperial Army

In 2007, then–Japanese Prime Minister Shinzo Abe stirred international interest in the controversy over Japanese military comfort women by denying that the military was responsible for the women's coercion. He defined *coercion* in a narrow sense as "government authorities breaking into private homes and taking [women] like kidnappers" and stated that "it is a fact that no evidence has been found to support coercion as initially defined." He asserted that private agents, not the military itself, had coerced the

Hirofumi Hayashi is a professor of politics and international relations at Kanto Gakuin University. He is the research director of the Center for Research and Documentation on Japan's War Responsibility (JWRC) and editor of Senso Sekinin Kenkyu. *He is the author of* Sabakareta Senso Hanzai (Tried War Crimes: British War Crimes Trials of Japanese), BC-kyu Senpan Saiban (Class B & C War Crimes Trials), *and* Singaporu Kakyo Shukusei (Massacre of Chinese in Singapore).

DOI: 10.1177/0002716208314191

women, stating that "in some cases the private go-betweens coerced the women, so in effect there was coercion in the broad sense." But Abe never admitted that the women were coerced by Japanese military personnel or officials.[1] Later, Abe said he would uphold the 1993 Kono Statement (by Yohei Kono, then chief cabinet secretary), which reported that "in many cases their recruitment, transfer, control, etc., were conducted generally against their will, through coaxing, coercion, etc." However, Abe did not take back his original comments.[2] He also failed to reprimand then–Deputy Chief Cabinet Secretary Shimomura, who had openly denied any military involvement.

In contrast, Abe has been a fierce critic of the abduction of Japanese citizens by North Korea. Had he applied the narrow sense of *coercion*, meaning only coerced abductions that were carried out by agents of the North Korean state, none of the Japanese citizens removed to North Korea would be considered abductees. Such views could be criticized for holding to a double standard, but to the regret of many researchers and advocates for historical truth, Japan's media have not been highly critical of Abe's statements.

Since his election as a member of the House of Representatives in 1993, Abe has joined several ultrarightist Diet members' groups related to the interpretation of history. Research and campaigns related to the issue of the Japanese military comfort women and other war crimes developed rapidly during this time (Tawara and Uozumi 2006). Abe's grandfather, ex–Prime Minister Nobusuke Kishi, was a confidant of Hideki Tojo and a minister in the Tojo cabinet. Abe stated that he believes that Japan's war and the behavior of the Japanese military were righteous, and hence he began efforts to recover his grandfather's honor by fighting back against new research and the subsequent campaigns. Some of the main arguments of these Diet groups are that the Nanjing Massacre was fabricated, that comfort women were regular prostitutes rather than victims of war crimes, and that Japan did not act aggressively. One of their targets is history textbooks, which currently contain some references to aforementioned Japanese military atrocities. In addition, the Diet groups' ultimate aim is to change the Constitution and, in particular, the war-renouncing Article 9 (Hayashi 2005).

Abe's recent position as prime minister demonstrates that ultrarightists have taken over the Liberal Democratic Party and the Japanese government. Key members of the cabinet are ultrarightist cronies of Abe. As for the conservative politicians of the mainstream Liberal Democratic Party (LDP), such as ex–Prime Ministers Kiichi Miyazawa and Kono Yohei, some have already retired or passed away, and the rest have lost their influence in the party. Although Abe's resignation means such a line has run into an impasse, the policy of the Fukuda cabinet is as yet uncertain.

Researchers Fight Back

Since the beginning of the twenty-first century, Japan's media have lost interest in historical issues and have seldom covered issues related to Japan's war compensation, such as the controversy over comfort women. The arguments of ultrarightists flood the mainstream mass media and few media sources cover research that contradicts them. However, the proposed resolution in the U.S. House of Representatives (H. Res. 121 [2007]) on the issue of Japanese military comfort women has changed circumstances to some degree (Yoshimi, Nishino, and Hayashi 2007).

Although this proposed resolution, submitted in January 2007, was almost completely ignored by the mass media in Japan, Abe's statements and the subsequent international response has reminded the Japanese people that this issue has not yet been settled. However, the Japanese media covered only events overseas and continued to ignore the domestic response. Under such circumstances the Center for Research and Documentation on Japan's War Responsibility (JWRC), in which most of the researchers on Japan's war responsibility are involved, felt it could not allow the Japanese government to ignore this resolution. The result of this rejection would not only be a distorted view of historical fact, but also a discrediting of the Japanese people as a whole in the eyes of the international community. This led to a public appeal by the JWRC on February 23, 2007: "Appeal on the Issue of Japan's Military Comfort Women" (JWRC 2007a).

The JWRC's appeal advocates certain facts as documented in various materials: the former Japanese Army and Navy created the comfort women system to serve their own needs; the military decided when, where, and how "comfort stations" were to be established and implemented these decisions, providing buildings, setting regulations and fees, and controlling the management of comfort stations; the military was well aware of the various methods used to bring women to comfort stations and of the circumstances these women were forced to endure. Furthermore, the JWRC concludes that while licensed prostitution in Japan may be called a de facto system of sexual slavery, the Japanese military comfort women system was literal sexual slavery in a far more thorough and overt form. Finally, the JWRC expressed the strong hope that the world should acknowledge these facts and that a fundamental and final resolution to the comfort women issue would soon be reached (JWRC 2007a).

[T]he military was well aware of the various methods used to bring women to comfort stations and of the circumstances these women were forced to endure.

In spite of such campaigns, the Japanese media ignored efforts of researchers and groups like the JWRC. It is for this reason that the JWRC decided to hold a press conference at the Foreign Correspondents' Club of Japan on April 19, 2007. At the press conference, researchers presented several documents submitted as evidence to the Tokyo war crimes tribunal showing that the Japanese military had kidnapped women to work as sex slaves. One of the exhibits, submitted by the Dutch prosecution from WWII war crimes trials of the Japanese, reads, "they arrested women on the streets and after a medical examination placed them in the brothels," as was the case in Pontianak in Borneo, Indonesia. Another exhibit relating to a case in East Timor reads, "I know of a lot of places where the Japanese forced the chiefs to send native girls to Japanese brothels, by threatening the native chiefs, telling them that if they did not send the girls, the Japanese would go to the chiefs' houses and take away their near[est] female relatives for this purpose." The JWRC stated that the Japanese government must admit to the coercion and criminality involved in the comfort women system, because it had accepted the war crimes trials, including the Tokyo Tribunal, in Article 11 of the peace treaty (JWRC 2007b).

While the overseas media gave heavy coverage to the press conference (such as the *New York Times* and the *Washington Post*, April 18, 2007), the Japanese media paid little attention; but they were unable to ignore it completely.

Prior to this press conference, at the end of March 2007, a collection of information about Yasukuni Shrine was released by the Diet Library. Among the material is a document that shows that a war criminal convicted and sentenced to ten years' imprisonment by the Dutch war crimes trial on a charge of forced prostitution was enshrined at Yasukuni because he died of illness while serving his sentence (*Senso Sekinin Kenkyu* 2007, 18-19). This enshrinement took place in 1967 by agreement between Yasukuni Shrine and the Health and Welfare Ministry, part of the Japanese government. Such honoring of a man convicted of war crimes suggests the Japanese government at that time had accepted that comfort women were coerced and that such coercion was done for the good of the nation (Yoshimi, Nishino, and Hayashi 2007, 39).

The Fruits of Research and the Ultrarightist Resurgence since the 1990s

The controversy over the Japanese military's comfort women began in the 1980s. Before the 1980s, most books published in Japan about the war had dealt with Japanese suffering, such as in Hiroshima and Nagasaki, and with the U.S. air raids against Japanese cities. However, the history textbook dispute of 1982, in which the Ministry of Education ordered the deletion from history textbooks of references to Japan's aggression and military atrocities, had a considerable impact on Japan. Fierce criticism came from other Asian countries, and many Japanese were made aware of the nature and extent of Japan's wartime aggression. In the wake of this dispute, more than a few veterans began to speak out truthfully about their own wartime actions. In addition, historians began to look into war crimes such as the Nanjing Massacre and the biological warfare experiments of

Unit 731. However, the comfort women issue was still ignored, although most historians knew about it.

[T]he history textbook dispute of 1982, in which the Ministry of Education ordered the deletion from history textbooks of references to Japan's aggression and military atrocities, had a considerable impact on Japan.

The situation changed dramatically in 1991 when a former comfort woman from South Korea, Kim Hak Sun, broke nearly half a century of silence and made her story public. She was followed by several more women, not only in South Korea, but in other Asian nations as well. Their bravery in stepping forward encouraged Japanese activists, especially female activists, to organize support groups. The first of many lawsuits against the Japanese government was filed by Kim Hak Sun and other Koreans in December 1991. The Japanese government denied any Japanese military involvement in the comfort women system and refused not only to apologize to or provide reparations for the women, but also to carry out any kind of investigation.

However, in January 1992 the historian Yoshimi Yoshiaki unearthed official documents in the Defense Agency's National Institute of Defense Studies that proved conclusively that the military had played a role in the establishment and control of comfort stations (Yoshimi 2000, 35). As a result, Prime Minister Kiichi Miyazawa publicly admitted that the Japanese military was involved, and he apologized for the comfort women system for the first time. Since then, research on the issue has been active, and popular movements demanding a formal state apology and reparations to the victims have developed very quickly.

It is not possible to describe in detail the process of this research and the history of the various movements. However, the following is a summary of research findings so far. First, it has been demonstrated that the Japanese government and military were fully and systematically involved in planning, establishing, and operating the comfort women system. Japanese officials involved were Home Ministry personnel, including prefectural governors and the police at all ranks; Foreign Ministry officials; and the governors-general of Korea and Taiwan (Yoshimi and Hayashi 1995; Yoshimi 2000). Second, the Japanese military set up so-called "comfort stations" in almost every area they occupied. In addition to Korean, Taiwanese, and Japanese women, local women in the occupied areas were victimized (Yoshimi and Hayashi 1995; Yoshimi 2000). Third, the military comfort women system was clearly sexual slavery, organized and controlled by the military, and it constituted sexual, racial, ethnic, and economic discrimination and the violation of the rights of women (Yoshimi and Hayashi 1995; Yoshimi 2000). Fourth, although one of the reasons given by the Japanese military for introducing the comfort women system was to prevent the rape of local women by soldiers, rape was not eliminated. Rape and comfort stations existed together (Yoshimi and Hayashi 1995; Yoshimi 2000). Fifth, it has been proven that the system of Japanese military comfort women violated numerous international laws, including laws against enslavement and the transportation of minors across national borders. Overwhelming evidence shows that the comfort women system constituted a war crime and a crime against humanity (Yoshimi and Hayashi 1995; Yoshimi 2000).

Finally, the suffering of the women involved did not end with liberation. Many comfort women were unable to return home. Some still remain where they were abandoned. Former comfort women have suffered the aftereffects of disease, injury, psychological trauma, and posttraumatic stress disorder, as well as social discrimination for their pasts (Yoshimi and Hayashi 1995; Yoshimi 2000).

As a result of these early efforts in the 1980s and 1990s to bring facts to light and increase public awareness, the Japanese public began to take note of the comfort women issue, and it has been taught as part of high school and junior high school history courses (Hayashi 2001). Ultrarightists, however, began a systematic counterattack in the mid-1990s. They attacked textbooks that dealt with Japan's various atrocities, including the comfort women system, demanding that such material be deleted to recover a sense of national pride. Under political pressure, publishers of textbooks began to restrain the descriptions used. The minister of education stated in 2004 that it was desirable for references to Japanese atrocities, such as the comfort women system, to be dropped (Hayashi 2005, 161).

In junior high school history textbooks approved by the Ministry of Education in April 2005 for use from 2006 on, a description of Korean forced labor was virtually deleted. Furthermore, the term "comfort women" can no longer be found in the textbooks. As a whole, mention of Japanese aggression and atrocities has been drastically cut under pressure from the Ministry of Education, the Liberal Democratic Party, and the right-leaning mass media (Hayashi 2005, 162-68).

Against a background of economic depression and a climate of prejudice against other Asians, particularly the Chinese and Koreans, many Japanese have been influenced by these xenophobic campaigns. It is well known that former prime minister Abe and key persons in the Abe cabinet have been core members of such campaigns (Tawara and Uozumi 2006, 85-91).

The U.S. House of Representatives' Resolution and the Japanese Response

The U.S. House of Representatives passed a resolution (H. Res. 121) on July 30, 2007, to the effect that the government of Japan "should formally acknowledge, apologize, and accept historical responsibility in a clear and unequivocal manner" for the military sexual slavery, known to the world as comfort women. However, the Japanese government refused to accept this resolution in any way.

In response to House Resolution 121, civic groups in Japan, including the JWRC, that have been campaigning on behalf of survivors of the comfort women system issued a statement on July 31, 2007: "What Would Make a Japanese Government Apology to Comfort Women Unequivocal?" (JWRC et al. 2007).

The statement's proposals are as follows:

1. The government of Japan must explicitly accept the fact that the government and military of Japan in the period from the onset of the Manchurian Incident to the end of the Asia-Pacific War made women from its colonies and occupied areas into comfort women against their will and forcibly put them under sexual slavery, and that these acts were illegal according to the human rights norms of the time.
2. Based on such acceptance, either the government or the parliament of Japan must issue, through an official and formal manner such as a cabinet decision or a parliamentary resolution, an apology in which the responsibility of the state of Japan is clarified.
3. The government of Japan must provide a letter of such apology to each and all of the individual survivors regardless of their countries or regions of origin or residence.
4. To show that this apology is genuine, the government of Japan must provide compensation to individual victims through new legislation.

In addition, the statement proposed the following measures to demonstrate to the world that the apology is genuine:

1. The government of Japan should fully disclose all documents in their custody that have not yet been released and conduct a full and thorough fact-finding effort and investigation. The facts of victimization should be investigated in all affected countries and regions, so as to obtain a full picture of the reality of all the different types of victimization of and damage inflicted upon women.
2. The government of Japan should implement suitable educational measures to ensure that accurate knowledge of this issue is passed on to future generations to ensure that such atrocities shall never be repeated.
3. The government of Japan should resolutely refute all and any word or deed aimed at denying the criminal and/or coercive nature of Japan's military sexual slavery and thus defend the dignity of the survivors and victims.

In spite of these efforts, most of the mass media in Japan responded unfavorably to the statement. Some claim that the Japanese military comfort women system did not constitute a crime but was a common occurrence during war (Yoshimi, Nishino, and Hayashi 2007, 50-51). Others claim that the Japanese government has already apologized several times (JWRC et al. 2007). People in Japan seem to have lost interest in Japan's war responsibilities. On the other hand, over the past decade the number of politicians of the younger generation in the LDP and the Democratic Party who admire prewar Japan, justify Japan's wars, and want to overturn the "renouncement of war" article of the constitution has been increasing, with former prime minister Abe one of their champions. They refuse to admit that the Japanese military was involved in atrocities or that Japan has responsibility for the war, with the aim of recovering state prestige and building a political regime under which Japan can enter wars abroad in alliance with the United States.

There is a link here with the current, international issue of human trafficking and prostitution. Japan is one of the main target countries for human trafficking. The Trafficking in Persons Report, issued in June 2007 by the U.S. government, states that "Japan is primarily a destination, and to a lesser extent a transit country, for men, women, and children trafficked for the purpose of commercial sexual exploitation" (U.S. Department of State 2007).

A great problem is that human trafficking (forcible in some cases) and prostitution seem to be tolerated even by some MPs, who, as illustrated below, have rationalized the system of military comfort women. In June 2007, an ultrarightist group took out advocacy advertising in the *Washington Post* rationalizing the Japanese military's use of comfort women (*Washington Post*, June 14, 2007). One of the signatories, an MP, claims in a book about comfort women and the Nanjing Massacre that "in countries where prostitution is legal, there are prostitutes some of who work against their will. Unfortunately this is necessary" (Nishimura 2007, 164). A former LDP MP who was a member of an ultrarightist group of MPs (whose secretariat general was Abe) also claimed it was commonplace that someone was taken against their will during wartime (Nihon no Zento to Rekishi Kyouiku wo Kangaeru Wakate Giin no Kai 1997, 435-36). Such advertising admits that women were taken against their will but tries to rationalize the fact by saying it is common during war.

Reconciliation?

The nationalistic atmosphere pervading Japan means that recent criticism from Asian countries, such as China and South Korea, has provoked antipathy among some Japanese. Citizens suffering from the economic depression and who feel vulnerable in a highly competitive society tend to display aggressive behavior against others. It seems that China and Korea are the main targets of recent Japanese aggression. In these circumstances, it is easy for antiforeign politicians to capture their sympathy. There is a tendency for younger politicians to be more antiforeign (Hayashi 2005). It appears that the government of South Korea is at a loss as to how to respond, while the Chinese government remains silent over the former prime minister's statements to give priority to improving China-Japan relations.

On the other hand, some people are beginning to realize that Japan has to come to terms with its neighbors. The U.S. House of Representatives' resolution can be construed as a message to this effect. As a result, the word "reconciliation" has recently become fashionable. Although reconciliation is essential, attempts are being made at reconciliation without a formal state apology or individual compensation to victims. The excuse is that Japan has already apologized on many occasions and that the countries that suffered, such as China and Korea, should stop bringing up past issues. This line is even followed by officials of the Japanese Foreign Ministry as well as by certain intellectuals in Japan and other Asian countries (Kim 2007). However, this approach may distract from what is currently going on in Japan. It might be a reflection of the mood of Japanese society, but pursuing this line will leave the victims behind, and a chance for reforming Japan might be missed. Reconciliation needs to be achieved among the ordinary people of the Asia-Pacific region, including the victims, not among those in power.

Surprisingly enough, Prime Minister Abe resigned suddenly in September 2007. His resignation seems to mean that the ultrarightist line has come to a deadlock. I expect this opportunity could be a turning point for a better future. Will Japan be a nation that truly promotes human rights and maintains a stance of renouncing war? The comfort women issue and other questions of Japan's war responsibilities are not only problems to be settled for the sake of victims of a war long past, but also issues closely related to Japan's future.

Notes

1. Abe's account at the Budget Committee of the House of Councilors, March 5, 2007.
2. Abe's answer to Ms. Kiyomi Tsujimoto, Member of the House of Councilors, March 16, 2007.

References

Hayashi, Hirofumi. 2001. The Japanese movement to protest wartime sexual violence: A survey of Japanese and international literature. *Critical Asian Studies* 33 (4): 572-80.

———. 2005. Nihon no Haigaiteki Nashonarizumu wa Naze Taito shitaka [Why Japanese chauvinistic nationalism has gained power]. In *Kesareta Sabaki: NHK Bangumi Kaihen to Seiji Kainyu Jiken* [Censored judgment: Interpretation of NHK's TV program and politicians' intervention], ed. VAWW-NET Japan, 160-86. Tokyo: Gaifusha. http://www32.ocn.ne.jp/~modernh/paper72.htm.

JWRC (The Center for Research and Documentation on Japan's War Responsibility). 2007a. Appeal on the issue of Japan's military comfort women. February 23. http://space.geocities.jp/japanwarres/center/english/appeal03.htm.

———. 2007b. Reference materials of the press conference on Japanese military sexual slavery ("comfort women"). April 17. http://space.geocities.jp/japanwarres/center/hodo/hodo38.pdf.

JWRC et al. 2007. What would make a Japanese government apology to comfort women unequivocal? July 31. http://space.geocities.jp/japanwarres/center/english/appeal05.htm.

Kim, Puja. 2007. "Ianfu" Mondai to Datsu-Shokuminnchi-shugi ["Ianfu" issue and de-colonialism]. *Inpakushon* [Impaction] 158 (July): 124-47.

Nihon no Zento to Rekishi Kyoiku wo Kangaeru Wakate Giin no Kai [Young Diet Member's League to Consider Japan's Future and History Education]. 1997. *Rekishi Kyokasho heno Gimon* [Doubts on history textbook]. Tokyo: Private Press.

Nishimura, Koyu, ed. 2007. *Johosen: Ianfu-Nankin no Shinjitsu* [Information warfare: Truth of comfort women and Nanjin]. Tokyo: Okura Shupan.

Senso Sekinin Kenkyu [Report on Japan's War Responsibility]. 2007. Feature: Frontline of comfort women issue. *Senso Sekinin Kenkyu* 56 (June). http://space.geocities.jp/japanwarres/center/somokuji.htm.

Tawara, Yoshifumi, and Akira Uozumi. 2006. *Abe Shinzo no Honsho* [Real character of Abe Shinzo]. Tokyo: Kinyobi.

U.S. Department of State. 2007. Trafficking in persons report. June 12. http://www.state.gov/g/tip/rls/tiprpt/2007/.

Washington Post. 2007, June 14. The Facts. Advertisement.

Yoshimi, Yoshiaki, 2000. *Comfort women: Sexual slavery in the Japanese military during World War II.* New York: Columbia University Press.

Yoshimi, Yoshiaki, and Hirofumi Hayashi, eds. 1995. *Nihongun Ianfu* [Japanese military comfort women]. Tokyo: Otsuki Shoten.

Yoshimi, Yoshiaki, Rumiko Nishino, and Hirofumi Hayashi. 2007. *Koko made wakatta Nihon-gun Ianfu Seido* [Clarified picture of Japanese military comfort women system]. Kyoto, Japan: Kamogawa Shuppan.

The Politics of History and Memory in Democratic Spain

By

CAROLYN P. BOYD

This article examines the political uses of history and memory in Spain since the death of General Francisco Franco in 1975. The myth of the war as a collective tragedy facilitated the democratic transition, as did the Amnesty Law of 1977, which applied to the agents of Franquist repression as well as its victims. Once democracy was consolidated, professional historians clarified military responsibility for the civil war and documented the extent of the repression; the right responded by reviving the Franquist myth of the civil war as a crusade against communism. "Memory" replaced history in public discourse with the breakdown of the transition consensus and the maturation of a generation with no recall of the war or the dictatorship. Demands for official condemnation of the dictatorship and public recognition of its victims culminated in the passage of the so-called Law of Historical Memory in October 2007.

Keywords: Spain; history; memory; historical memory; civil war; dictatorship; democratic transition

A t the end of October 2007, the Spanish parliament began to debate the so-called "Law of Historical Memory." Although its passage was a foregone conclusion, the law will probably never lay completely to rest the profound disagreements—over national history and identity and the claims of memory, both individual and "collective"—that have preoccupied Spaniards since the death of General Francisco Franco in 1975. This article traces the evolution of the political uses of history and memory in democratic Spain, focusing in particular on the space each has occupied in political discourse and practical politics over the past thirty years.

Carolyn P. Boyd is a professor of history and dean of the Graduate Division at the University of California, Irvine. She is the author of Praetorian Politics in Liberal Spain (1979) and Historia Patria: Politics History and National Identity in Spain, 1875-1975 (1997) and the editor of Religión y política en la España contemporánea (2007). She is currently writing a book on the politics of commemoration in modern Spain.

DOI: 10.1177/0002716207312760

"History" and "memory" are terms often used interchangeably in popular discourse, despite the large and ever-growing body of literature whose purpose is to distinguish between them (Halbwachs 1980; Le Goff 1992; Fentress and Wickham 1992; Olick and Robbins 1998; Bell 2003). Indeed, in Spain the word "memory" has become the preferred locution in many contexts, including nominally neutral ones. While this is not the moment for an extensive review of that literature, a brief definition of the terms "history," "memory," "historical memory," and "collective memory" as I will use them in this article is probably in order, if only to clarify the degree to which contemporary political usage has distorted, confounded, or instrumentalized them.

What is memory? For both individuals and groups, it is the process by which people construct personal narratives supportive of integrated and efficacious identities in the present. Without memory—that is to say, without a past—individuals and groups can neither make sense of their current existence nor plot their futures. Individual and group memories, like individual and group identities, are the product of active creation, not passive inheritance; through selective remembering and forgetting, people construct out of the randomness and fragmentation of human experience comprehensible stories in which past events cumulatively determine present existence and provide signposts to guide future action.

Technically speaking, real remembering is a psychological process that takes place only in the individual mind and involves only those events that the individual has experienced directly. Outside of individual experience, "memory" is a metaphor for mediated knowledge of past events. It is therefore inaccurate and misleading to refer to "collective memory," except in those instances where all members of a collectivity who have lived through the same event perform an act of collective remembrance. But even though memory is experientially based and unique to the individual, it is socially framed. As Maurice Halbwachs (1980) has argued, individual memory is structured by the groups—family, class, religion, nation—to which an individual belongs. Symbolic or mnemonic cultural practices, such as oral traditions, sacred texts, rituals, commemorations, monuments, museums, and archives, create a social memory, or set of narratives about the past, that are typically not based on direct experience but that provide a matrix for individual identities and shape and sustain collective identities. As a group adjusts its identity in response to changing political and social circumstances, social memory evolves, altering the frame through which individual experience is understood.

Historical memory is a form of social memory in which a group constructs a selective representation of its own imagined past (Lavabre 2006). Historical memory may legitimate or challenge the status quo, teach a lesson, validate a claim, consolidate an identity, or inspire action—that is, it typically has a social or political purpose. There is no single historical or collective memory, but rather there are as many stories about the past as there are social or political groups vying for power (Sevillano Calero 2003). History, on the other hand, may be defined as a system of critical inquiry bound by rules that govern the use of evidence and argumentation. Like other forms of social memory, history provides a "genealogy of the present" (Fontana 1982) and is thus susceptible to change over time. Nevertheless, the historian is governed by the principle of disciplinary autonomy—that is, he or she is professionally obligated to put distance between the object of study and his or her own subjectivity and to resist the temptation to view present circumstances in essentialist or deterministic terms.

History and Memory in the Transition

Political scientists and historians have tended to view the Spanish transition to democracy as a "model" transition because of its consensual, nonviolent character and positive outcome (Gunther, Montero, and Botella 2004). As Paloma Aguilar Fernández (1996) first argued, the sociocultural basis of the transition was the shared memory of the civil war as a fratricidal tragedy for which responsibility was equally shared, a social memory summed up in the slogans "never again" and "we were all guilty." Fearful of reopening the political and social cleavages that had produced the bloody civil war of 1936 to 1939, the political elites who negotiated the constitutional compromise agreed to "forget" the past in order to create a new political order based on mutual tolerance and respect (Juliá 2006). The legal codification of this act of forgetting was the Amnesty Law of 1977, which encompassed acts of political violence committed during the civil war and the forty-year Franquist dictatorship that followed (Aguilar Fernández 1997). The law included both those victimized by Franquist repression and the agents of that repression, a concession to the right that reflected the balance of political forces at the time.

As Santos Juliá (2003, 2006, 2007) has forcefully argued, "amnesty" should not be confused with "amnesia"; nor is active forgetting the same thing as failing to remember. On the contrary, the agreement among political elites to put the past behind them derived from their collective memory of the violence of the 1930s. Although there was much less agreement on collective responsibility for the dictatorship, democratic reform from within the prevailing regime structures was deemed feasible only if a blanket amnesty was extended to all political crimes. The transition to democracy in Spain thus rested on a de facto "pact of silence" that avoided confrontation with those responsible for the dictatorship and denied public recognition of its victims. To avoid arousing the ire of the right, the first governments of the transition avoided purging the state administration and the judiciary of Franco loyalists. Statues and other symbolic tributes to the victors in the war continued to occupy public spaces. As numerous public opinion surveys indicated throughout the 1980s, a large majority of Spaniards supported the decision to avoid an official reckoning with the past. Fear of military reaction and their own complicity in sustaining the dictatorship justified to many Spaniards the pact of silence (Aguilar Fernández 2006).

Official silence on the civil war and the dictatorship did not mean censorship, however, nor did it indicate lack of popular or scholarly interest in the war. By 1986, the bibliography of the civil war included some fifteen thousand titles

(Blanco Rodríguez 2006). Although the Socialist government of Felipe González abstained in 1986 from official commemoration of what the prime minister termed an "uncivil war," scholars were less inhibited, organizing dozens of conferences and collective publications whose primary purpose was to disseminate the results of scholarly research on the war (Aróstegui 1988). Meanwhile, ordinary Spaniards' apparently insatiable curiosity about the war was satisfied by a deluge of popular publications, television programs, and films.

For the generation of historians who came to professional maturity in the 1960s and early 1970s, scholarly research was a form of political activism whose target was the official Franquist memory of the war as a crusade against the godlessness, anarchy, and antipatriotism of the Second Republic. The quest for accurate historical information was facilitated during the transition by the opening of archives—in particular, the Civil War Section of the Archivo Historico Nacional in Salamanca, which made available the masses of documents confiscated by the Nationalists during and after the war for use in the subsequent prosecution of "masonry and communism." Historians also benefited from the opening of private archives and study centers by those who lost the war,[1] although the rich documentation in the Francisco Franco Foundation remained off-limits to most researchers.

With their research on the origins and conduct of the civil war, Spanish historians took ownership of a field of inquiry that had been ceded to foreigners during the dictatorship. They also reoriented historical studies in the universities, where contemporary history had been marginalized since the end of the war. Whereas Franquist historiography had attributed Spain's "decline" after 1700 to the betrayal of the nation's Catholic identity by modernizing elites, the new paradigm, based on Marxian and structuralist analyses, blamed Spanish backwardness on the failure of the bourgeois revolution in the nineteenth century. The civil war was accordingly seen as the result of a prolonged structural crisis, an interpretation that sustained the myth of the war as an inevitable collective tragedy (Pérez Ledesma 2006; Ruiz Torres 2002).

By the 1990s, however, historians felt able to dispense with the myth of collective responsibility that had facilitated the transition. New research rescued the Second Republic from the infamy into which it had been cast by Franquist historiography and modified the image of dysfunctionality inherited from liberal and Marxist scholarship; Spanish democracy thereby acquired a respectable ancestry. Democratic consolidation also made it politically possible to assign responsibility for the civil war to its most proximate cause, the military rising against the Republic in July 1936. In this reconceptualization of the Spanish past, the war and the dictatorship represented anomalous interruptions of Spain's entirely normal, if somewhat tardy, path to modernity (Bernecker and Brinkmann 2005).

At the same time, historians began to investigate the policies and politics of the Franco regime, particularly its first phase. Overcoming bureaucratic obstructionism and the intentional destruction of some military and police records (González Quintana 2007; Espinosa Maestre and Reig Tapia 2006), persistent scholars began to document and quantify the human costs of the Franquist repression.

The new statistics, which demonstrated conclusively that the victims of Nationalist repression vastly outnumbered those killed by the revolutionary left at the outbreak of the war, dealt another blow to the myth of equal responsibility (Juliá 1999; Casanova 2002).

Archival research on the dictatorship formed part of a more general shift of historiographical focus away from national-level politics to the local and regional levels, a development that added depth and complexity to earlier accounts of the Republic and the civil war. While the emphasis on local history reflected the new accessibility of municipal and provincial archives, the principal impetus came from resurgent nationalist movements in Catalonia, the Basque Country, and Galicia. Writing history from the "periphery" was a form of identity politics whose target was not only the National-Catholic myth of "eternal Spain," but also the teleological narrative of national unification that liberal historians had crafted in support of Spanish nationhood in the nineteenth century. The peripheral nationalists' challenge to the mythscape of Spanish nationalism provoked a defensive reaction from traditionalists in the Royal Academy of History (Real Academia de la Historia 1998, 2000a) and also stimulated research by cultural historians into the processes by which the idea of "Spain" had been historically constructed and transmitted.

Tensions between center and periphery played out symbolically in the 1990s in the conflict over the 507 bundles of official papers belonging to the Generalitat of Catalonia that were housed in the civil war archive in Salamanca. Responding to demands for the repatriation of Catalonia's "historical memory," the Socialist government agreed in 1995 to return the documents. Soon thereafter, the mayor of Salamanca collected ninety-seven thousand signatures on a petition opposing the measure. With its electoral victory in March 1996, the rightist PP (Popular Party) halted the transfer, but to mollify its Catalanist coalition partner Convergència i Unió (CiU), it agreed to further study of the issue. Over the next decade a series of expert commissions considered the disposition of the civil war "papers" amid vociferous public debate that not only divided the PP and the PSOE (Spanish Socialist Workers' Party) but provoked a quarrel over the respective claims of Catalonia, the city of Salamanca, and the Autonomous Community of Castilla y León (*El Mundo* 2005). In January 2006, the Socialists transferred the documents to the Generalitat and incorporated the civil war archive in Salamanca into a Center for the Documentation of Historical Memory. Salamanca has appealed the transfer. The intensity of the struggle registers the degree to which history and historical memory are perceived to hold the key to collective identity and political justice.

History Teaching and Textbooks in the Transition

Textbooks written for the secondary school market during and after the transition reflected the political and historiographical trends discussed above. In modern societies, history as a school subject is an important vector of social memory, the function of which is to provide future citizens with a frame for civic behavior. Through symbols and stories, or governing myths, history teaching and textbooks legitimate existing political arrangements and provide clues to national identity and destiny. Not surprisingly, under the Franco regime state control of the history curriculum and textbooks reached its highest levels since the creation of the public school system in the 1850s.

[R]eflecting the commitment to consensus among Spanish political and cultural elites, most [history textbooks] registered the hegemonic memory of the civil war as a fratricidal tragedy and remained silent on events whose recollection might serve to revive the profound conflicts that had led to war in 1936.

With the loosening of centralized state control after the transition, history textbooks presented a greater variety of ideological perspectives on the Spanish past (Boyd 2006). Nevertheless, reflecting the commitment to consensus among Spanish political and cultural elites, most of them registered the hegemonic memory of the civil war as a fratricidal tragedy and remained silent on events whose recollection might serve to revive the profound conflicts that had led to war in 1936. The texts of the 1980s responded to Santayana's dictum that "those who do not learn from the past are condemned to repeat it." They located the Republic, civil war, and dictatorship in the broader context of a "difficult modernization," with emphasis on the political and social conflicts engendered by economic transformation. Although they differed in their evaluation of the reforms of the Second Republic, nearly all texts transmitted the dominant historical memory of the 1930s as a period when the political center was overwhelmed by extremists on left and right. The failure of mutual respect, the absence of a "democratic culture," and the resulting disorder led first to military intervention and then to war. By privileging the memory of democratic failure while silencing the memory of authoritarianism and repression, the texts prioritized the political values of tolerance and stability over those of freedom and justice, with at least short-term benefits for the process of democratic change. Their relative silence on political violence of all kinds rested on the politically useful assumption that "all of us were guilty." The textbooks thus reinforced the policy of "wiping the slate clean" that made possible the negotiated transition to liberal democracy.

By the 1990s, with democracy fully consolidated, the Socialists envisioned a new purpose for history education: the creation of "ethical and engaged citizens." According to the pedagogical guidelines associated with their educational reform law (the LOGSE; General Organic Law of the Educational System), history should enable students to "analyze and critically evaluate the realities of the contemporary world and the antecedents and factors that influence it" and to recognize "the plurality of perceptions and interpretations of the same historical reality" (RD 1007/1991, June 14, 1991; RD 1178/1992, October 2, 1992). Accordingly, the official curriculum focused almost exclusively on modern history, while earlier historical periods were given short shrift, and history itself was subsumed in the larger category of the social sciences. By encouraging students to see history as a process of inquiry and dialogue rather than as an immutable set of facts to be memorized, the LOGSE sought to instill the habits of mind and behavior appropriate to a democratic society.

The textbooks published in the wake of the LOGSE reflect the gradual breakdown of the elite consensus of the transition and the consequent erosion of the "pact of silence" regarding the dictatorship. For the first time, a majority of textbooks explain the origins, evolution, and significance of the dictatorship in terms of the relations of power in Spanish society, both in the past and, by implication, the present. But whereas books edited by conservative publishers retained the myth of the war as a collective tragedy in which moral culpability was evenly distributed, left-of-center publishing houses discarded it in favor of an honest account of the military rebellion and detailed comparisons of political violence on each side. Treatment of the dictatorship also varied: progressive texts focused on the postwar Franquist repression, while conservative texts emphasized economic and social mobility in the second phase of the regime.

Although the LOGSE gave autonomous communities control over 35 percent of the school curriculum (45 percent in the communities with their own language), in practice, regional editions of the textbooks distributed by large national publishers were essentially identical, varying only in the addition of a few pages or paragraphs that illustrated the local experience of larger historical processes (Valls Montés 2004, 145). Publishers whose market was primarily regional, on the other hand, offered identity-driven narratives in which the history of "the Spanish state" was subordinated to the history of the region or national community. In the most extreme examples, history textbooks vilified the centralizing Spanish state for its continuous repression and victimization of the Catalan and Basque peoples (Prades 1997a; 1997b).

Most history textbooks written after passage of the LOGSE prioritized historical knowledge over mythmaking and historical distance over passionate moralizing. Even though they offered selective and divergent interpretations of the past, they explicitly endorsed the scholarly values of objective analysis and argument from evidence. Guided by the premise that the present cannot be separated from the recent past, they no longer attempted to draw a veil of silence over the violence and injustices committed by Spaniards against one another. In revising the historical memory of the war to include its forgotten victims, they helped close the chasm that during the dictatorship divided individual memories from official memory.

History Wars of the 1990s

Shortly after its electoral victory in 1996, the PP took aim at the LOGSE. In a speech delivered at the annual opening of the Royal Academy of History in October, the new minister of education, Esperanza Aguirre, criticized the "calamitous state" of history education (Ortiz de Orruño 1998, 11). The ill-advised policies of the previous government, she claimed, had diluted history's formative value. By depriving children of traditional historical knowledge—especially chronology and biography—the Socialists were guilty of "one of the most subtle forms of the political utilization of history" (*El Mundo* 1996). Shortly thereafter, Aguirre announced the appointment of a committee of thirteen respected university and secondary school professors to advise on the complete reform of humanities at the secondary level.

Despite its grand title, the Plan for Improving the Humanities announced in October 1997 focused exclusively on history. The detailed syllabus developed by the committee restored the traditional balance between premodern and modern history and assigned priority to the study of the "unitary character of the histori-cal trajectory of Spain" (Almuiña 1998). As the minister noted a few days later, the goal was for all students to "learn the same thing, independently of the autonomous community in which they reside" (Ruiz Torres 1998, 69). In the ensuing furor, less attention was paid to the syllabus itself than to the underlying assumption of a common "Spanish" historical trajectory. The public remarks of the minister and conservative supporters like Federico Jiménez Losantos, who praised the plan as an effort "to recover at least a part of the terrain lost in edu-cation and in national feeling" (Culla and Riquer 1998, 161), confirmed the worst fears of the Catalans and Basques, whose representatives in the Cortes immedi-ately announced their determined opposition to the proposed reform.

The next two months saw the publication of 650 essays and editorials dealing with the Aguirre reform (*El País* 1998). As the historian José Alvarez Junco pointed out (Junco 1997), what was really at stake was not the transmission of historical knowledge but rather "control of the myths upon which the legitimacy of our institutions is based." For many commentators, the debate was over the purposes of history as a school discipline. Should history instill a shared civic or national identity, or did assigning it a "formative" role violate both the integrity of the discipline and the liberty of the individual student? Were the "memoristic" methods and traditional subject matter championed by Aguirre appropriate for future citizens in a democracy? Was it possible to agree on a single "history of Spain"? As the Catalan Socialist Jordi Sole Tura noted, there were as many histories as there were interest groups, and "the Government that is now trying to regulate knowledge of history has its principal roots in one of the darkest sides of that same history" (Tura 1997). The Aguirre plan was finally tabled in December after all of the parliamentary groups except the PP refused to support it.

Armed with a report on existing history textbooks prepared by the Real Academia de la Historia (2000b), the PP resurrected its reform plan after winning an absolute majority in the general elections. Written on the basis of a cursory review of textbooks seemingly selected for the extremism of their content (Valls Montés 2004), the report concluded that secondary level history books were contaminated with "sociologism, pedagogism and political circumstances." It criticized the LOGSE for emphasizing process and values over factual knowledge and for privileging contemporary history over the more distant past. Most controversial, however, was its condemnation of the textbooks used in the autonomous communities, particularly those used in the Basque *ikastolas*, where "the history that is taught is partial and tendentious, inspired in nationalist ideas that favor racism and that exclude everything that might signify common ties." The academy insisted that the "the history of Spain is an undeniable reality that must be present in the curriculum, even if not in a dominant form." The Catalan nationalist parties labeled the report "a further step towards the xenophobic, nationalist and españolista vortex" (*El Mundo* 2000); but in fact many Spaniards were shocked by the egregious examples of nationalist schoolbook rhetoric unearthed by the academy and the right-wing press. Taking advantage of the widespread indignation, the Ministry of Education enacted the new curricular guidelines in January 2001 (a measure rescinded by the Socialists when they returned to power in 2004).

Meanwhile, the right also sought to reshape historical memory of the civil war and the dictatorship. The sixtieth anniversary of the war in 1996 marked the reappearance of the ideologically charged narratives of the Franco decades. Led by the prolific journalist Pío Moa (1999), popular historians revived the Franquist interpretation of the war as a patriotic crusade against the anarchy of the Republican period. The revisionists exonerated the military from responsibility for the civil war, arguing instead that its origins could be traced to the leftist revolution of October 1934, which opened a period of growing violence and disorder that ultimately required a military response. Although Moa's books, along with those by Ricardo de la Cierva and César Vidal, lacked historical rigor, they satisfied the undiminished consumer demand for books about the war (Aróstegui 1997).

The neo-Franquist interpretation of the civil war was inserted into a revisionist grand narrative that depicted the Second Republic as a radical interruption of the gradual democratization of the liberal parliamentary monarchy founded by Antonio Cánovas del Castillo in 1876. Ignoring the authoritarianism and corruption of the restoration political system, the Aznar government took advantage of the centenary of Cánovas's assassination in 1997 to relocate its own historical antecedents in nineteenth-century liberalism (Ruiz Torres 2002). In the same vein, right-wing revisionism justified Franco's dictatorship as a necessary period of recuperation from the chaotic interlude of the republic and civil war.

According to this account, the political stability, economic growth, and social order that were the fruits of the "Franquist peace" made possible the resumption of the democratization process initiated by Cánovas after 1875. The PP, as heir to this political lineage, could thus claim to embody the true spirit of constitutional liberalism whose culmination was the Constitution of 1978.

The revisionists exonerated the military from responsibility for the civil war, arguing instead that its origins could be traced to the leftist revolution of October 1934, which opened a period of growing violence and disorder that ultimately required a military response.

The "Memory Boom"

Although "history" provided a focal point for partisan politics in the late 1990s, after the turn of the century "memory" began to occupy a larger share of public discourse on the past (Ruiz Torres 2007). The shift in preference for memory over history tracked the continuing shift in the balance of political power toward the right; attacking the PP where it was most vulnerable, the left depicted the right as the enemy of "historical memory." But equally important was the international debate over how democratic or democratizing societies should confront histories of violence, repression, and genocide. In Germany and France, the silence and omissions that had eased the postwar reconstruction of democracy were increasingly intolerable to younger generations untainted by wartime complicity (Judt 2005, 803-31). In emerging democracies in Eastern Europe, South Africa, and Latin America, the victims of repression demanded justice and public acknowledgement of their suffering. The revision of official memory to include the individual memories of those previously silenced was understood to be a necessary first step toward reconciliation and democratic consolidation (Winter 2007).

At the turn of the twenty-first century, 45 percent of the Spanish population was too young to recall either the war or the dictatorship. For this generation—the grandchildren of those who had endured the war and the children of those who had agreed to "forget" the past to make possible the transition—recovery of the memories of those previously silenced was a way of satisfying their curiosity about the past (Juliá 2006; Aróstegui 2006). In 2000, after uncovering the unmarked common grave of his grandfather, a victim of Falangist violence in 1936, the journalist Emilio Silva Barrera founded the Association for the Recuperation of Historical Memory (ARMH), which soon boasted a network of local and provincial branches dedicated to the excavation of mass graves and the identification and reburial of remains (Silva Barrera 2003; Ferrándiz Martín 2007). This grassroots movement soon developed ties to the left and the nationalist parties. Organizations like the Forum for Memory, linked to the Spanish Communist Party (PCE), and the Labor Group organized in Euskadi by the Aranzadi Scientific Society undertook excavations in areas occupied by Franquist forces during the war.

Professional historians had been publishing detailed, archive-based accounts of the executions and purges for years, but their scholarship had reached a limited audience. In contrast, images of mass graves and mutilated cadavers, fully exploited by the media, reached millions and clarified, for the first time for many Spaniards, the scope and brutality of the repression. The emotive phrase "Recuperation of Historical Memory" reflected the depth of the social trauma that still lingered sixty years after the end of the civil war. At the same time, the charge that historical memory had been suppressed, only to be recently recuperated, had a political intent—to discredit the PP, which continued to insist that "reopening old wounds" jeopardized the consensus upon which Spain's democratic constitution depended.

Meanwhile, the "model transition" lost some of the moral authority it had previously enjoyed, at least among left-wing intellectuals, who now blamed the negotiated transition for an alleged "democratic deficit" that explained the persistence of authoritarianism and apathy in the Spanish electorate. The "politics of forgetting," "amnesia," and "disremembering" had damaged the democracy they were intended to fortify (Reig Tapia 1999, 2006; Resina 2000; Espinosa Maestre 2007); as Vicenç Navarro, a professor of public policy in Barcelona, put it, "There cannot be an authentically democratic culture in Spain until there is an antifranquist culture, for which we need a vivid historical memory" (Navarro 2001). Spain's "amnesia" was compared unfavorably to recent French and German efforts to confront the past—somewhat unfairly, given that postwar political democratization in both nations had involved a similar process of active forgetting. But even public intellectuals willing to concede the functionality of "forgetting" during the transition now insisted that Spain's European identity depended upon official acknowledgement of the crimes of the dictatorship.

Open condemnation of the dictatorship was a step the PP was unwilling to take. In 1999, despite PP objections, opposition members of the Cortes Commission on Foreign Affairs approved a resolution condemning the "military rising against the constituted legality embodied in the political institutions that represented the Second Spanish Republic" (Aguilar Fernández 2006, 287). The unanimous Cortes resolution of November 20, 2002 (DSC, 20/11/2002: 20511) that condemned political violence and expressed moral support for the victims of the civil war, the exile, and the dictatorship declined to assign responsibility for the war. Public opinion surveys suggested that a slight majority of Spaniards still shared the PP's desire to avoid the issue, out of fear that instrumentalizing the past risked a recurrence of political violence. Significantly, young Spaniards were least likely to hold this view (Aguilar Fernández 2006).

[P]ublic intellectuals willing to concede the functionality of "forgetting" during the transition . . . insisted that Spain's European identity depended upon official acknowledgement of the crimes of the dictatorship.

The Socialist victory in the general elections of March 2004 only intensified the memory boom. As a result of its electoral pact with its coalition partners, the PSOE appointed an "Interministerial Commission for the Study of the Situation of the Victims of the Civil War and Franquism," whose charge was to recommend measures to compensate and provide for the "moral and juridical rehabilitation" of the victims of political repression (RD 1891/2004, September 4, 2004). The creation of the commission triggered a massive controversy over who was a victim, what forms of symbolic recompense were due them, and whether restitution should involve derogation of the sentences handed down by the military courts of the dictatorship. The government of José Luis Rodríguez Zapatero had opened a Pandora's box of competing "memories" and claims that threatened the stability of his government and deepened the ideological cleavages in Spanish society.

The "fever for remembering" (Erice 2006) climaxed in 2006—the seventy-fifth anniversary of the proclamation of the republic and seventieth anniversary of the outbreak of the civil war—when the Congress of Deputies endorsed a bill proclaiming the "Year of Historical Memory" (Ley 24/2006, July 7, 2006). Public commemorations of those victimized under Franco dotted the calendar (Egido León 2006.) For many, remembering was a question of equity and justice: for more than thirty years, only the Franquist war dead had been publicly memorialized; now there was a moral obligation to honor the fallen republicans. Monuments to Franco were dismantled in Madrid and La Coruña, although in many localities Franquist symbols, street names, and statues were left undisturbed (Andrés Sanz 2006). The newly created Center for the Documentation of Historical Memory in

Salamanca was charged with "assessing and cooperating in the location of infor-mation to make reparations to the memory of and aid the victims of repression" (RD 697/2007, June 1, 2007). In July, the battle shifted for six months to the pages of the two largest national dailies, *El País* and *El Mundo*, where descendents of civil war dead on both sides sought to shape historical memory through the so-called "war of the death notices" (de la Cal 2006).

Although most of the commemorative activity originated on the left, the increasingly conservative Catholic hierarchy in Spain practiced its own brand of memory politics, refusing to allow the eradication of Falangist and Franquist symbols on its property while petitioning the papacy to beatify priests, monks, and nuns who had fallen victim to anticlerical violence during the 1930s. In March 2001, Pope John Paul II beatified 233 "martyrs"; on October 28, 2007, his successor beatified 498 more, including a group of priests killed during the Asturian revolution of October 1934. Critics pointed out the disproportion between these grand, quasi-official ceremonies, sponsored by an institution that has never acknowledged its complicity in the dictatorship, and the unassisted efforts of ordinary Spaniards to locate the remains of their Republican ancestors in unmarked graves.

The virulence of the memory wars made it difficult to craft the "Law of Historical Memory," as it was popularly known.[2] Although the government wanted unanimous approval, the controversy that immediately erupted after its introduc-tion indicated that consensus was probably irretrievable, even though the bill was intentionally modest in its ambitions. It pointedly avoided references to historical or collective memory, recognizing only each citizen's right to "personal and family memory." The bill laid out the process whereby individuals sanctioned for political commitments and/or their cultural or sexual identities could seek a "Declaration of Reparations and Personal Recognition"; it enhanced the pensions of survivors of Republican soldiers and Franquist political prisoners; and it instructed local admin-istrative units to facilitate the location and identification of those buried in common graves. It also stipulated the removal of partisan commemorative symbols and pro-hibited political acts at the Valley of the Fallen (the Franquist monument to the regime's war dead). But it stopped well short of a "truth and reconciliation" process and the nullification of the summary judgments handed down by military tribunals during the dictatorship, a principal demand of the left.

It soon became apparent that the law intended to resurrect the "spirit of recon-ciliation and concord . . . that guided the transition" had achieved just the oppo-site. While it failed to satisfy the expectations of the left and the nationalist parties, the PP objected to the entire proposal and accused the Socialists of wishing to "bury the democratic transition" (Cué and Díez 2007). Public opinion polls indi-cated a similar split among ordinary citizens (*El País* 2006). The PP's continuing refusal to compromise, however, cleared the way for serious negotiations among the coalition partners, who agreed on a revised version of the legislation in October 2007 (Congreso de los Diputados 2007). The bill as it was proposed more clearly condemns the Franco regime, and it declares the "illegitimacy" (but not the nullification) of all judicial sentences imposed for political or ideological commitments, including religious beliefs, during the war and the dictatorship. The provisions requiring removal of Franquist symbols from the public sphere and the depoliticization of the Valley of the Fallen are strengthened. The bill was expected to receive the support of all parties except the Catalan Republican Left; even the PP had endorsed some of the articles, if not the entire law.

Most tellingly, the bill explicitly refuses to define or impose a common historical memory for all Spaniards. Instead, it guarantees the right of each individual or group to remember the past in their own way, while asserting a governmental role in the search for historical knowledge and the promotion of "democratic memory"—presumably, a public sphere open to competing "memories." It may be that the new law will mark the beginning of the end of the memory obsession, the divisive political consequences of which have given rise to a new appreciation for the virtues of forgetting in the interest of social harmony. It has seemingly clarified the relationship between history and memory for many professional historians, who are reasserting the independence of their discipline from the demands of politics, nation building, and moral judgment (Molinero 2006). History cannot administer justice; its moral authority comes from its regard for truth seeking and its social utility from its power to explain and interpret. The recent turn to cultural history suggests a politically attractive avenue of research. Drawing on both archival evidence and individual memories to recreate the symbolic language, values, and subjectivities of the men and women who experienced the civil war and the dictatorship, it may illuminate the distance that separates twenty-first-century Spaniards from their predecessors (Pérez Ledesma 2006; Izquierdo Martín and Sánchez León 2006). By historicizing the past and differentiating it from the present, historians may make the "past that does not pass" less the source of continuing friction than the reason for a renewed commitment to democratic coexistence.

Notes

1. These included the Pablo Iglesias Foundation (Spanish Socialist Workers' Party, or PSOE, 1977), the Salvador Seguí Foundation (libertarian movement, 1986), and the History of Labor Archive in the 1st of May Foundation (Communist Party Workers' Commissions, 1992).

2. The technical name of the proposed law is "Proposal for a Law in Which Rights Are Recognized and Broadened and in Which Measures Are Established in Favor of Those Who Suffered Persecution of Violence during the Civil War and the Dictatorship" (Ministerio de la Presidencia 2006).

References

Aguilar Fernández, P. 1996. *Memoria y olvido de la guerra civil española*. Madrid, Spain: Alianza.
———. 1997. Collective memory of the Spanish Civil War: The case of the political amnesty in the Spanish transition to democracy. *Democratization* 4 (4): 88-109.
———. 2006. La evocación de la guerra y del franquismo en la política, la cultura y la sociedad españolas. In *Memoria de la guerra y del franquismo*, ed. S. Juliá, 279-318. Madrid, Spain: Fundación Pablo Iglesias/Taurus.
———. 2006. Presencia y ausencia de la guerra civil y del franquismo en la democracia española: Reflexiones en torno a la articulación y ruptura del "pacto de silencio." In *Guerra civil. Mito y memoria*, ed. J. Aróstegui and F. Godicheau, 245-94. Madrid, Spain: Marcial Pons Historia/Casa de Velázquez.

Almuiña, C. 1998. Humanidades e Historia de España en la ESO: La propuesta de la Fundación Ortega y Gasset. *Ayer* 30:25-62.

Andrés Sanz, J. de. 2006. *Los símbolos y la memoria del franquismo*. Estudios de Progreso 23. Madrid, Spain: Fundación Alternativa. www.falternativas.org.

Aróstegui, J., ed. 1988. *Historia y memoria de la guerra civil: Encuentro en Castilla y León: Salamanca, 24-27 de septiembre de 1986*. 3 vols. Valladolid, Spain: Junta de Castilla y León, Consejería de Cultura y Bienestar Social.

———. 1997. La guerra de Don Ricardo y otras guerras. *Hispania* 57/2, (196): 777-87.

———. 2006. Traumas colectivos y memorias generacionales: El caso de la guerra civil. In *Guerra civil: Mito y memoria*, ed. J. Aróstegui and F. Godicheau, 57-92. Madrid, Spain: Marcial Pons/Casa de Velázquez.

Bell, D. S. A. 2003. Mythscapes: Memory, mythology, and national identity. *British Journal of Sociology* 54 (1): 63-81.

Bernecker, W. L., and S. Brinkmann. 2005. La difícil identidad de España: Historia y política en el cambio de milenio. *Ideas (FH-Heilbronn)* 1:1-10.

Blanco Rodríguez, J. A. 2006. El registro historiográfico de la guerra civil, 1936-2004. In *Guerra civil. Mito y memoria*, ed. J. Aróstegui and F. Godicheau, 373-406. Madrid, Spain: Marcial Pons/Casa de Velázquez.

Boyd, C. P. 2006. De la memoria oficial a la memoria histórica: La guerra civil y la dictadura en los textos escolares de 1939 al presente. In *Memoria de la guerra y del franquismo*, ed. S. Juliá, 79-100. Madrid, Spain: Fundación Pablo Iglesias/Taurus.

de la Cal, Juan C. 2006. La guerra civil de esquelas se dispara. *El Mundo*, Crónica supplement. September 3.

Casanova, J., ed. 2002. *Morir, matar, sobrevivir: La violencia en la dictadura de Franco*. Barcelona, Spain: Editorial Crítica.

Congreso de los Diputados, Comisión Constitucional. 2007. Dictamen. Proyecto de ley por la que se reconocen y amplían derechos y se establecen medidas en favor de quienes padecieron persecución o violencia durante la guerra civil y la dictadura (10.10.07).

Cué, Carlos E., and Anabel Díez. 2007. PSOE e IU-ICV dan un vuelco total a la Ley de Memoria y declaran ilegítimos los juicios de Franco. *El País*. April 20.

Culla, J. B. , and B. de Riquer. 1998. La enseñanza de la historia desde una perspectiva catalana. *Ayer* 30:159-69.

Egido León, Á. 2006. La historia y la gestión de la memoria: Apuntes para un balance. *Hispania Nova. Revista de Historia Contemporánea* 6. http://hispanianova.rediris.es/6/dossier/6d008.pdf.

El Mundo. 1996. Esperanza Aguirre deplora el estado de los estudios de historia. October 11.

El Mundo. 2000. Campaña dirigida desde el gobierno. June 28.

El Mundo. 2005. Los "papeles de Salamanca": Del Franquismo a la actualidad. June 6.

El País. 1998. 650 artículos de opinión sobre humanidades. January 13.

El País. 2006. El aniversario de la guerra civil, entre la memoria y el olvido. 20 minutos.es. July 18.

Erice, F. 2006. Combates por el pasado y apologías de la memoria, a propósito de la represión franquista. *Hispania Nova. Revista de Historia Contemporánea* 6. http://hispanianova.rediris.es/6/dossier/6d008.pdf.

Espinosa Maestre, F. 2007. De saturaciones y olvidos. Reflexiones en torno a un pasado que no puede pasar. *Hispania Nova. Revista de Historia Contemporánea* 7. http://hispanianova.rediris.es/6/dossier/6d008.pdf.

Espinosa Maestre, F., and A. Reig Tapia. 2006. *Contra el olvido: Historia y memoria de la guerra civil*. Barcelona, Spain: Crítica.

Fentress, J., and C. Wickham. 1992. *Social memory*. London: Basil Blackwell.

Ferrándiz Martín, F. 2007. Exhumaciones y políticas de la memoria en la España contemporánea. *Hispania Nova. Revista de Historia Contemporánea* 7. http://hispanianova.rediris.es/6/dossier/6d008.pdf.

Fontana, J. 1982. *Historia: Análisis del pasado y proyecto social*. Barcelona, Spain: Crítica.

González Quintana, A. 2007. La política archivística del gobierno español y la ausencia de gestión del pasado desde el comienzo de la transición. *Hispania Nova. Revista de Historia Contemporánea* 7. http://hispanianova.rediris.es/6/dossier/6d008.pdf.

Gunther, R., J. R. Montero, and J. Botella. 2004. *Democracy in modern Spain*. New Haven, CT: Yale University Press.

Halbwachs, M. 1980. *The collective memory*. Trans. V. D. Ditter and F. J. Ditter Jr. New York: Harper & Row.

Izquierdo Martín, J., and P. Sánchez León. 2006. *La guerra que nos han contado: 1936 y nosotros*. Madrid, Spain: Alianza.

Judt, T. 2005. *Postwar: A history of Europe since 1945*. London: William Heinemann.

Juliá, S., ed. 1999. *Víctimas de la guerra civil*. Madrid, Spain: Temas de Hoy.

————. 2003. Echar al olvido: Memoria y amnistía en la transición. *Claves de Razón Práctica* 129:14-24.

————. 2006. Memoria, historia y política de un pasado de guerra y dictadura. In *Memoria de la guerra y del franquismo*, ed. S. Juliá, 27-78. Madrid, Spain: Fundación Pablo Iglesias/Taurus.

————. 2007. De nuestras memorias y de nuestras miserias. *Hispania Nova. Revista de Historia Contemporánea* 7. http://hispanianova.rediris.es/6/dossier/6d008.pdf.

Junco, José Álvarez. 1997. De historia y amnesia. *El País*. December 29.

Lavabre, M. C. 2006. Sociología de la memoria y acontecimientos traumáticos. In *Guerra civil. Mito y memoria*, ed. J. Aróstegui and F. Godicheau. Madrid, Spain: Marcial Pons/Casa de Velázquez.

Le Goff, J. 1992. *History and memory*. New York: Columbia University Press.

Moa, P. 1999. *Los orígenes de la guerra civil española*. Madrid, Spain: Encuentro Ediciones.

Ministerio de la Presidencia. 2006. Reconocimiento y ampliación de derechos y establecimiento de medidas a favor de quienes padecieron persecución o violencia durante la guerra civil y la dictadura. July 28. www.mpr.es.

Molinero, C. 2006. ¿Memoria de la represión o memoria del franquismo?" In *Memoria de la guerra y del franquismo*, ed. Santos Juliá, 219-46. Madrid, Spain: Fundación Pablo Iglesias/Taurus.

Navarro, Vicenç. 2001. Los costes de la desmemoria histórica. *El País*. June 16.

Olick, J. K., and J. Robbins. 1998. Social memory studies: From "collective memory" to the historical sociology of mnemonic practices. *Annual Reviews in Sociology* 24:105-40.

Ortiz de Orruño, J. M., ed. 1998. Historia y sistema educativo. *Ayer* 30.

Pérez Ledesma, M. 2006. La guerra civil y la historiografía: No fue posible el acuerdo. In *Memoria de la guerra y del franquismo*, ed. S. Juliá, 101-34. Madrid, Spain: Fundación Pablo Iglesias/Taurus.

Prades, Joaquina. 1997a. La historia ¿Era ESO? *El País*. November 2.

Prades, Joaquina. 1997b. Sabino Arana en la "iskastola." *El País*. November 2.

Real Academia de la Historia. 1998. *España: Reflexiones sobre el ser de España*. 2nd ed. Madrid, Spain: Real Academia de la Historia.

————. 2000a. *España como nación*. Barcelona, Spain: Planeta.

————. 2000b. Informe sobre los textos y cursos de historia en los centros de enseñanza media. June 23. www.filosofia.org/his/h2000ah.htm.

Reig Tapia, A. 1999. *Memoria de la guerra civil: Los mitos de la tribu*. Madrid, Spain: Alianza.

————. 2006. *La cruzada de 1936: Mito y memoria*. Madrid, Spain: Alianza.

Resina, J. R. 2000. *Disremembering the dictatorship: The politics of memory in the Spanish transition to democracy*. Atlanta, GA: Rodopi.

Ruiz Torres, P. 1998. La historia en el debate político sobre la enseñanza de las Humanidades. *Ayer* 30:63-111.

————. 2002. Political uses of history in Spain. In *Political uses of the past: The recent Mediterranean experience*, ed. J. Revel and G. Levi, 95-116. Portland, OR: Frank Cass.

————. 2007. Los discursos de la memoria histórica en España. *Hispania Nova. Revista de Historia Contemporánea* 7. http://hispanianova.rediris.es/6/dossier/6d008.pdf.

Sevillano Calero, F. 2003. La construcción de la memoria y el olvido en la España democrática. *Ayer* 52:297-319.

Silva Barrera, E. 2003. *Las fosas de Franco: Los republicanos que el dictador dejó en lac cunetas*. Madrid, Spain: Temas de Hoy.

Tura, Jordi Solé. 1997. ¿Qué historia? *El País*. November 6.

Valls Montés, R. 2004. La enseñanza de la historia: Entre polémicas interesadas y problemas reales. In *Miradas a la historia: Reflexiones historiográficas en recuerdo de Miguel Rodríguez Llopis*, ed. E. Nicolás Marín and J. A. Gómez Hernández, 141-54. Murcia, Spain: Universidad de Murcia. www.um.es/campusdigital/.

Winter, J. M. 2007. The generation of memory: Reflections on the "memory boom" in contemporary historical studies. *Archives & Social Studies* 1:363-97.

Australia's History under Howard, 1996-2007

ANDREW BONNELL
and
MARTIN CROTTY

This article argues that since the election of his Coalition government in 1996, John Howard and his conservative allies in government and the media have waged a long campaign to influence the representation and public understanding of Australian history. They have sought to play down the historical harm done to Indigenous Australians and to emphasize more affirming stories of the rise of a new, democratic nation. The conservatives' waging of the "history wars" has been motivated by neoconservative ideology imported from the United States, the political interests of the Coalition government, and the personal background and convictions of the prime minister. Despite sustained criticism of the Australian Broadcasting Corporation as well as the National Museum of Australia and many academic historians, and despite attempts to institute a national history curriculum, this article concludes that the history wars, for all their smoke and fury, have had only transient effects on the practice of Australian history.

Keywords: John Howard; Australia; history wars; Aboriginal; National Museum of Australia

The conservative Coalition government led by Prime Minister John Howard has been in power in Australia since March 1996 when it displaced Paul Keating's Labor government in a landslide election. More than a decade later,

Andrew Bonnell is a senior lecturer in history at the University of Queensland. Publications include The People's Stage in Imperial Germany. Social Democracy and Culture, 1890-1914 *(London: IB Tauris, 2005) and* Shylock in Germany: Antisemitism and the German Theatre from the Enlightenment to the Nazis *(London: IB Tauris, 2008). He is history editor of the* Australian Journal of Politics and History.

Martin Crotty teaches Australian history at the University of Queensland. He is author of Making the Australian Male: Middle-Class Masculinity in Australia 1875-1920 *(MUP, 2001); coeditor of* The Great Mistakes of Australian History *(UNSW Press, 2006); and is currently writing a history of the Returned and Services League of Australia (RSL), the largest exservicemen's body in Australia. He is also the coeditor of the* Journal of Australian Studies.

DOI: 10.1177/0002716207310818

Australian history has frequently been a battleground between the government and its supporters on one hand, and academic historians and other members of the so-called "left-wing intellectual elite" on the other. The debates have been wide-ranging. The nature of Australia's relations with its Indigenous people has been the most emotive and controversial topic, but other aspects of Australian social and political history have also been subjects of contention. The debates have played out in a wide variety of forums: prime ministerial speeches, the National Museum of Australia (opened in 2001), a History Summit convened in 2006 to advance proposals on a national history curriculum, the mainstream media (particularly News Limited newspapers such as the *Australian*), and Internet blogs.

Howard has often been reflexively derided by his critics as a knee-jerk reactionary, nostalgic for the 1950s. However, while Howard's attachment to conservative social values is no doubt sincere, he has also shown himself to be a highly strategic and purposive political operator, who has sought to entrench and extend the hegemony of the right in the Australian political landscape. Although a constitutional monarchist who cherishes Australia's traditional ties to Britain, Howard has borrowed much from the arsenal of the contemporary U.S. Republican right, as far as political strategy and tactics are concerned, including sometimes racially tinged "wedge politics" and the technique of branding political opponents as agents of a supposed "left-liberal elite," even as he advances the interest of the power elites in the corporate sector. Borrowings from American conservative discourse have included attacks on "political correctness" in universities and the media and U.S.-style "cultural wars." These semantic wars serve multiple political purposes: they distract from material economic issues that might focus voters' discontent on government policy; they constitute a potential wedge between elements of the opposition Labor Party's lower-income base (viewed as susceptible to appeals to nationalism) and more cosmopolitan or pro-multicultural progressive intellectuals; and they assert the dominance of conservative cultural values in an attempt to shift the center of gravity of public debate further to the right. In various ways, the field of Australian history has become a battleground for the "culture wars" of the past decade as Howard has sought to use it as a tool to advance his political agendas.

Howard's advancement of a particular understanding of Australian history has also been guided by personal conviction and background. His father and grandfather both fought in the Australian Imperial Forces in France in World War I, an event central to the national historical imagination. Howard's father, Lyall, was a small businessman with a dislike for unions. His mother was a Methodist, and the young John Howard was an enthusiastic participant in Methodist Sunday School. His mother often refused permission for her son to attend school camps and vetted their associates in a bid to protect him from what she regarded as undesirable influences. Howard was born and raised in Sydney, grew to adulthood in Sydney, studied law in Sydney, and after graduating entered legal practice in Sydney until entering politics—as member for Bennelong, an electorate in Sydney. Apart from a short period in 1964 and 1965, spent largely in the United

Kingdom, he did not travel extensively, and he lived at home with his mother until he married in 1971 (Errington and Van Onselen 2007, 1-46; Barnett and Goward 1997, 1-16). Marion Maddox (2004) has recently thrown doubt on how much of Howard's conservatism can be explained by his Methodist upbringing as the church was then much more liberal—at times even radical—than most people looking for the roots of Howard's social conservatism have imagined. Nonetheless, by most measures, Howard's upbringing was conservative and insular, and his understanding of Australian history reflects this. It is a background he has used to connect himself with the Australian "mainstream" and to pillory his ideological opponents.

Howard is by no means the first Australian prime minister to seek to instrumentalize Australian history for political ends. Most notably, his predecessor, Paul Keating (treasurer in the Labor government of Bob Hawke from 1983 to 1991, prime minister from 1991 to 1996) explicitly invoked his own interpretation of Australian history to promote his political objectives in the areas of Australia's closer engagement with Asia, his drive to make Australia a republic instead of a monarchy under the British crown, and his desire for a process of "reconciliation" between Australians of European origins and Indigenous Australians (Macintyre and Clark 2003, 123-28; Watson 2002). Keating's public commemorations of Australian military history stressed the campaigns fought by Australians in defense of their own region in Southeast Asia and New Guinea, rather than the traditional focus on the more imperial and remote Gallipoli campaign of 1915, thereby emphasizing the importance of Australia's regional environment. In support of his drive to break the residual connection with the British throne he criticized British policy in the first half of the twentieth century for neglecting Australian security; and in a memorable speech in the inner-city Sydney suburb of Redfern, Keating delivered the most candid speech to date by an Australian prime minister acknowledging the historic wrongs inflicted on Indigenous Australians by white settlers:

> The starting point might be to recognise that the problem starts with us non-Aboriginal Australians.
> It begins, I think, with the act of recognition. Recognition that it was we who did the dispossessing. We took the traditional lands and smashed the traditional way of life. We brought the diseases. The alcohol. We committed the murders. We took the children from their mothers. We practised discrimination and exclusion. It was our ignorance and our prejudice. And our failure to imagine these things being done to us. (Keating 1992/1995, 228)

Keating also used history in distinctly partisan ways, quite separately from any attempt to advance a particular national agenda. He portrayed Howard's political hero, Sir Robert Menzies (prime minister from 1939 to 1941 and from 1949 to 1966, and founder of the Liberal Party) as an Anglophile who lacked pride in Australia; and he attempted to portray John Howard and the then-leader of the Liberal Party, John Hewson (leader 1990 to 1994), as throwbacks to an illusory golden age of the 1950s (*Hansard*, February 27, 1992). It was Keating who made

Australian history a political issue; but it was Howard on the conservative side who appreciated the centrality of history to the "battle of ideas" he believed, and still believes, needed to be waged by the Liberal/National Party Coalition.

Howard's use of Australian history was, however, radically different from Keating's. While Keating sought to accompany his modernizing economic project with measures to modernize Australia's polity and cultural life, Howard has sought to implement reassuringly conservative social and cultural policies, while continuing to pursue neoliberal economic reform. In a television interview a month before his election in March 1996, Howard said that he wanted Australians to "feel comfortable and relaxed about three things: I would like to see them comfortable and relaxed about their history; I would like to see them comfortable and relaxed about the present and I'd also like to see them comfortable and relaxed about the future" (Australian Broadcasting Corporation 1996).

In his first year of office, John Howard denounced the so-called "black arm-band view" of Australian history (a term coined by the eminent conservative historian Geoffrey Blainey [1993, 11]) in his programmatic statement of the guiding values of his government in the 1996 Sir Robert Menzies lecture. The lecture gave the interpretation of history a key role in his government's self-image. The challenge, said Howard,

> is to ensure that our history as a nation is not written definitively by those who take the view that Australians should apologise for most of it.
> This "black armband" view of our past reflects a belief that most Australian history since 1788 has been little more than a disgraceful story of imperialism, exploitation, racism, sexism and other forms of discrimination.
> I take a very different view. I believe that the balance sheet of our history is one of heroic achievement and that we have achieved much more as a nation of which we can be proud than of which we should be ashamed. (Howard 1996)

For more than a decade, the Howard government's efforts on the terrain of the so-called "history wars" have followed this broad statement of the prime minister's historical orientation and have served two combined purposes: to contest the supposed hegemony in public debate of an unpatriotic and negative liberal-left intelligentsia in universities and the media; and to assert a positive, nationalistic view of Australian history that would enable Australians to feel "comfortable and relaxed" while they endured more potentially unsettling economic reform. The subjects that have been contested or embraced have been wide-ranging—race relations, the "stolen generations," the influence of the British legacy, the achievements of past prime ministers such as Sir Robert Menzies, the Anzac legend, and the White Australia policy—but the philosophy, ideologies, and politics underlying the Howard government's attempts to shape Australian history as practiced, disseminated, and understood have been enduring and consistent since Howard's election.

Among the means at the federal government's disposal for influencing public debate, the Howard government used its control over funding for the higher education system and public broadcasting. There has been a tendency for the Liberal and National parties to view universities and the Australian Broadcasting Commission (ABC) as harboring left-wing intellectual "elites" hostile to both conservative politics and the Australian "mainstream." Academics and public broadcasters have frequently come under rhetorical attack from Howard, other members of the government, and their supporters in the mainstream media, but they have also, more seriously, been weakened by funding cuts. From 1995 to 2003, Australia was the only Organization for Economic Cooperation and Development (OECD) country to reduce public spending on tertiary education as a proportion of GDP. Australian public investment declined by 7 percent, while other OECD countries increased public expenditure on tertiary education by an average of 48 percent over the same period (OECD 2006, 208, Table B2.2).

[T]he Howard government's efforts on the terrain of the so-called "history wars" have followed this broad statement of the prime minister's historical orientation and have served two combined purposes: to contest the supposed hegemony in public debate of an unpatriotic and negative liberal-left intelligentsia in universities and the media; and to assert a positive, nationalistic view of Australian history that would enable Australians to feel "comfortable and relaxed" while they endured more potentially unsettling economic reform.

Corporate universities seeking to maximize their income, and university students being encouraged to view higher education as a financial investment that should yield a financial return, have both served to weaken the humanities. The slide in student and staff numbers in history, already apparent after a switch to a more "user pays" funding model under Keating, accelerated sharply in the first years of the Howard government. Despite the public disinvestment in higher education, the federal education ministry has become more aggressively interventionist in universities, forcing changes in governance and workplace relations onto universities (see Marginson 2004; Macintyre 2007). Most disturbing has been the government's corruption of the peer-review processes of the Australian Research Council through vetoing specific research grant applications (see Haigh 2006).

The ABC, also identified as an aberrant left-wing redoubt, had its budget cut by A$55 million, about 10 percent, within months of the conservative coalition's election victory in 1996 (Inglis 2006, 383), and the Howard government has since appointed right-wing media commentators, such as News Limited columnist Janet Albrechtsen, conservative anthropologist Ron Brunton,[1] and right-wing historical polemicist Keith Windschuttle,[2] to the corporation's board of directors. Notably, all three have been prominent in the history wars. In considering the role of the national public broadcasting network in Australia, it should be noted that the only national daily broadsheet newspaper in the country is produced by the Murdoch concern, News Limited, which also owns the only state-based daily newspapers in Brisbane, Darwin, and Adelaide and the highest-selling newspapers in Melbourne and Sydney. Seventy percent of Australia's metropolitan newspapers are News Limited–controlled, and they tend to adopt a similar editorial line (Young 2007, 4-6). The Murdoch press has been a vigorous proponent of the "culture wars" from the right, and its columnists have been a vocal cheer squad in support of the government's positions in the history wars (McKnight 2005). Government policies toward higher education and public broadcasting essentially had two functions: they reflected an ideological preference for private enterprise versus the public sector, and they also attempted to tilt the playing field of public debate by exerting financial and ideological pressure on institutions perceived as critical of government policy or subversive of conservative understandings of Australian history.

Within this broader pattern of attempting to influence and direct the understanding, promulgation, and reception of Australian history, the breadth of topics addressed and the range of mediating agencies upon which influence has been brought to bear have both been considerable. But the most passionately fought-over topics and institutions have been "national" in their import and scope, as befitting the concerns of a national government and an instinctively centrist prime minister operating in a climate of heightened conservative nationalism. Questions concerning the treatment of Australia's Indigenous people have gone to the legal and moral core of the nation's foundations; the National Museum was understood as an embodiment of the nation's past; and the question of a national history curriculum has clear connections with a conservative "politics of memory" concerned with how "our history" is being taught to "our children" and the effects on national identity and a sense of national pride and belonging (Clark 2006, 1-4).

There are two main issues on which the Howard government has taken a markedly different position from its predecessor with regard to Indigenous people: native title and restitution for past wrongs, especially those suffered by Aborigines forcibly removed from their parents as children. In both cases the Howard government has sought to justify less generous "special" treatment for Indigenous Australians through, and concurrently with, a broader project of espousing a more affirming view of Australian history that has included minimizing the wrongs committed by the colonizers and seeking to discredit those historians who have focused on the negative sides of colonization.

During the twentieth century, many thousands of Aboriginal children were removed from their parents, to be raised in orphanages or by white adoptive families (Haebich 2000). In most cases, the children's welfare was the ostensible reason for the removal, but racist social-engineering agendas are considered by most historians to have played a part. Given the then widely prevalent assumption that the "full-blood" Aboriginal population was destined to die out, it was believed by some officials that it was imperative to prevent the emergence of an anomalous "half-caste" population, with the result that lighter-skinned children in Aboriginal communities were often targeted for removal and assimilation into white society (Haebich 2000, 271-87). After a Royal Commission into Aboriginal Deaths in Custody reported in 1991 that a high proportion of Indigenous people who committed suicide while in prison or police custody had histories of institutionalization and separation from their families, the Human Rights and Equal Opportunity Commission undertook an investigation into the experience of forced removal of Indigenous children. The inquiry resulted in the publication in 1997, after the change of government, of a long report titled *Bringing Them Home*, in which many Indigenous people who had experienced separation from their families and severance from their communal identities related their experiences (Human Rights and Equal Opportunity Commission 1997). The report came as a revelation to many non-Aboriginal Australians, who had generally failed to realize the extent of the practices of child removal and the dimensions of suffering that they had caused. The *Bringing Them Home* report contributed to a growing grassroots movement for reconciliation between Indigenous and non-Indigenous Australians and called for official apologies to Indigenous Australians from Australian governments and the churches involved. The churches and state governments duly apologized.

John Howard, however, resisted the calls for a Commonwealth government apology on the basis that this generation could not be held responsible for well-intentioned errors of previous generations (though he has encouraged Australians to remember and take pride in less controversial aspects of Australian history), and his government devoted considerable legal resources to opposing claims for compensation from members of what became known as the "stolen generations." Howard was also a notable absentee from the "reconciliation marches" that took place in Australian cities in late 2000, and he has instead preferred to concentrate on what he has termed "practical reconciliation" measures, such as improving health and educational outcomes for Indigenous people (Errington and Van Onselen 2007, 262-64). Such positions suited Howard's personal and political preferences for maintenance of Australian national pride, eulogizing of Australia's settlers and founders, and defense of what he repeatedly defines as the "mainstream." To the many Australians who were deeply troubled by the stories of the stolen generations, Howard offered comfort and legitimation and reaped the political dividend.

A concerted campaign against the use of the term "stolen generations" and the argument that the removal of Aboriginal children from their families called out for reparations and an apology from the government was conducted by right-wing commentators, some linked to privately funded think tanks, others writing in the Murdoch press (Manne 2001). These included Ron Brunton, of the right-wing think tank the Institute of Public Affairs, who attacked the Human Rights and Equal Opportunity Commission for suggesting that the policy of forced removal of children amounted to genocide under the terms of the 1948 United Nations Convention on Genocide (Article 2[e] of which specifically refers to "forcibly transferring children of the group to another group," a point not addressed by Brunton's article) (see Brunton 1998). Andrew Bolt, a columnist with the Murdoch-owned Melbourne tabloid *Herald Sun*, was a particularly vociferous critic of the concept of the stolen generations (see Manne 2001, 1-4). When the film *Rabbit Proof Fence* appeared in 2002, directed by Philip Noyce and based on the memoir by Doris Pilkington (Nugi Garimara), Bolt attacked the film for alleged inaccuracies and included references to the "lies of the 'stolen generations' activists," the "silly compensation cases that collapse," and "the slick claims of genocide" (Bolt 2002). Bolt has since claimed on a number of occasions that the stolen generations "myth" is killing Aboriginal children because it has made authorities more reluctant to remove Aboriginal children from dysfunctional or dangerous environments (Bolt 2006-2007). In Bolt's neat political inversion, it is the left-wing historians who are now responsible for the suffering of Aboriginal children.

Bolt has since claimed on a number of occasions that the stolen generations "myth" is killing Aboriginal children because it has made authorities more reluctant to remove Aboriginal children from dysfunctional or dangerous environments. In Bolt's neat political inversion, it is the left-wing historians who are now responsible for the suffering of Aboriginal children.

The question of how to come to terms with the history of the stolen generations also caused divisions within conservative opinion. In 1997, Robert Manne, the editor of the conservative monthly journal *Quadrant* (once a cold war product of the Congress for Cultural Freedom) resigned, after coming under heavy criticism from the board of directors of the magazine. Manne had exhibited impeccable anticommunist credentials during the cold war, but he and the philosopher Raymond Gaita were troubled by the revelations of the *Bringing Them Home* report and argued that conservatives needed to take the moral implications of this history seriously, including the extent to which child removals may have amounted to genocide (see Gaita 1999, 107-30). Manne was effectively ousted from the editorship of *Quadrant* and replaced by the veteran right-wing libertarian newspaper columnist P. P. McGuinness, under whom *Quadrant* engaged in a series of aggressively revisionist forays into Aboriginal history (Manne 2001, 57-60), including a symposium held in September 2000 on "Truth and Sentimentality in Aboriginal History," which was not only devoted to the debunking of the history of the stolen generations, but included a presentation by freelance writer Keith Windschuttle accusing left-wing historians such as Stuart Macintyre and Henry Reynolds of promoting the "break-up of Australia" through their advocacy of Aboriginal land rights and political self-determination (Windschuttle 2000). Prime Minister John Howard has expressed his strong approval of the post-Manne *Quadrant*, with particular reference to its engagement in historical revisionism as especially "close to [his] heart":

> Of the causes that *Quadrant* has taken up that are close to my heart none is more important than the role it has played as counterforce to the black armband view of Australian history. Until recent times, it had become almost de rigueur in intellectual circles to regard Australian history as little more than a litany of sexism, racism and class warfare.
>
> Again, it would take the brave voices of a few individuals to take a stand against the orthodoxies of the day. And again *Quadrant* has been an outpost of lively nonconformity in its willingness to defend both Geoffrey Blainey and Keith Windschuttle against the posses of political correctness. (Howard 2006b)

Another unwanted legacy in Indigenous affairs (as far as the incoming Howard administration was concerned) was in the area of native title. In 1992, the High Court of Australia handed down the *Mabo* judgment, which essentially found that under common law, a residual form of native title to traditional lands still existed under strictly defined conditions: principally, that the land had not passed into freehold title since European settlement, which would have the effect of extinguishing native title, and that the relevant Aboriginal or Torres Strait Islander group could demonstrate a continuing link to the land in question. These were difficult tests to meet in practice, after more than two centuries of dispossession. After complex negotiations with Indigenous spokespeople and other stakeholders, and in the face of a scare campaign from conservative commentators, who attacked the historical basis of the concept of native title and sought to arouse unfounded fears that citizens' backyards would be at risk from native title claims, the Keating government passed the Native Title Act in 1993 to provide a legislative framework for the implementation of the *Mabo* judgment. The incoming Howard government promised to roll back native title and provide certainty of tenure for rural landholders, the core constituency of the agrarian-based

National Party. The issue of native title was revived in December 1996 by the High Court decision in the case of the *Wik Peoples v. Queensland*, which determined that pastoral leases did not extinguish native title rights, although in the case of a conflict of rights between the rights of native title holders and the rights of the pastoralist, the rights of the pastoralist prevailed. Despite the very narrow scope of native title rights under the two High Court decisions, agrarian interests and conservative commentators were vocal in their condemnation of "judicial activism" and the very notion of native title, and the Howard government's 1998 amendments to the Native Title Act hedged native title with even more restrictive conditions.

The debate over *Mabo* and native title became as much an argument over Australian history as one about the common law—and one in which the "history warriors" (a term coined by Stuart Macintyre—see Macintyre and Clark 2003) have supported the Howard government with considerable fervor. One of the speakers at the 2000 *Quadrant* symposium, Keith Windschuttle, referred to Henry Reynolds as "the brains behind Eddie Mabo's eventually successful claim for native title to the High Court in 1992" (Windschuttle 2000, 9). Reynolds had long been a pioneering scholar in the field of Australian Indigenous history. Reynolds did important and innovative work on Aboriginal resistance to European settlement, or invasion (Reynolds 1982), and later researched the historical basis of native land title (Reynolds 1987) and the question of Aboriginal sovereignty in a colonized country in which, unlike New Zealand and North America, there were no treaties between the colonizing power and Indigenous groups (Reynolds 1996). In much of the media commentary on the *Mabo* case, Reynolds was credited with having simultaneously popularized and debunked the concept of *"terra nullius,"* shorthand for the body of legal opinion holding that land in presettlement Australia had been without owners and that there were no prior claims on land before European settlement. The extent to which High Court judges were influenced by Reynolds's historical research on the ancestry of native title in Australia, and how much they were guided by their own reading of common law as it affected native title claims, has been the subject of some controversy (van Krieken 2000). There is a respectable body of legal opinion to support the view that the High Court *Mabo* decision represented a "cautious correction," based on "long established common law doctrines, amply supported by precedents" (Nettheim 1993, 10), rather than a "judicial revolution" by activist judges based on novel doctrines promulgated by radical historians. This has not stopped some writers launching an attack on Henry Reynolds's historical work, apparently guided by the belief that if Reynolds's work can be discredited, the legal basis of native title would be undermined. Thus in 2005, a Tasmanian historian, Michael Connor, wrote a lengthy attack on the concept of *terra nullius*, including ad hominem recriminations against Reynolds and other historians putatively guilty of "Australiaphobia." Connor's polemic was published by Keith Windschuttle's own publishing house, Macleay Press (Connor 2005; see Warden 2006; Ritter 2007, 146-48) and was given wide and sympathetic coverage by News Limited newspapers such as the *Australian*.

Keith Windschuttle, who had been a dogmatic leftist in the late 1960s and into the 1970s, and whose polemic against postmodernism titled *The Killing of History* (1994) had met with a warm reception from conservative opinion both in Australia and the United States, had launched his own assault on left-leaning practitioners of Australian Indigenous history. Windschuttle's *The Fabrication of Aboriginal History* (2002) made two central arguments. First, widely accepted accounts of massacres by European settlers in colonial Van Diemen's Land (Tasmania) were exaggerated, and the death toll of frontier violence in colonial Tasmania, where the near-extinction of the Indigenous population was sometimes characterized as "genocide," was actually relatively small. Second, errors allegedly made by prominent scholars of Aboriginal history and frontier violence in Tasmania were part of a deliberate campaign by left-leaning historians to foist a false picture of colonization onto the public for ideological purposes. These left-leaning historians supposedly constituted an "orthodoxy," which Windschuttle sought to discredit.

Windschuttle's (2002) book was the subject of considerable media controversy as well as scholarly criticism. It was criticized on empirical grounds for naïve overreliance on official sources that could not be expected to report fully the reality of the frontier (Boyce 2003) and on the grounds that his low estimate of Aboriginal deaths from frontier violence was based on a standard of proof that was unfeasibly high under frontier conditions (Attwood 2005, 117-21). The contention that a few footnote errors in works published more than twenty years previously amounted to a conspiracy to falsify history was also rejected, with one of the historians accused by Windschuttle of deliberate fabrication, Lyndall Ryan, complaining of a media witch hunt in the wake of Windschuttle's charges (Ryan 2003). Windschuttle was also charged with misrepresenting academic historians with his claim that they advanced a united "orthodox" thesis that the Tasmanian Aborigines had been the victims of a policy of genocide. Lyndall Ryan's work, in fact, emphasized the survival of an Aboriginal population in Tasmania, arguing against the popular view that the population had been wholly exterminated, and Reynolds's work considered the question of genocide but concluded that the term was not an accurate descriptor of the colonial government's policies (Ryan 1981; Reynolds 2001). Notwithstanding the "straw man" nature of Windschuttle's charges, a vigorous debate took place in the media and among scholars over the applicability of the concept of genocide to Australia (Bonnell and Crotty 2004; Moses 2004; Levi 2007). The debate partly turned on the extent to which the term "genocide" could be decoupled from the paradigm of the Holocaust and be used in ways that nonetheless reflected the UN Convention on Genocide, and the extent to which the cumulative effects of dispossession and frontier violence by white settlers could amount to genocide, even in the absence of any explicitly genocidal intent on the part of the colonial authorities. Raymond Evans and Bill Thorpe (2001) suggested the formulation "indigenocide" to describe a process of "developmental genocide," the outcome of the wholesale supplanting of Indigenous people, even without state-organized mass killing.

To conservative media commentators, any discussion of the possibility of genocide in Australia was offensive and seemed like an attempt by leftists to besmirch and discredit Australia's national history. News Limited newspapers, especially the *Australian*, gave considerable column space to Windschuttle and his claims, defended him from his critics, and at times launched their own attacks on those who attempted to expose Windschuttle's errors and misinterpretations. Windschuttle was widely and frequently praised, his critics derided cruelly and often.

While issues concerning Australian Aboriginal history were among the most politically and emotionally charged subjects of the Howard years' history wars, debate was not confined to these topics. The Howard government also expressed concern with the way in which Australian history was represented to the public in, for example, the new National Museum of Australia, and taught to students in schools. Both areas became targets for government intervention.

The National Museum of Australia was opened in 2001, coinciding with the centenary of the Federation of the Australian States to form the Commonwealth of Australia. The plan for a national museum had been two decades in the making but had mostly been met with indifference from the federal government, and the project had languished on the back burner before John Howard came to power in 1996. The council overseeing the National Museum was chaired by former Liberal Party Federal President Tony Staley and has included Prime Minister Howard's authorized biographer and former journalist David Barnett, conservative columnist Christopher Pearson (a former speechwriter for John Howard who has a weekly opinion column in the Murdoch-owned *Weekend Australian*), and respected conservative historian John Hirst. With the exception of Hirst, a number of members of the council seem to have been selected more for reasons of political affiliation and ideological reliability than for expertise in museology or history.

In 2000, not long before the museum was due to open, David Barnett, as one of the members of the council, instigated a major review of the museum's displays, claiming that too many of the exhibits reflected "political correctness" and/or "Marxist claptrap." Among many other complaints, including an alleged bias in favor of Indigenous activists, Barnett argued that Australian corporate leaders should be given greater prominence. A detailed report by Monash University history professor Graeme Davison did not reveal any systematic political bias (Macintyre and Clark 2003, 191-94). The National Museum remained a target of conservative attacks, however: Keith Windschuttle claimed that the zigzag ground plan of the museum's building echoed Daniel Libeskind's new Jewish Museum in Berlin—conveying a subliminal message that Australia had a genocidal past (Macintyre and Clark 2003, 196). A second review, this time headed by conservative La Trobe University sociologist John Carroll, again found no "systemic problem" of "cultural or political bias" at the National Museum (Macintyre and Clark 2003, 196-97). The director of the museum, one of Australia's most experienced and professional Aboriginal bureaucrats, Dawn Casey, was given only a one-year extension of her term in 2002, which was not renewed at the end of 2003, resulting in her being made redundant from the public service (Kremmer 2003). The whole affair smacked of churlishness dressed up as a noble commitment to evenhandedness.

In terms of the teaching of Australian history, Howard has long expressed concerns that Australian children were being denied their rightful heritage of pride in their country's achievements and were too often finishing their secondary school years without a clear sense of the overall national historical narrative (Errington and Van Onselen 2007, 188; Clark 2006, 2, 33-34). It was not, however, until 2006 that Howard entered the debate in full swing, perhaps in the interests of providing a distraction from controversial industrial relations laws for which the government was being severely criticized at the time. On the eve of Australia Day 2006, John Howard used his speech to the National Press Club in Parliament House to call for a "root and branch renewal of the teaching of Australian history in our schools." Not only were too few school students studying Australian history, he maintained, but the way in which it was taught aroused concern:

> Too often, it is taught without any sense of structured narrative, replaced by a fragmented stew of "themes" and "issues." And too often, history, along with other subjects in the humanities, has succumbed to a postmodern culture of relativism where any objective record of achievement is questioned or repudiated. (Howard 2006a)

The federal education minister, Julie Bishop, duly convened a national "history summit" in August 2006, at which conservative historians (described by the minister as representing the "sensible center" in the national history debate) predominated. Notwithstanding, the summit's results still fell short of Prime Minister Howard's intentions. In a measure widely viewed as indicative of Howard's desire for a more decisively conservative outcome to the national history curriculum, the conservative historian Blainey and a former Howard staffer, right-wing political commentator Gerard Henderson, were in 2007 appointed to a panel to help develop the national history curriculum for secondary schools. The debate around the national history curriculum showed that for some on the right, like Keith Windschuttle, "reviving national history as a political narrative" was seen as a vital means to "combat the long campaign waged by the intelligentsia to undermine the nation" (Windschuttle 2007, 18, 22).

Again, Howard has received strong support from conservative newspaper columnists and editors in relation to Australian history in the school curriculum. Two days after Howard's National Press Club address of January 2007, the *Australian* editorialized that "young Australians are growing up completely clueless about how their country came to be the prosperous democracy they are proud of." The *Australian* blamed the lack of interest in history at secondary school level on curriculum planners whose bleak outlook on the past was "out of sympathy with popular patriotism" and whose emphasis on a thematic approach destroyed any coherent narrative, resulting in children being taught "bits and pieces of the past" (*Australian*, January 27, 2006). Columnists such as Janet Albrechtsen also attacked leading "left" historians such as Robert Manne and Stuart Macintyre in an often willfully deceptive fashion and gave strong support to more narrative-based and affirming versions of Australian history (*Australian*,

August 23, 2006). The general thrust of their arguments has been that historians are so politically biased they will corrupt the younger generation of Australians unless, startlingly, politicians intervene.

In the almost twelve years since John Howard became Australian prime minister, he and his allies have fought the history wars constantly, if not consistently. As well as decrying the black armband version of the past that Howard believes to have received too much attention, he and his allies have consistently argued for more emphasis on Australian achievements. They have fought the campaign through attacks on liberal institutions such as the ABC and Australian universities, through attempts to have the National Museum conform to a more celebratory agenda, and through attempts to impose a national history curriculum. Most recently, Howard has instituted the Prime Minister's Prize for Australian History, worth A$100,000. In June 2007 the first award was made jointly to Les Carlyon for his history of Australians fighting on the Western Front in World War I (*The Great War*, 2006) and to Peter Cochrane for a history of Australian democracy (*Colonial Ambition: Foundations of Australian Democracy*, 2006). Both, predictably, are books about Australian achievement and concern politics and war—the "stuff" of history, and the essence of conservative historical narratives.

> *In the almost twelve years since John Howard became Australian prime minister, he and his allies have fought the history wars constantly, if not consistently. As well as decrying the black armband version of the past that Howard believes to have received too much attention, he and his allies have consistently argued for more emphasis on Australian achievements.*

Undoubtedly, the politicization of Australian history has been detrimental to academic and public debate. Historians have had their integrity called into question, and the merit of any historical writing is publicly assessed by whether it is affirming on one hand or "black armband" on the other. Considerations of how enlightening, instructive, or original the work is take second place in a "culture wars" environment. Moreover, the reputation of academic historians has been tarnished by the constant vituperative attacks from conservation opinion writers, a development that has assisted, or at the very least hindered resistance to, the downgrading of the humanities in the tertiary education sector.

And yet it would be easy to exaggerate the effects of Australia's history wars. The West German historians' dispute (*Historikerstreit*) of the mid-1980s generated a bibliography of hundreds of articles, but arguably resulted in little or no advance in historical knowledge per se. The Australian history wars have had a similarly thin outcome in terms of the advancement of historical scholarship. They have sparked a flurry of footnote-checking. At best, some lacunae in documentation have been identified, which may result in more thorough primary source–based publications in the future. Staff numbers in universities were in decline before John Howard came to power, undergraduate enrollments have not suffered as much as has at times been feared, and historians are going about their business as they always have.[3] The National Museum made only a few changes to some exhibition labels, and a national history curriculum appears little closer to realization. While the history wars have provided background noise for the depletion of humanities faculties in Australian universities, and have accompanied the frustration of Indigenous hopes for more emancipatory government policies and a genuine reconciliation process, their influence has hardly been decisive. The history wars have been loud, long, and often bitter, but have fundamentally changed very little about the practice of Australian history. It is some cause for comfort to Australian historians that their commitment to liberal democratic humanism, to scholarship, and to their students has transcended the politics of their calling for the past decade. It is, ultimately, as it should be.

Notes

1. Ron Brunton was a senior fellow of the Institute of Public Affairs from 1995 to 2001, was a regular columnist with the Murdoch-owned Brisbane *Courier Mail* from 1997 to 2003, and was appointed a director of the Australian Broadcasting Commission by the Howard government in 2003.

2. Keith Windschuttle, writer and frequent media commentator (especially in *Quadrant* magazine and the Murdoch press), was appointed a director of the Australian Broadcasting Commission by the Howard government in 2006.

3. Since the completion of this article, the Howard government was defeated in the general election of November 24, 2007. Prime Minister Howard lost his own seat in Parliament, only the second time in Australian history this has happened. The new Labor Party government of Kevin Rudd has so far demonstrated no inclination to become involved in any "culture wars." It has, however, signaled an intention to revise the national history curriculum developed in the last year of the Howard government to make it less nationalistic. The full effects of the Labor government's election on historical teaching and research in Australia will not be clear for some time yet.

References

Attwood, Bain. 2005. *Telling the truth about Aboriginal history*. Crows Nest, NSW, Australia: Allen & Unwin.

Australian Broadcasting Corporation. 1996. Transcript of interview of John Howard by Liz Jackson, broadcast on *Four Corners* program, February 19. http://www.abc.net.au/4corners/content/2004/s1212701.htm (accessed July 17, 2007).

Barnett, David, and Pru Goward. 1997. *John Howard, Prime Minister*. Melbourne, Australia: Viking.

Blainey, Geoffrey. 1993. Drawing up a balance sheet of our history. *Quadrant* 37 (July/August): 10-15.

Bolt, Andrew. 2002. Rabbit proof myths. http://members.optushome.com.au/jimball/Rabbitproofmyth.html (accessed July 23, 2007). (Originally published in *Herald Sun*, Melbourne, Australia)

———. 2006-2007. http://blogs.news.com.au/heraldsun/andrewbolt/ (accessed September 21, 2007).

Bonnell, Andrew G., and Martin Crotty. 2004. An Australian *"Historikerstreit"*? *Australian Journal of Politics and History* 50:425-33.

Boyce, James. 2003. Fantasy island. In *Whitewash: On Keith Windschuttle's fabrication of Aboriginal history*, ed. Robert Manne, 17-78. Melbourne, Australia: Black Inc.

Brunton, Ron. 1998. Betraying the victims of the "stolen generations." *Courier Mail* (Brisbane, Australia), February 26. http://www.ipa.org.au/files/news_786.html (accessed July 23, 2007).

Carlyon, Les. 2006. *The Great War*. Sydney, Australia: Pan Macmillan.

Clark, Anna. 2006. *Teaching the nation: Politics and pedagogy in Australian history*. Melbourne, Australia: Melbourne University Press.

Cochrane, Peter. 2006. *Colonial ambition: Foundations of Australian democracy*. Melbourne, Australia: Melbourne University Press.

Connor, Michael. 2005. *The invention of Terra Nullius: Historical and legal fictions on the foundation of Australia*. Paddington, NSW, Australia: Macleay Books.

Errington, Wayne, and Peter Van Onselen. 2007. *John Winston Howard*. Melbourne, Australia: Melbourne University Press.

Evans, Raymond, and Bill Thorpe. 2001. The massacre of Australian history. *Overland* 163:21-39.

Gaita, Raymond. 1999. *A common humanity*. Melbourne, Australia: Text Publishing.

Haebich, Anna. 2000. *Broken circles. Fragmenting Indigenous families, 1800-2000*. Fremantle, WA: Fremantle Arts Centre Press.

Haigh, Gideon. 2006. The Nelson touch—Research funding; the new censorship. *The Monthly* 12:20-29.

Howard, John. 1996. The liberal tradition: The beliefs and values which guide the federal government. Sir Robert Menzies Lecture, November 18. Media Transcript. Web site of Prime Minister John Howard, http://web.archive.org/web/19970212063226/http://www.nla.gov.au/pmc/pressrel/menzies.html (accessed July 19, 2007).

———. 2006a. Address to the National Press Club, Great Hall, Parliament House, January 25. http://www.pm.gov.au/media/Speech/2006/speech1754.cfm (accessed August 20, 2007).

———. 2006b. Address to the Quadrant Magazine 50th anniversary dinner, Four Seasons Hotel, Sydney, Australia, October 4. Speech Transcript. http://www.pm.gov.au/media/speech/2006/speech2165.cfm (accessed July 23, 2007).

Human Rights and Equal Opportunity Commission. 1997. *Bringing them home: Report of the National Inquiry into the Separation of Aboriginal and Torres Strait Islander Children from Their Families*. Sydney, Australia: HREOC.

Inglis, Ken. 2006. *Whose ABC? The Australian Broadcasting Corporation 1983-2006*. Melbourne, Australia: Black Inc.

Keating, Paul. 1992/1995. The Redfern Park Speech, December 10, 1992. In *Advancing Australia. The speeches of Paul Keating, prime minister*, ed. Mark Ryan. Sydney, Australia: Big Picture Publications.

Kremmer, Christopher. 2003. History wars claim a casualty. *The Age* (Melbourne, Australia), December 6. http://www.theage.com.au/articles/2003/12/05/1070351786939.html (accessed July 30, 2007).

Levi, Neil. 2007. "No sensible comparison?" The place of the Holocaust in Australia's history wars. *History & Memory* 19 (1): 124-56.

Macintyre, Stuart. 2007. Universities. In *Silencing dissent*, ed. Clive Hamilton and Sarah Maddison, 41-59. Crows Nest, Australia: Allen & Unwin.

Macintyre, Stuart, and Anna Clark. 2003. *The history wars*. Carlton, Victoria, Australia: Melbourne University Press.

Maddox, Marion. 2004. Howard's methodism: How convenient?! *Journal of Australian Studies* 83:1-11.

Manne, Robert. 2001. In denial. The stolen generations and the right. *Australian Quarterly Essay* 1(1): 1-113.

Marginson, Simon. 2004. Higher education. In *The Howard years*, ed. Robert Manne. Melbourne, Australia: Black Inc. Agenda.

McKnight, David. 2005. The Murdoch press and the culture war. In *Do not disturb. Is the media failing Australia?* ed. Robert Manne, 53-74. Melbourne, Australia: Black Inc.

Moses, A. Dirk, ed. 2004. *Genocide and settler society: Frontier violence and stolen Indigenous children in Australian history*. New York: Berghahn Books.

Nettheim, Garth. 1993. Judicial revolution or cautious correction? *Mabo v Queensland*. *UNSW Law Journal* 16 (1): 1-26.

Organization for Economic Cooperation and Development (OECD). 2006. *Education at a glance*. OECD Indicators 2006 Edition. Paris: OECD.

Reynolds, Henry. 1982. *The other side of the frontier: Aboriginal resistance to the European invasion of Australia*. Ringwood, Victoria, Australia: Penguin Books.

———. 1987. *The law of the land*. Ringwood, Victoria, Australia: Penguin Books.

———. 1996. *Aboriginal sovereignty. Reflections on race, state and nation*. St. Leonards, NSW, Australia: Allen & Unwin.

———. 2001. *An indelible stain: The question of genocide in Australia's history*. Ringwood, Victoria, Australia: Penguin.

Ritter, David. 2007. Myths, truths and arguments: Some recent writings on Aboriginal history. *Australian Journal of Politics and History* 53 (1): 138-48.

Ryan, Lyndall, 1981. *The Aboriginal Tasmanians*. St. Lucia, Australia: University of Queensland Press.

Ryan, Lyndall. 2003. Reflections by a target of a media witch hunt. *History Australia* 1 (1): 105-9.

van Krieken, Robert. 2000. From Milirrpum to Mabo: The High Court, Terra Nullius and moral enterpreneurship. *UNSW Law Journal* 23 (1): 63-77.

Warden, James. 2006. Atramentous history. *History Australia* 3 (2, item 49): 1-8.

Watson, Don. 2002. *Recollections of a bleeding heart: A portrait of Paul Keating PM*. Milsons Point, NSW, Australia: Random House.

Windschuttle, Keith. 1994. *The killing of history: How a discipline is being murdered by literary critics and social theorists*. Sydney, NSW, Australia: Macleay Press.

———. 2000. The break-up of Australia. *Quadrant* 44 (September): 8-16.

———. 2002. *The fabrication of Aboriginal history*. Paddington, NSW, Australia: Macleay Press.

———. 2007. The nation & the intellectual left. *New Criterion* 26 (January): 15-22.

Young, Michael, 2007. *Death, sex and money: Life inside a newspaper*. Melbourne, Australia: Melbourne University Press.

Democracy and Memory: Romania Confronts Its Communist Past

By
VLADIMIR TISMANEANU

All postcommunist societies face major dilemmas in confronting their traumatic past. A functional democracy cannot be based on lies, denial, and amnesia. Romania's exit from communism has resulted in a hybrid quasi-democratic regime, with former communists like Ion Iliescu maintaining influential positions and opposing a genuine break with the past. In 2006, President Traian Băsescu established a Presidential Commission for the Analysis of the Communist Dictatorship in Romania; the author of this article was selected as its chair. The commission's *Final Report* was the basis for President Băsescu's condemnation of the communist dictatorship as illegitimate and criminal. Offering a comparative perspective, the author focuses on the debates that led to the creation of the commission, the commission's activity and the fierce attacks on it by nostalgic communists and xenophobic nationalists, and the impact of moral justice on Romania's democratic political culture.

Keywords: postcommunist stocktaking; communist nostalgia; resistance to facts

In January 2007, Romania acceded to the European Union, a few years after having entered the North Atlantic Treaty Organization (NATO). This was a watershed in Romania's history, a significant moment in the history of Eastern Europe, and a test for the European Union's commitment to accepting problematic

Vladimir Tismaneanu is a professor of government and politics at the University of Maryland and chair of the Editorial Committee of East European Politics and Societies. In 2006, he served as chairman of the Presidential Commission for the Analysis of the Communist Dictatorship in Romania and, since April 2007, as chairman of the Presidential Advisory Commission for the Analysis of the Communist Dictatorship in Romania. He is the author of numerous books, including Fantasies of Salvation: Democracy, Nationalism, and Myth in Post-Communist Europe *(Princeton, 1998) and* Stalinism for All Seasons: A Political History of Romanian Communism *(University of California Press, 2003). The University of Maryland awarded him its Distinguished International Service Award in 2007.*

DOI: 10.1177/0002716207312763

candidates as long as they have complied with the major accession requirements. A few years ago, in a controversial article published in the *New York Review of Books*, historian Tony Judt argued that the real test for the European Union was Romania's accession, considering its pending structural problems (2001). At the time, the article generated anger among Romanian intellectuals and produced reactions both pro and con.[1] Nevertheless, one cannot deny the nature of the difficulties with which Romania is faced, among them that of an unmastered past. This article proposes to document and critically examine, in a comparative perspective, Romania's efforts to assume and judge its communist past. The starting point for the analysis is Romania's decision to work through its communist past, a late decision that came about in a convoluted fashion. Still, once the process started in late 2005 and early 2006, it gathered a tremendous momentum and resulted in the first categorical state condemnation of the communist dictatorship as illegitimate and criminal.

The questions I try to answer with this article are as follows: Why did Romania engage so late in the effort to assume its communist past? What were the main obstacles that prevented this historical catharsis for almost seventeen years after the December 1989 revolution? Why did this catharsis occur precisely in 2006? How does Romania compare to other East European countries in terms of mastering its dictatorial past? What political and cultural conditions explain the resurgence and intensification of the anticommunist sentiment after a long period of relative indifference or even torpor regarding this topic? To elaborate on all these points would require a whole book. The most important item is that the belated nature of Romania's decision to confront its communist totalitarian past was predominantly the consequence of obstinate opposition to such an undertaking from parties and personalities directly or indirectly linked to the ancien régime. The elections of November and December 2004 resulted in the victory of an anticommunist coalition and the election of Traian Băsescu as the country's president. In spite of political rivalries and the disintegration of the initial government coalition, both the National Liberal and the Democratic Parties understood the importance of coming to terms with the past. Especially after January 2006, both the liberal prime minister, Călin Popescu-Tăriceanu (head of the Liberal Party), and President Băsescu (linked to the Democratic Party) have championed de-communization. At the other end of the political spectrum, in an effort to boycott Traian Băsescu's initiatives, former president Ion Iliescu and other leaders of the Social Democratic Party (in many respects still dominated by former *nomenklatura* figures) allied themselves with the ultrapopulist, jingoistic, and anti-Semitic "Greater Romania Party," which is headed by the notorious Corneliu Vadim Tudor, a former Nicolae Ceausescu sycophant. The condemnation of the communist dictatorship has become one of the most hotly debated political, ideological, and moral issues in contemporary Romania. Unlike Germany, where a parliamentary consensus (minus the radical left) allowed for the relatively peaceful activity of the Enquete Commission headed by former dissident pastor Reiner Eppelmann, the Presidential Commission for the Analysis of the

Communist Dictatorship in Romania (PCACDR), which I chaired, was continuously attacked from the extreme left, the nationalist right, and Orthodox clericalist and fundamentalist circles (the daily newspaper *Ziua* was the most vocal).

As chairman and coordinator of the PCACDR, I witnessed the historical event on December 18, 2006, when the Romanian President, Traian Băsescu, presented and adopted before Parliament the conclusions and proposals of the PCACDR's *Final Report*. The behavior of those present could be divided into two categories: those who acted like hooligans, vehemently denying the importance and legitimacy of official reckoning with the communist past; and those who, imbued with the solemnity of the event, reacted in a dignified manner. The next day, in an interview with the BBC, the president insisted that the hysteria of the crypto-communists and the nationalists was no reason to be deterred from continuing along the line of working through Romania's traumatic dictatorial past. On the contrary, their attitude was a sign that the path chosen was the right one, from an academic and moral point of view. A functional and healthy democratic society cannot endlessly indulge in politics of oblivion and denial. Reconciliation remains spurious in the absence of repentance. In the short term, the politics of forgetfulness (what former Polish prime minister Tadeusz Mazowiecki once called "the thick line with the past") can have its benefits if one takes into account the newly born and fragile social consensus. In the long term, however, such policies foster grievous misgivings in relation to collective values and memory, with potentially disastrous institutional and psychoemotional consequences.

The condemnation of the communist regime in Romania can be integrated, from a historical standpoint, into the space circumscribed by two factors that marked the post-1989 period. On one hand, there is former president Ion Iliescu's politics of amnesia over his three mandates, 1990 to 1992, 1992 to 1996, and 2000 to 2004 (which was also a regrettable characteristic for the Democratic Convention during the Emil Constantinescu administration from 1997 to 2000). On the other, there are the constant attempts from civil society to speed up the process of de-communization. The latter is defined by several original movements: the Timişoara proclamation in March 1990 that advocated lustration and the June 1990 student protest movements spearheaded by the Civic Alliance. Also encompassed within this framework are various attempts to rehabilitate certain periods of Romanian communism, along with campaigns aimed at recycling aspects of the country's authoritarian past (e.g., numerous initiatives to "restore the name" of pro-Nazi Marshal Ion Antonescu or to sanitize the murderous history of the fascist Iron Guard[2]). In contrast, there were attempts at a "memory regime," that is, an effort to recuperate "a shattered past" (Jarausch 2003), in addition to movements that demanded other sorts of clarifications—particularly legal ones on the basis of the gradual opening of the *Securitate* archives and of other institutions that had a crucial role in the functioning and reproduction of the regime—and obtaining moral and material compensations for suffering inflicted by the twentieth-century totalitarian experience in Romania.

In the early 1990s, the issue of de-communization was a hot one, in Romania and throughout Central and Eastern Europe. But as the process of these societies' normalization progressed, de-communization gradually faded into the background. Only recently, first and controversially in Poland, and now in Romania, has it come back to the forefront of civic and political agendas. Traian Băsescu, during his electoral campaign in 2004, neither placed de-communization prominently in his platform nor pretended to have been a victim of communism.[3] However, the specific dynamics of Romanian politics and the mobilization of civil society acted as catalysts for a strong return into the public debate of topics related to the communist dictatorship. In March 2006, the Group for Social Dialogue (a major civil society organization of some of the country's most famous intellectuals) as well as the leaders of the main trade unions endorsed an Appeal for the Condemnation of the Communist Regime, launched by prominent Civic Alliance personality Sorin Iliesiu, which accelerated the process by which the Romanian state finally took an official attitude toward its traumatic past. In April 2006, convinced by now of the urgent necessity of such an initiative, President Băsescu decided to create the PCACDR. His position at the time, and during the entire period of de-communization, proves the importance of political will and determination in the attempt to initiate and sustain a potentially centrifugal endeavor. President Băsescu entrusted me with selecting the members of the commission. In so doing, I took into account the scholarly competence and moral credibility of the people invited to join this body. Among the commission members figured well-known historians, social scientists, civil society personalities, former political prisoners, former dissidents, and major figures of democratic exile. President Băsescu charged the commission with the task of producing a rigorous and coherent document that would examine the main institutions, methods, and personalities that made possible the crimes and abuses of the communist regime. In addition to its academic tasks, the work of the commission was meant to pass moral judgment on the defunct dictatorship and invite a reckoning with the past throughout a painful, albeit inevitable, acknowledgement of its crimes against humanity and other forms of repression. This was a revolutionary step in Romanian postcommunist politics: neither ex-communist president Ion Iliescu nor anticommunist president Emil Constantinescu had engaged in such a potentially explosive undertaking. From the very outset, immediately after the commission's creation was announced, radical-nationalist and nostalgic-communist circles issued attacks. Much of the verbal assault, including scurrilous slanders and vicious anti-Semitic diatribes, targeted the commission's president.[4]

The PCACDR was the first such state body created in the countries of the former Soviet bloc. The only precedent could be found in unified Germany, where the Bundestag created, between 1992 and 1998, two successive Enquete Commissions that investigated the history of the SED (Socialist Unity Party) Dictatorship and its effects on German unity (McAdams 2001). At the end of the mandate of the second Enquete Commission, on the basis of its activity and practice, a foundation was established: the Stiftung zur Aufarbeitung der SED-Diktatur (June 5, 1998). The creation of the German commissions represents, however, a different situation under circumstances of unification, institutional absorption, and value transference on the West-East axis. There are nevertheless a series of similarities between the Enquete Commissions and the PCACDR, particularly in what concerned the mandates. Both the Romanian and the German mandates understood the analysis of their communist pasts along the lines of the study of the structures of power and mechanisms of decision making during the history of the regime; the functions and meaning of ideology, inclusionary patterns, and disciplinary practices within the state and society; the study of the legal and policing system; the role of the various churches during the various phases of state socialism; and finally, the role of dissidence, of civil disobedience, and, in Romania's case, of the 1989 revolution. Both in Romania and Germany, the commissions were meant to provide evaluations related to problems of responsibility; guilt; and continuity of political, cultural, social, and economic structures from the communist through postcommunist periods. The overall purpose of both bodies was to establish the basis for what Avishai Margalit (2002) called an ethics of memory. The PCACDR activity was generally guided by Hannah Arendt's (1994, 405) vision of responsibility and culpability: "What is unprecedented about totalitarianism is not only its ideological content, but the *event* itself of totalitarian domination."

In addition to its academic tasks,
the work of the commission was meant
to pass moral judgment on
the defunct dictatorship and invite
a reckoning with the past throughout
a painful, albeit inevitable, acknowledgement
of its crimes against humanity and other
forms of repression.

The difference between the German and Romanian commissions is that the Enquete Commissions of the SED Dictatorship and the subsequent foundation were created in a unified Germany with the massive support of the Bundestag, under circumstances of thorough de-legitimation of the communist party and state, and in the context of a national consensus regarding the criminal nature of the Stasi. In contrast, in Romania there was a flagrant absence of expiation, penance, or regret. Without such premises, any act of reconciliation draws dangerously close to whitewashing the past. In Germany, the parliament's mandate was the obvious sign of a political consensus over the necessity of mastering and overcoming the totalitarian past. At the same time, it also meant a serious commitment on the part of the state for purposes of investigating and researching the complexities of the communist phenomenon in the country. In Romania, the PCACDR lacked legislative backing and had minimum financial support, its members working mostly pro bono. The parliament proved to be a site of outward and tacit opposition and subversion to the president's initiative to investigate the history of the communist regime. Moreover, various political factions promoted institutional parallelisms by continuous fueling of opposite, nostalgic, and even negationist interpretations from budget-dependent bodies such as the Institute of the Romanian Revolution (chaired by Ion Iliescu) or the Institute for the Investigation of Totalitarianism (created in the early 1990s and dominated by nationalist politicians and historians). Therefore, the PCACDR lacked the infrastructure, the resources, and the consensus for a countrywide, state-supported campaign for implementing the *Final Report* (with its conclusions and policy recommendations). The permanent squabbles between parties and their representatives and the strong negationist trend characterizing Romania's political realm prevented the *Final Report* and the PCACDR from having a structural impact similar to that of the Stiftung zur Aufarbeitung der SED-Diktatur.

In a sense, the PCACDR comes close to the commissions for truth and reconciliation created in countries such as South Africa, Chile, Argentina, and Rwanda. One has to mention, though, that in contrast to these commissions, the PCACDR had no decision-making power and no subpoena prerogative. Moreover, it should be stressed that the PCACDR's activities and research took place under the pressure of a constrained time period (April-December 2006). The project and activities of the PCACDR benefited from the previous experience of the International Commission on the Holocaust (ICHR) in Romania, chaired by celebrated writer and Nobel Peace Prize laureate Elie Wiesel. The main difference between the two endeavors is that the proceedings of the ICHR could not be perceived, as in the PCACDR's case, as a direct threat or involving a personal stake in contemporary society and politics, since the three historical groups involved in the Holocaust (the victims, the perpetrators, and the bystanders) had mostly disappeared. As far as the communist past is concerned, many of the perpetrators, victims, and witnesses of the regime's crimes are still alive and involved in societal dynamics, some of them even holding seats in the Romanian parliament. The moment on December 18, 2006, when exponents of the radical left and right booed President Băsescu's delivery of the findings of the PCACDR, demonstrated that a genuine democracy cannot function properly in the absence of historical consciousness. No viable democracy can afford to accept amnesia, forgetfulness, and the loss of memory. An authentic democratic community cannot be built on the denial of past crimes, abuses, and atrocities. The past is not another country. It cannot be wished away—the more that is attempted, the more we witness the return of repressed memories (for example, consider the recurring efforts to prosecute former Mexican president Luis Echeverria for his involvement in the bloody repression of student demonstrations of the early 1970s). For the first time in post-1989 Romania, the PCACDR rejected outright the practices of institutionalized forgetfulness and generated a national conversation about long-denied and occulted moments of the past (including instances of collaboration and complicity).[5]

No viable democracy can afford to accept amnesia, forgetfulness, and the loss of memory. An authentic democratic community cannot be built on the denial of past crimes, abuses, and atrocities.

In January 2007, President Băsescu visited the Sighet Memorial (a museum dedicated to the victims of communism) in northern Romania. This institution, because of poet Ana Blandiana's and writer Romulus Rusan's dedications and because of the diligence of historians from the research center affiliated with the memorial, is the most important *lieu de mémoire* dealing with Romania's tragic communist past. By January 2007, immediately after having posted the PCACDR's *Final Report* on the president's Web site, there were some reactions that signaled what I consider a false problem. It has been argued that the PCACDR document exonerates certain political figures murdered by communists, but who themselves could hardly be considered democrats. To this I would first say that the presidential commission did not intend *any* exoneration. The introduction of the *Final Report* clearly states its purpose:

> The condemnation of the communist regime is today first of all a moral, intellectual, social and political obligation. The Romanian democratic and pluralist state can and must do it. The acknowledgement of these dark and tragic pages of our national recent history is vital for the young generations to be conscious of the world their parents were forced to live in. Romania's future rests on mastering its past, henceforth on condemning the communist regime as an enemy to human society. If we are not to do it today, here and now, we shall burden ourselves with the further complicity, by practice of silence, with the totalitarian Evil. In no way do we mean by this collective guilt. We emphasize the importance of learning from a painful past, of learning how was this possible, and of departing from it with compassion and sorrow for its victims. (*Raport Final* 2006).

The PCACDR aimed at a synthesis between understanding the traumatic history through an academic praxis that presupposes distance from the surveyed subject and empathizing with the people who suffered from the crimes and abuses of the dictatorship. The commission pursued a reconstruction of the past along the dichotomy of distance-empathy, focusing upon both general and individual aspects of the past. The *Final Report*'s transgressive intentionality lies in the facts,[6] in the more or less familiar places of Romanian's communist history. The PCACDR first identified victims, regardless of their political colors, for one cannot argue that one is against torture for the left while ignoring such practices when it comes to the right. The militants of the far right should have been punished on a legal basis, but this was not the case for the trials put forth by the Romanian Communist Party (RCP). The communists simply shattered any notion of the rule of law. The *Final Report* identifies the nature of abuses and its victims, though it does not leave aside the ideological context of the times. For the PCACDR, the communist regime represented the opposite of rule of law, an *Unrechtsstaat*. However, any attempt at "discovering" a Bitburg syndrome (Maier 1988; Baldwin 1990) in the PCACDR document is a malevolent, biased statement more than a pointed academic argument.

I consider that there is an overlying conceptualization of memory in the pages of the *Final Report*, one that puts together what Richard S. Esbenshade (1995) identified as the two main paradigms in Eastern Europe, shaped before and after the fall of communism, for the relationship between memory and communal identity. On one hand, there is the "Milan Kundera paradigm," according to which "man's struggle is one of memory against forgetting" (that is, instrumentalized amnesia vs. individual, civic remembrance). On the other, there is the "George Konrad paradigm," where "history is the forcible illumination of darkened memories," presupposing a "morass of shared responsibility" (Esbenshade 1995; Kundera 2005; Konrad 1982). In this way, the PCACDR attempted to answer to Tony Judt's (2002a) "double crisis of history" in former Eastern Europe.[7] As the reactions to the *Final Report* show, the formation and employment of a society-wide "critically informed memory" (Dominick LaCapra 1998) is challenged by widespread cynicism and distrust at all sociopolitical levels and by multiple historical myths, anxieties, expectations, illusions, and memories (developed during the communist period as resistance to the ubiquitous ideological discourse of the RCP dictatorship) that claim legitimacy because of their private and unofficial character (Deak, Gross, and Judt 2000; Judt 2000). Dealing with both the communist and fascist past (and implicitly Romania's responsibility for the Holocaust) must become a factor of communal cohesion as it imposes the rejection of any comfortably apologetic historicization. The *Final Report*'s conclusions postulate the moral equivalence of the two extremisms that caused such trauma: "the far left must be rejected as much as the far right. The denial of communism's crimes is as unacceptable as the denial of those of fascism. As any justification for the crimes against humanity performed by the Antonescu regime ought not to be tolerated, we believe that no form of commemoration of communist leaders/representatives should be allowed" (*Raport Final* 2007, 637). Subsequently, the main instrument for the process of mastering the past, employed by the PCACDR, was the deconstruction of the ideological certainty

established by the communist regime upon which the latter founded its legitimacy and that it creatively instrumentalized in its attempt to encompass the
entire society. From the appearance of antifascism to the discourse of the "socialist nation," the *topoi* (traditional theme or motif) of Romanian Stalinism permeated public consciousness, simultaneously maiming collective memory and
significant chunks of the country's history. The post-1989 period in Romania was
dominated by an absence of expiation, of penance, or of a mourning process in
relation to the trauma of communism. Therefore, reconciliation was impossible,
for it lacked any basic truth value.

Taking into account all of the above, it can be argued that the condemnation of
the communist regime was based upon a civic-liberal ethos and not, as some commentators stated, on a moral-absolutist discourse, as legitimization for a new power
hierarchy in the public and political space. In the following lines, I will provide an
extensive quote from President Băsescu's December 18, 2006, speech to clarify the
conceptual and discursive complex that lies at the core of the communist regime's
condemnation. During a joint session of the Romanian parliament, President
Băsescu accepted the conclusions and recommendations of the PCACDR's *Final
Report*. His address became an official document of the Romanian state, published
in the country's *Official Monitor*, no. 196, on December 28, 2006.

> As Head of the Romanian State, I expressly and categorically condemn the communist
> system in Romania, from its foundation, on the basis of dictate, during the years 1944 to
> 1947, to its collapse in December 1989. Taking cognizance of the realities presented in
> the Report, I affirm with full responsibility: the communist regime in Romania was ille-
> gitimate and criminal. . . . In the name of the Romanian State, I express my regret and
> compassion for the victims of the communist dictatorship. In the name of the Romanian
> State, I ask the forgiveness of those who suffered, of their families, of all those who, in
> one way or another, saw their lives ruined by the abuses of dictatorship. . . . Evoking
> now a period which many would wish to forget, we have spoken both of the past and of
> the extent to which we, people today, wish to go to the very end in the assumption of the
> values of liberty. These values, prior even to being those of Romania or of Europe, flow
> from the universal, sacred value of the human person. If we now turn to the past, we do
> so in order to face a future in which contempt for the individual will no longer go unpun-
> ished. This symbolic moment represents the balance sheet of what we have lived
> through and the day in which we all ask ourselves how we want to live henceforward.
> We shall break free of the past more quickly, we shall make more solid progress, if we
> understand what hinders us from being more competitive, more courageous, more con-
> fident in our own powers. On the other hand, we must not display historical arrogance.
> My purpose is aimed at authentic national reconciliation, and all the more so since
> numerous legacies of the past continue to scar our lives. Our society suffers from a gen-
> eralized lack of confidence. The institutions of state do not yet seem to pursue their real
> vocation, which relates to the full exercise of all civil liberties. . . . Perhaps some will
> ask themselves what exactly gives us the right to condemn. As President of Romanians,
> I could invoke the fact that I have been elected. But I think that we have a more impor-
> tant motive: the right to condemn gives us the obligation to make the institutions of the
> rule of law function within a democratic society. We cannot be allowed to compromise
> these institutions. They cannot be allowed to be discredited by the fact that we approach
> them with the habits and mentalities of our recent past. . . . The condemnation of
> communism will encourage us to be more circumspect towards utopian and extremist
> projects, which want to bring into question the constitutional and democratic order.

Behind the nostalgic or demagogic discourses, there lies more often than not the temptation of authoritarianism or even totalitarianism, of negation of the explosion of individual energies, of inventiveness and creativity which has taken place since December 1989. We have definitively escaped terror, we have escaped fear, in such a way that no one has the right to bring into question our fundamental rights. The lesson of the past proves that any regime that humiliates citizens cannot last and does not deserve to exist. Now, all citizens can freely demand that their inalienable rights should be respected, and the institutions of state must work in such a way that people will no longer feel humiliated. During this period of transition, much has been said about the moral crisis of society. It relates to numerous aspects of daily life. I am certain that we shall leave behind the state of social mistrust and pessimism in which we have been submerged by the years of transition if, together, we undertake a genuine examination of the national conscience. (Băsescu 2006)

The above excerpt indicates several directions along which the meaning of the act of condemning the communist regime was drawn. First of all, this initiative is a fundamentally symbolic step toward national reconciliation by means of clarifying and dealing with the past. Only in this way can Romanian society overcome the fragmentation typical of the "legacy of Leninism."[8] President Băsescu advocated a reinstitutionalization freed from the burden of the party-state continuities and the possibility for laying the foundation of a "posttotalitarian legitimacy."[9] It is his belief that only in such fashion can one develop the not-yet-attained national consensus. At this point, one cannot but stop and wonder whether such a project falls in line with what Adam Michnik called the "mantra of anticommunism" postcommunism. In some of his writings, Michnik noted quite a few similarities between some forms of anticommunism, especially in Poland, with the former antifascism of the Comintern and post-1945 periods. He saw both as mere forms within which a deeper structure, focused upon political bickering and neoauthoritarian tendencies, is hidden.

Anticommunism, like antifascism, does not itself attest to anyone's righteousness. The old lie—the lie of communists settling scores with fascism—has been replaced by a new lie: the lie of anticommunists settling scores with communism. . . . Communism froze collective memory; the fall of communism, therefore, brought with it, along with a return to democracy, paratotalitarian formations, ghosts from another era. . . . The debate about communism has thus become, through blackmail and discrimination against political enemies, a tool in the struggle for political power. (Michnik 2002, 516-25; see also Michnik 1998)

In Romania, the condemnation of the communist regime has taken place with a consistent view to reconciliation, consensus, reform, and working through the past. It did not serve either as a weapon of President Băsescu against his enemies or as a means of rehabilitating any xenophobic and/or antidemocratic, precommunist movements (as in the case of Poland with Roman Dmowski's ultranationalist Endecja). Starting in late April 2006, some sections of the Romanian mass media indulged in an abuse of Michnik's ideas. Many individuals with hardly liberal-democratic pedigrees, such as former president Ion Iliescu, former prime minister Adrian Năstase, and Social Democratic Party ideologue Adrian Severin, used the principles professed by former Polish dissident Michnik to justify their lack of penance, their amnesia, and their opportunism.[10]

The reverberations of the past are part of contemporary polemics and define competing visions of the future. It is quite often in relation to the past, especially a traumatic one, that political actors identify themselves and engage in competitions with their opponents. Reviewing Jan T. Gross's book *Fear* (2006), David Engel (2007, 538-39) wrote,

> Unless Polishness, whatever its constituent characteristics, is transmitted from generation to generation through mother's milk, as it were, nothing that Gross or anyone else might say about any part of the Polish community in 1946, 1941, or any other year more than six decades in the past *necessarily* reflects upon any part of the community today. It can do so only to the extent that the present community continues to affirm the values implicated in past events. Thus *Fear* or any other work of history can legitimately be neither offered nor read as a vehicle for contemporary self-examination except insofar as it prompts contemporaries to question strongly whether they remain committed to those values.

The postcommunist debates on the past should be seen as indicators of contemporary ideological cleavages and tensions, confirming Jürgen Habermas's (1989, 232-33) analysis of the public use of history as an antidote to oblivion, denial, and partisan distortions: "It is especially these dead who have a claim to the weak anamnestic power of a solidarity that later generations can continue to practice only in the medium of a remembrance that is repeatedly renewed, often desperate, and continually on one's mind." Attitudes toward the *Final Report* are therefore suggestive of ostensibly implausible political and symbolic alliances (former apparatchik Ion Iliescu and xenophobic demagogue Corneliu Vadim Tudor have vied in vilifying the document).[11] The report was written neither from a conservative nor a populist standpoint, and this was one of the main points of contention in the attacks rejecting the validity of the document. Another obstacle on the road to reconciliation is the fact that the perpetrators of Romania's communist regime have not been confronted, legally and institutionally, with their crimes. They enjoy great material and status benefits, being allowed to basically laugh in the faces of their victims. Individuals whom the *Final Report* identifies as guilty of crimes against humanity or as former members of Nicolae Ceausescu's last Politburo, directly involved in the bloody crackdown against demonstrators in Timisoara and Bucharest in 1989, have long been pardoned and continue to defend the old regime. Ion Dinca, former secretary of the RCP's Central Committee, first vice-prime-minister, Elena Ceausescu's right hand, and a political general in the Romanian communist army, was buried on January 2007 (a month after the publication of the *Final Report*) with military honors like a hero of the Romanian state. The president, however, reacted by demanding and receiving the resignations of all responsible for this blunder.

President Băsescu created, on April 11, 2007, the Consultative Commission for the Analysis of the Communist Dictatorship (CCACDR), which is composed of twelve experts (I serve as chair). The main function of this body is to provide the specialized knowledge for the legal initiatives promoted by the executive branch in relation to the overall effort of dealing with the communist past (e.g., lustration law; commemorations; textbooks; laws regarding the victims, survivors, and perpetrators). At the same time, the CCACDR is meant to be the academic backbone of two other important projects: the *Encyclopedia of Romanian Communism* and the high school textbook for the study of the communist historical experience in Romania. Another significant development is the fact that the Institute for the Investigation of the Crimes of Communism in Romania (chaired by historian Marius Oprea, a member of the PCACDR), mandated by the Romanian prime minister with a considerable yearly budget, took on some of the main policy recommendations of the *Final Report* and initiated both the campaign and the research that are aimed at their realization (e.g., issues related to the outrageously high pensions of former secret police officers). In conclusion, I consider that President Băsescu's condemnation of the communist regime in Romania was a moment of civic mobilization. Generally speaking, de-communization is, in its essence, a moral, political, and intellectual process. These are the dimensions that raise challenges in contemporary Romanian society. The PCACDR's *Final Report* answered a fundamental necessity, characteristic of the postauthoritarian world, of moral clarity. The moral-symbolic action is, according to McAdams (2001), one of the four types of retributive justice (the others being the criminal, the noncriminal, and the rectifying aspects). I would even argue that it is the most important, especially if one is to take the model of Jan Kubik's (1994) book on the influence of civic countersymbols in opposition to the hermeneutic routine inherent to a political establishment. The *Final Report* identified many features of guilt, in relation to the communist experience, that have never before been under scrutiny. It offers a framework for shedding light upon what Jaspers (2001) called "moral and metaphysical guilt"—the individual's failure to live up to his or her moral duties and the destruction of solidarity of social fabric (see also Liiceanu 2007). This, in my opinion, is the angle from which one can see to the connection between condemnation initiative and politics. In the words of Charles King (2007), "The commission's chief tasks had to do with both morality and power: to push Romanian politicians and Romanian society into drawing a line between past and present, putting an end to nostalgia for an alleged period of greatness and independence, and embracing the country's de facto cultural pluralism and European future." Such matters considered, the PCACDR was indeed a political project through which both the acknowledgement and conceptualization of the 1945 to 1989 national traumatic experience were accomplished, whilst those responsible for the existence of communism as a regime in Romania were identified.

The PCACDR, relying on President Băsescu's political commitment, created a document where responsibility for the past was claimed and individualized. There are hardly other ways of reconstructing *Gemeinsamkeit*, that is, the social cohesion and communion destroyed by the atomization brought about in the communist regime. As I have already stated, the *Final Report* was written with analytical rigor, with compassion for the victims, and in full awareness of the trauma both incumbent in the past and in the act of remembrance itself. The PCACDR had to listen to what Frankfurt School philosopher Theodor W. Adorno (1984) referred to as "the voice of those who cannot talk anymore." The commission and the symbolic act undertaken by the Romanian president are the premises for reconciliation. But both the commission and the president could not impose reconciliation in the absence of repentance. The commission's work and the intense debates surrounding it highlight one of the most vexing, yet vitally important tensions of the postcommunist world: the understanding of the traumatic totalitarian past and the political, moral, and intellectual difficulties, frustrations, hopes, and anxieties involved in trying to come to grips with it.

Notes

1. Tony Judt's article "Romania: Bottom of the Heap," *New York Review of Books*, November 1, 2001, came out in Romanian in a volume edited by Mircea Mihaies, including various polemical responses by influential Romanian intellectuals—see Tony Judt (2002b); see also Tony Judt's discussion of Eastern Europe in his masterful *Post-War: A History of Europe Since 1945* (2005). I discussed the moral and political dilemmas of de-communization in *Fantasies of Salvation: Nationalism, Democracy, and Myth in Postcommunist Europe* (Tismăneanu 1998).

2. See my Romanian-language volume *Spectrele Europei Centrale* (Tismăneanu 2001). I extensively discuss this interesting process of recycling (neo/proto/crypto) fascism by means of integrating it into the identitarian discourse legitimizing the communist regime. In the "Lessons of 20th Century" chapter, I argue that "the Ceausescu regime was, at its most basic level, a very interesting mix that brought together both the legacy of militarist authoritarianism from the 1941-1944 period, which was celebrated in myriad ways, and the degraded mystic inspired by the extreme-right, which was grafted upon the institutional body of Romanian Stalinism" (pp. 246-47).

3. Born in 1951, Traian Basescu graduated from the Naval Institute in Constanţa and spent most of his life under communism as a sea captain for the Romanian commercial fleet. After 1990, he became a member of the Petre Roman government, minister of transportation, then mayor of Bucharest and head of the Democratic Party. In 2004, he won the presidential elections against former prime minister and social-democratic leader Adrian Nastase.

4. See my books *Democratie şi memorie* (Tismăneanu 2006) and *Refuzul de a uita* (Tismăneanu 2007).

5. See Bogdan Cristian Iacob (2007a, 2007b, 2007c, forthcoming); and Cosmina Tanasoiu (2007).

6. See A. D. Moses (1998). Dominick LaCapra (1992, 127) similarly pointed to the distance-empathy synthesis, as a valid method of approaching recent history, in his argument for reconstruction and electivity on the basis of fact within a democratic value system: "A reckoning with the past in keeping with democratic values requires the ability—or at least the attempt—to read scars and to affirm only what deserves affirmation as one turns the lamp of critical reflection on oneself and one's own." See also LaCapra (1998).

7. I also dealt with this topic in detail in *The Crisis of Marxist Ideology in Eastern Europe: The Poverty of Utopia* (Tismăneanu 1988).

8. Kenneth Jowitt (1992) defined Eastern Europe as a "brittle region" where "suspicion, division, and fragmentation predominate, not coalition and interrogation," because of lasting emotional, ethnic, territorial, demographic, and political fragmentation from the (pre-)communist period. For a recent discussion of this thesis, also see Tismăneanu, Howard, and Sil (2006).

9. Bogdan Iacob (2007a), in the first article of his series in *Idei in Dialog*, argued that the nature and profile of the condemnation of Romanian communist regime comes close to what Jan-Werner Müller (2000, 258) coined as the *Modell Deutschland*.

10. Adam Michnik was shocked upon being informed that his ideas on "Bolshevik-style anticommunism" (which cannot be understood without the context of the Polish debates and without taking into account the post-1989 tribulations of Solidarity) were invoked by various former *nomenklatura* members

in Romania, with the purpose of blocking the clarification of the past (personal conversation with Adam Michnik, Bucureşti, Romania, June, 9, 2007).

11. See Iliescu (2007). For an excellent analysis of various vitriolic attacks on the *Final Report*, see Gallagher (2007). As for Greater Romania Party chairman and vice president of Romania's Senate Corneliu Vadim Tudor, suffice it to mention his reference to the "crazy Tismăneanu Report" produced by "two Jews" whose parents allegedly brought communism to Romania on Red Army tanks (Tismăneanu and PCACDR member, philosopher H.-R. Patapievici), *Tricolorul*, September 18, 2007.

References

Adorno, Theodor W. 1984. *Modèles critiques*. Paris: Payot.

Arendt, Hannah. 1994. *Essays in understanding 1930-1954*. New York: Harcourt Brace.

Baldwin, Peter, ed. 1990. *Reworking the past: Hitler, the Holocaust and the historians' debate*. Boston: Beacon.

Băsescu, Traian. 2006. Speech given with the Occasion of the Presentation of the Report by the Presidential Commission for the Analysis of the Communist Dictatorship in Romania. December 18. www.presidency.ro.

Deak, Istvan, Jan T. Gross, and Tony Judt, eds. 2000. *The politics of retribution in Europe: World War II and its aftermath*. Princeton, NJ: Princeton University Press.

Engel, David. 2007. On continuity and discontinuity in Polish-Jewish relations: Observations on fear. *East European Politics and Societies* 21 (3): 538-39.

Esbenshade, Richard S. 1995. Remembering to forget: Memory, history, national identity in postwar East-Central Europe. *Representations* 49 (Winter): 72-96.

Gallagher, Tom. 2007. In ochiul furtunii. *România Libera*, September 14.

Gross, Jan T. 2006. *Fear: Anti-Semitism in Poland after Auschwitz—An essay in historical interpretation*. New York: Random House.

Habermas, Jürgen. 1989. *The new conservatism: Cultural criticism and the historians' debate*. Cambridge, MA: MIT Press.

Iacob, Bogdan Cristian. 2007a. O clarificare necesară: Condamnarea regimului comunist din România între text şi context. I. *Idei in Dialog* 9 (36, August): 1-15.

———. 2007b. O clarificare necesară: Condamnarea regimului comunist din România între text şi context. II. *Idei in Dialog* 9 (36, September): 37-39.

———. 2007c. O clarificare necesară: Condamnarea regimului comunist din România între text şi context. III. *Idei in Dialog* 9 (36, October): 33-34.

———. 2007d. O clarificare necesară: Condamnarea regimului comunist din România între text şi context. IV. *Idei in Dialog* 9 (36, November): 22-24.

Iliescu, Ion. 2007. Nişte scribălăi ne dau lecţii [Some scribblers give us lessons]. *Jurnalul National*, August 22.

Jaspers, Karl. 2001. *The question of German guilt*. New York: Fordham University Press.

Jarausch, Konrad H. 2003. Introduction. In *Shattered past: Reconstructing German histories*, ed. Konrad H. Jarausch and Michael Geyer. Princeton, NJ: Princeton University Press.

Jowitt, Kenneth. 1992. *New world disorder: The Leninist extinction*. Berkeley: University of California Press.

Judt, Tony. 2000. *Europa Iluziilor*. Iaşi, Romania: Polirom.

———. 2001. Romania: Bottom of the Heap. *New York Review of Books*, November 1.

———. 2002a. The past is another country: Myth and memory in postwar Europe. In *Memory and power in post-war Europe: Studies in the presence of the past*, ed. Jan-Werner Müller, 157-84. New York: Cambridge University Press.

———. 2002b. *Romania: La Fundul Grămezii*. Polemici, Controverse, Pamflete. Iaşi, Romania: Polirom.

———. 2005. *Post-war: A history of Europe since 1945*. New York: Penguin.

King, Charles. 2007. Review of Comisia Prezidenţială pentru Analiza Dictaturii Comuniste din România, *Raport Final* (Bucharest, 2006). www.presidency.ro. (Forthcoming in *Slavic Review*)

Konrad, George. 1982. *The loser*. San Diego, CA: Harcourt Brace Jovanovich.

Kubik, Jan. 1994. *The power of symbols against the symbols of power: The rise of Solidarity and the fall of state socialism in Poland*. University Park: Pennsylvania State University Press.

Kundera, Milan. 2005. *Cartea Râsului şi a Uitării*. Bucureşti, Romania: Editura Humanitas.

LaCapra, Dominick. 1992. Representing the Holocaust: Reflections on the historians' debate. In *Probing the limits of representation—Nazism and the "Final Solution,"* ed. Saul Friedländer, 108-27. Cambridge, MA: Harvard University Press.

———. 1998. Revisiting the historians' debate—Mourning and genocide. *History and Memory* 9 (1-2): 80-112.

Liiceanu, Gabriel. 2007. *Despre ura*. Bucureşti, Romania: Ed. Humanitas.

Maier, Charles S. 1988. *The unmasterable past: History, Holocaust, and German national identity*. Cambridge, MA: Harvard University Press.

Margalit, Avishai. 2002. *The ethics of memory*. Cambridge, MA: Harvard University Press.

McAdams, A. James. 2001. *Judging the past in unified Germany*. New York: Cambridge University Press.

Michnik, Adam. 1998. *Letters from freedom*. Translated by Jane Cave. Forward by Kenneth Jowitt. Berkeley: University of California Press.

———. 2002. Mantra rather than discourse. Peace and Mind Symposium. *Common Knowledge* 8 (3): 516-25.

Moses, A. D. 1998. Structure and agency in the Holocaust: Daniel J. Goldhagen and his critics. *History and Theory* 37 (2): 194-219.

Müller, Jan-Werner. 2000. *Another country: German intellectuals, unification, and national identity*. New Haven, CT: Yale University Press.

Raport Final—Comisia Prezidentiala pentru Analiza Dictaturii Comunisteiîn Romania. 2006. Introducere. www.presidency.ro.

———. 2007. Bucureşti, Romania: Editura Humanitas.

Tanasoiu, Cosmina. 2007. The Tismaneanu Report: Romania revisits its past. *Problems of Post-Communism* 54 (4): 60-69.

Tismăneanu, Vladimir. 1988. *The crisis of Marxist ideology in Eastern Europe: The poverty of utopia*. New York: Routledge.

———. 1998. *Fantasies of salvation: Nationalism, democracy, and myth in post-communist Europe*. Princeton, NJ: Princeton University Press.

———. 2001. *Spectrele Europei Centrale*. Bucureşti, Romania: Polirom.

———. 2006. *Democratie şi Memorie*. Bucureşti, Romania: Curtea Veche.

———. 2007. *Refuzul de a uita*. Bucureşti, Romania: Curtea Veche.

Tismăneanu, Vladimir, Marc Howard, and Rudra Sil, eds. 2006. *World order after Leninism*. Seattle: University of Washington Press.

Can Truth Be Negotiated? History Textbook Revision as a Means to Reconciliation

By
FALK PINGEL

International school textbook revision and research became a professional academic activity after the First World War. It broadened its scope and methodological approaches considerably after the collapse of the bipolar world. Today, a number of different agencies, such as international governmental institutions, NGOs, and academic as well as pedagogical institutions, are involved in projects on the revision of history teaching in postconflict societies. This article examines the pros and cons of different project designs, focusing on the sometimes contradictory aims projects are expected to achieve and on the interplay between the various agencies. Examples highlighting the reconstruction and reconciliation process are taken from Bosnia and Herzegovina, Israel-Palestine, and Rwanda and South Africa.

Keywords: international school textbook revision; reconciliation; history teaching; remembrance

Changing Patterns of International Textbook Revision

Textbooks matter. Every week, newspaper headlines all over the world refer to them. Besides issues related to new areas of learning, like Internet technology (IT), the topic most frequently raised in textbook studies is the ideology that textbooks convey. In this regard, textbooks for the humanities, in particular on language and literature, history and civics, and more recently, religion, stand out.[1] Some core problems and geographical areas on which articles focus include

Falk Pingel, PhD, is deputy director of the Georg Eckert Institute for International Textbook Research in Braunschweig, Germany. In 2003, he was the first director of the Organization for Security and Cooperation in Europe's (OSCE) Education Department in Sarajevo, Bosnia and Herzegovina. He formerly taught contemporary history as well as theory and didactics of history at Bielefeld University. Among his publications are Häftlinge unter SS-Herrschaft *(Hamburg, 1978);* Holocaust und Nationalsozialismus *(ed., Wien, 2002); and* The European Home: Representations of 20th Century Europe in History Textbooks *(Strasbourg, 2000).*

DOI: 10.1177/0002716207313087

- controversies between two or more nations, peoples, or states about the presentation of each other's history;
- clashes between the historical narratives of different ethnic groups within a state or society; and
- the role of religious instruction in multireligious settings.

In the decades following the Second World War, Europe was the main theater of textbook debates and bilateral or multilateral research projects, but more recently the focus has shifted to Asia and the Middle East. In East Asia, the Second World War still provides the crucial point of reference for most history textbook controversies, whereas in Southeastern Asia, the legacy of a colonial past or current internal tensions between different population groups come to the fore. The Middle East attracts attention because the so-called cultural dialogue between Western European states and Muslim societies focuses on this region.

Besides content-related problems, methodological issues of learning history and civics are frequently raised. There is an ongoing, almost worldwide, debate on whether the history curriculum should define a body of knowledge, unquestioned values, and moral judgments that represent the shared historical memory of a given society or whether students should be trained in skills that allow them to compare different interpretations, to develop critical thinking, and to form their own judgments. Generally speaking, the debate on textbooks concentrates on contesting a multicultural or multiperspective approach on one hand, or an ethnically/nationally centered view on the other.

The transfer of knowledge from one generation to the next through textbooks is controlled not only by scholarly quality criteria and by pedagogical standards, but also by political interests. To overcome narrow national and nationalistic approaches to historical interpretations and geopolitical visions of the world, international textbook revision became a politically acknowledged and scholarly activity after the shock of the First World War, performed under the umbrella of international organizations such as the League of Nations and, after the Second World War, the United Nations Educational, Scientific, and Cultural Organization (UNESCO.) The well-known traditional model of interstate textbook projects created in the 1920s, which is still in use today, is characterized by bilateral or multilateral cooperation on equal terms such as the German-Polish or the Italian-Slovenian Textbook Commission, to mention two contemporary examples (Pingel 1999). This model represents a somewhat ideal approach where all partners recognize each other and meet in a symmetrical dialogue.

After the dissolution of the communist system and the opening of borders, the topics and methods of international textbook revision underwent remarkable changes that can be characterized as follows:

- from bilateral, quasi-official commissions set up by educational authorities to groups of experts linked to nongovernmental organizations (NGOs) and agencies of civil society;
- from controversies over the past to debate about current, open, and often still violent conflicts; and
- from conflicts between states to conflicts between groups within a state or society (or from war to civil war).

Therefore, two phases of international or intercultural textbook revision can be identified:

- Initially, bilateral or multilateral commissions agreed on a more or less harmonious version of the shared history, which sometimes showed features of a "diplomatic" agreement, as the commission members were obliged to find a compromise.
- At present, projects focus on developing principles and methods with which a disputed issue can be presented without necessarily writing a joint, ultimate narrative.

Consequently, the forms of textbook projects have changed over time. To find a middle ground between direct intervention and programs negotiated on equal terms, which are often not feasible in postconflict areas where there is a lack of infrastructure and stability, international organizations now employ a gradual model of education reform

- starting with short-term emergency reconstruction measures;
- followed by midterm constructive and systematic ground work;
- leading to the final stage of long-term sustainable education toward peace, tolerance, and international understanding (Smith and Vaux 2002).

The implementation of these measures may also be conceived of as an advancement from reconstruction to reconciliation. Such a process is often initially characterized by external control and intervention, by which power is gradually handed over to internal agencies until full local "ownership" is achieved. As a rule, only medium- and long-term measures have attracted the attention of research. However, the impact of direct emergency measures should not be underestimated, for they often produce the only tangible result in cases when the second or third steps have been omitted. An interventionist program on a large scale is currently being conducted in Iraq (and in Afghanistan).[2] International organizations such as UNESCO, the World Bank, and the United Nations Development Program (UNDP) produce new teaching materials in countries in which the local government can neither fully control its education system nor provide sufficient financial means for the required reform. Although foreign powers and international organizations seek the approval of local governments for their actions, their dominant position when providing expertise and funding arouses skepticism among the indigenous population, who suspect that a new cultural bias will permeate the reformed curriculum and thus alienate young people from local traditions, values, and way of life.

The original idea behind binational or multinational textbook commissions was based on a consensual model. Two or more conflicting partners compare divergent interpretations and try to forge a version accepted by all sides involved, which may then be published, disseminated, and translated into the teaching process. Although international textbook projects increasingly deviate from this model, many of the elements of this model still prevail in current projects.

The traditional, consensual projects are often financed and backed by governments. The firm institutional structure endows them with undeniable strengths.

They are provided with a clear agenda and work with clear goals in mind. The most obvious disadvantage is that they are often conceived as representatives of state ideology and do not dare to break political taboos or argue against issues of national pride. Such projects are feasible only if stable political structures are already in place. Hence, this model has lost ground in cases where violence is ongoing. Likewise, when partners do not even recognize each other diplomatically, "official" textbook commissions cannot be established and groups representing civil society have to pave the way for encounters and steps toward reconciliation to take place.

In many postconflict societies like Rwanda and Bosnia and Herzegovina, for example, work in civil society with the grass roots, combined with domestic reconstruction policy and international assistance or intervention, culminates in a mixture of tools designed to promote pacification and reconciliation in which textbook revision is only one aspect, if still an important one. Even though this article focuses on the revision of history textbooks as a means of reconciliation, it also examines the interplay of local and international actors, as well as the role played by textbook and curriculum development within the overall framework of peace-building measures, including truth commissions and trials, and so on. To identify factors that influence the potential success or failure of these processes, it will deal in particular with the cases of Rwanda, South Africa, the Middle East, and Bosnia and Herzegovina (BaH).[3] The findings drawn from these examples will be compared with the structures of more traditionally designed international textbook projects such as the German-Polish textbook consultations and the textbook debate in East Asia.

History Education in Postconflict Societies: A Neglected Factor and a Guarantor of Sustainable Peace?

Education, in particular history education, plays an ambiguous role in measures designed to resolve conflict. On one hand, it is striking that education is not a high priority when it comes to redistributing political power and economic resources after conflict and that sometimes education is hardly mentioned in peace settlements (Arlow 2004). On the other hand, implicitly or expressly, education is expected to secure the sustainability of peace and contribute to fostering attitudes toward peaceful cohabitation in the future.

Curriculum experts and teachers who work under poor material conditions are overburdened by high expectations to inculcate new values and attitudes in the students. But it is not only the tension between their weak position in society and the ambitious tasks society demands from them that puts them in a difficult position. The educational objectives they have to accomplish are also often contradictory. History education is expected to serve two aims: (1) to explain why the conflict happened and (2) to deliver a new narrative that consolidates the rifts of the past and strengthens inner cohesion in a shattered society. Although both aims seem to be acceptable and honorable at first glance, they appear to be incompatible in practice. Laying bare possible reasons for the conflict is painful and controversial and may divide rather than unite society. Thus, before history instruction has really started and can draw on viable research or documentation, governments often anticipate the challenge of an open, serious, and in-depth historical debate and either prescribe a new core narrative or put aside history instruction altogether. In the following paragraphs, the endangered and over-burdened role of history education in Rwanda, South Africa, and BaH will be examined.

The Rwandan government built reconciliation by inventing a new narrative that stated that Rwandan society was united and harmonious in the precolonial past and thereby neglected functional differences between groups that already existed before the colonialists arrived. The new narrative placed responsibility for "racism" and ethnic discrimination solely on the colonial powers. Education was expected to disseminate the message of the unifying powers that the people of Rwanda had inherited from their forefathers, and therefore it became the main tool for estab-lishing social cohesion (Rutayisire, Kabano, and Rubagiza 2004). Longman and Rutagengwa (2004, 164) called this "creating an official narrative of memory." The value-oriented approach of the new pedagogical agenda glosses over the problem-atic period of the massacres to find consolation and consolidation in a more distant, harmonious, and "indigenous" past. With this historical interpretation, the govern-ment in fact skipped the teaching of Rwandan history at school. Although a "National Conference on Educational Policy and Planning" decided in 1995 to pro-duce a "Textbook on the History of Rwanda," no such book is available as of November 2007, and Rwandan history cannot be taught without such a book. No agreement could be reached about how to write this book, since a history book would inevitably address the heart of the conflict and could not avoid offering explanations and reasons that might be understood to put the blame or responsi-bility for the crimes on a particular group (Tawil and Harley 2004). The aims were so high and unrealistic that this book will most likely never be written. Since his-tory teaching appeared infeasible under these premises, the government devel-oped social remembrance programs that gather young people in "solidarity camps" and official remembrance ceremonies (Longman and Rutagengwa 2004). Thus, the genocide is officially remembered, the victims are mourned, but *history teaching*—as opposed to *history education*—is not implemented to serve this objective.

Although the abolition of the apartheid system in South Africa was accompa-nied by an in-depth debate about innovative approaches to constructing a new, integrated South African history, the significance of history teaching for the rec-onciliation process diminished in the course of the reorientation process. The strong commitment to a postapartheid concept of history lost its appeal when it became obvious that the construction of a new master narrative—which went against the international trend in historiography—would take time and would open up strong and painful controversies before something that came close to an agreed corpus of content and interpretation could be outlined.

Two factions put forward their vision of a revised South African historiography: African teachers placed great hopes on the political change and expected a new and uncontested "black" history that would tell the one and only true story in contrast to the distorted one they had been exposed to for so many years. However, this story could never emerge overnight and would not be regarded as an appropriate way of building education for a multicultural, integrated South Africa. A pluralistic model was favored by a group of historians who worked at universities long since known for their antiapartheid position. They advocated the use of new source materials about African history, innovative methodological approaches such as multiperspective interpretations, group discussion, oral history, and testimonies; however, these methods were almost unknown to normal teachers in a township classroom and could hardly be transformed into a manageable pedagogical format under the prevailing material conditions and with such a lack of trained authors and teachers. As the government concentrated intellectual as well as material investments on new sectors like economics, sciences, and IT and tried to foster social sciences modeled on the old history curriculum on the pretext that this was a modern interdisciplinary approach combining geography, civics, and history, the reputation of history teaching decreased considerably in the second half of the 1990s (Johannesson 2002, 92). History courses were no longer regarded as helpful for fostering economic growth and accelerating the integration of society. "The irrelevance of the history argument" (Giroux 1997) correctly and surprisingly described the situation in South African schools where many teachers, in particular in poor township schools, still relied on old apartheid history textbooks, since the government was not willing to put alternative complementary material produced by the History Workshop and other initiatives onto the list of approved books (Reid and Siebörger 1995). Consequently, history was removed from the compulsory curriculum for several years, only to regain its former position gradually following renewed steps toward reform after the year 2000.

BaH may stand out as the country where history education suffers most from the legacy of a peace settlement. The Dayton Agreement of 1995 confirmed the separate education system for the three "constituent peoples"—Serbs, Croats, and Bosniaks—that had already been established in wartime. It federalized and "provincialized" education and made it the playground for cultural separatism. As the international peacemakers considered the political and security sectors to be much more important areas in which overarching institutions could be established, they left responsibility for education totally to the regional units: the Republika Srpska and the ten "cantons" of the ethnically mixed Federation of BaH, which were invested with rights to develop their own curriculum and textbooks. Furthermore, when a community is ethnically divided, schools may even teach different curricula, each of which emphasizes "one's own" history, society, geography, and culture while neglecting or disparaging those of the "others." Local politicians instrumentalized the educational institutions in their respective spheres of influence along lines that emphasized cultural differences as boundary markers for the concept of separate nationhood. Academics were instrumental in providing this process with a mantle of legitimacy (Pingel 2006). In spite of considerable efforts to reform curricula and textbooks made by the international community and local institutions since 2000 (before that time material reconstruction enjoyed absolute priority) and efforts designed to overcome barriers to a more integrative cultural policy, these institutions could not change the main parameters of the education system set out by the Dayton Agreement. The case of BaH is probably the most salient example of the often contradictory forces that define the place of history education in the reconstruction and reconciliation process.

In sum, it can be said that history *education* or history *politics* are seen as important factors for rebuilding society; however, this does not imply that disciplinary history *instruction* is allotted a prominent place. The initial interest in finding out the historical reasons why violence and conflict broke out in society is quickly overshadowed by a policy of remembrance that encapsulates or neutralizes the contested past.

Should Time, rather than History Teaching, Heal the Wounds?

The generation that is expected to create new curricula and textbooks has, as a rule, been involved in the conflict that they must deal with in a pedagogical context. It is because of this entanglement in a history that has not yet become a past that the Parliamentary Assembly of the Council of Europe passed a resolution on "Education in Bosnia and Herzegovina" in the year 2000 that proposed a moratorium on the teaching of the last war of 1992 to 1995. The moratorium is designed to give historians of all three ethnic groups the opportunity to develop a common approach to the topic, with the help of international experts. This moratorium is still in force. Contrary to the expectations of its creators, it has not stimulated enquiries into the war and its causes, but only created a vacuum that offers very little scope for intellectual curiosity and the development of new approaches to teaching issues of contemporary history (Pingel 2006). The same logic underpinned the Rwandan government's decision to abandon history teaching altogether until a new consensual concept had been developed. However, this is not likely to happen within one generation, for the wounds are still fresh. Recalling the conflict will stir emotions and controversy because perpetrators and victims can hardly have the same memories.

Surveys from BaH and Rwanda show that pupils want to know about war and genocide; they want proof of the stories they are confronted with in their families and in the media; but these stories are not permitted within the classroom, and students cannot examine them in a rational environment. In particular, the generation of older teachers tends to opt for the official moratoria and accepts the government's argument that scholars first have to collect clear documentation that "tells the truth" and does not leave room for different interpretations to arise (Freedman et al. 2004; Gasanabo 2002). However, the majority of people interviewed, be it parents, teachers, or students, in principle are in favor of teaching history to better understand the roots of the conflict—although they wish to avoid tackling the conflict itself. Psychologically speaking, this attitude may be categorized as an approach-avoidance conflict. The concept of the one and only truth that is based on a preordained political consensus is the major stumbling block that has to be overcome to give way to innovative teaching approaches.

[Pupils] want proof of the stories they are confronted with in their families and in the media; but these stories are not permitted within the classroom.

The controversy over the recent conflict, even if it is excluded from the curriculum, nevertheless also shapes—unconsciously or wittingly—the interpretation of the more distant past. The factions who fought the "recent war" in BaH are identified with those of the Second World War—Ustasha and Chetniks alike. Dealing with them in a lesson about the Second World War triggers uncontrolled associations with the recent war. As the genocide of Srebrenica cannot yet be dealt with in Bosniak history textbooks, massacres committed by Serbs in former times are now called "genocide," and everyone should understand that this Serbian "genocidal" attitude toward the Bosniak population extends to the last war—thus, the students are familiarized with a static image of the "other" that corroborates rather than refutes biased views (Pingel 2004). During the debate about a new textbook on Rwandan history, it became obvious that almost the whole history of Rwanda before the conflict was permeated by the differences that existed between the Hutus and the Tutsi. Teachers searched for periods or topics free from this bias and proposed that they should focus on cultural history (poems, customs, etc.), religion, and economic history (agriculture). But to treat Rwandan history without touching on the relationship between the different population groups does not contribute to reconciling them. As Gasanabo (2002, 83) put it, "You can't talk about 'us' without talking about 'me.'"

One may say that time heals all wounds and makes scars invisible, but it does not make them disappear. International nongovernmental organizations (INGOs) meanwhile offer platforms for a rational debate and offer programs for new teaching approaches such as drama, role-play, and art, which allow pupils to express emotions as well; they have been applied successfully in postconflict and posttrauma situations. Teachers are often not sufficiently familiar with these methods. In his teacher survey conducted in Rwanda, Gasanabo (2002) could only quote a few teachers who were open to innovative ways of teaching history through radio features, out-of-classroom meetings, and dialogue. Ministries of education are, as a rule, skeptical toward extracurricular activities, and INGOs are likewise obsessed with maintaining regular curricula and textbooks with which "official" guidelines for pedagogy may be applied.

Discovering Truth in a Communication Process

Whereas the strengthening of cohesive elements within divided societies makes sense, a preordained consensual approach to history textbook issues does not offer a sustainable solution to the problem of how violent or fresh conflicts should be tackled. To open up new horizons, an Israeli-Palestinian textbook project will be referred to here. In view of the ongoing armed clashes and irreconcilable territorial claims, the Peace Research Institute in the Middle East (PRIME) based in Beith Jala near Bethlehem/Palestine renounced the idea of presenting a joint narrative harmonizing the views of both sides when developing teaching materials about the Israeli-Palestinian relationship in the twentieth century. On one hand, the group of teachers and university historians working in the project recognizes that each side has its own narrative that is firmly anchored in a long history and strongly linked to a set of national feelings, religious beliefs, and cultural traditions that cannot be neglected. On the other hand, each side tries to understand the other's narrative, to discuss both narratives, and to subject both versions to scientific scrutiny. Critical questioning of the other's interpretation involves being critical of oneself. Truth turns out to be a communication process. Thus, the material consists of two "national" narratives presented on the left and right side of a double page, leaving blank space in between where teachers and students can write down their own interpretation and comments (*Learning Each Other's Historical Narrative* 2003).

The PRIME group had the ingenious idea of acknowledging, on one hand, the duality of the narrative as the point of departure, but, on the other hand, of encouraging recognition between each group as a legitimate bearer of opposed narratives. By contrast, in most other cases in which narratives of reciprocal exclusion meet, their legitimacy is mutually contested. However, the point of departure should not be mixed up with the final destination. Through in-depth, self-critical discussion, each "national" group revises its "own" narrative, which is then translated into English (as the working language of the project) and into the "other's" language, then discussed again both jointly and in separate groups. In the end, both sides come closer without merging or harmonizing their narratives; but the versions to be published and tried out through experimental teaching in selected schools in Palestine and Israel are recognized by both sides as legitimate views of a partially shared history that nevertheless cannot be interpreted in the same way. Although the project aims to produce a practical result, its core objective is the process of communication and mutual recognition that brings forth the product. The concept is open-ended. Moreover, the final publication should offer blank spaces in between the two narratives. Teachers, students and scholars are expected to write down their commentaries or even formulate a third version. Two points are of particular interest here:

1. Through the process of communication, each "national" narrative becomes estranged from the official mainstream version and so refutes the notion of a fixed "national narrative" altogether. This effect makes the approach vulnerable to conservative critique as it makes it obvious that by taking into account the other's viewpoint, one changes one's own viewpoint. In concrete terms: presenting the Palestinian narrative (or part of it) to Israeli students (and vice versa) not only offers the students insight into the thinking of the "adversary," it also tends to change students' self-perception and devaluate a consensual approach to the historical tradition of one's own people.
2. The draft version of the dual narrative produced by the PRIME project has already been published in French and Italian editions and been taught in schools of the two countries. Both books left out the blank space in between and thus missed the crucial point of the project: to constantly work on bringing both versions closer to each other. The presentation of two opposing interpretations fits into the Western European concept of multiperspective teaching that teachers put stress on, juxtaposing the two versions and gathering arguments for pros and cons rather than exposing themselves to an exercise of rapprochement. Teachers fall into a didactical trap inherent to the model (and that students voluntarily follow) if they neglect the challenge of the blank space: they train their students to confront views and conduct a controversial debate that may strengthen extreme positions but that does not necessarily help them engage in a process of critical self-reflection and revision of preconceived opinions.

Critical questioning of the other's interpretation involves being critical of oneself.

Projects conducted by NGOs often aim expressly to break down from the very outset communication barriers that politicians could not or did not want to overcome. The working procedures of NGO projects differ considerably from those applied by official bilateral or multilateral commissions. In traditional projects, the comparison of scientific concepts and their evaluation according to rational categories, based on academic research, is the medium of mediation. The scientifically mediated product will then be delivered or handed over to politicians and pedagogues to be put into practice, to be rejected, or to be molded. The establishment of the commission is already based on a political agreement defining tasks and procedures, such that such a commission usually can work for a certain time period—with luck until it presents a joint product—without political interference, as long as the members themselves do not express their dissent to politicians or in public. Only after having handed over the result of their work to the responsible educational agencies may a political debate be initiated and their work examined. In any case, responsibility for implementation lies with political institutions and educationalists on the ground. The German-Polish textbook conferences often serve as a model for the successful application of a consensus-driven, bilateral approach. However, the duration of such a reconciliation process through text-book revision is often underestimated. Despite the overall positive result, one should not forget that approximately fifteen years elapsed since the commission began work in 1970 before acceptance on both sides outweighed protest against and rejection of the joint textbook recommendations published in 1976. The publication triggered fierce public debates that were fought over even in the parliaments of these countries. Only after the political dispute had been settled could pedagogical consequences be drawn that led to the production of a number of teaching units and, finally, a joint resource book (*Gemeinsame Deutsch-Polnische Schulbuchkommission* 1977/1995; Becher, Borodziej, and Maier 2001). Accordingly, the working process can be divided into different stages:

- initial political founding agreement,
- disciplinary scholarly work,
- publication of a joint result,
- political approval (or rejection) of the result,
- public debate, and
- pedagogical implementation.

The working process of projects conducted by NGOs in conflict areas in which the violence has not abated is less easily defined, because the political, academic, and pedagogical levels cannot be clearly distinguished. The project may come under political fire from the outset and have to find means to tackle this threat. Professional mediation is needed to keep current politics out of the group meetings. The mediation not only has to guarantee a high academic standard of textbook analysis and methodological approach but also create an atmosphere of confidence, without which no fruitful results can be expected. The work of NGOs or expert groups, which are composed of devoted intellectuals, teachers, and parents, helps to create a nucleus for a civil society that can, in the long run, counterbalance backward-oriented political agencies. However, the implementation of products often turns out to be the Achilles' heel of projects conducted by NGOs. Ministries are not obliged to follow their advice and can ban their materials from schools. As a rule, the teaching units produced by NGOs are meant to provide additional material that does not replace regular textbooks. Teachers need training to become amenable to this kind of material and to the new methods it offers.

The crucial point is that at the start of the unifying or reconciliation process, the concept of the one and only truth is still prevalent and cannot be changed rapidly. The development of the new narrative has to acknowledge the longing for unity and a harmonized interpretation of the past. A strong multiperspective approach from the outset is, in most cases, not feasible, for teachers cannot implement it, scholars are not sufficiently trained to develop it, and politicians are not ready to accept it.

Furthermore, official reform projects carried out either between states or within a state frequently adhere to a hierarchy of implementation measures: from curriculum to textbooks to teacher training. If authorities strictly follow this hierarchy, reform efforts reach schools with a delay of up to five years. Such a long process can cause the reform to be diluted and prevent practical teaching from ever being brought into line with the curriculum or vice versa. Under these conditions, NGO projects are often marginalized.

From Reconstruction to Recognition: The Open-Ended Process in Bosnia and Herzegovina

In BaH, almost all the different stages and methods of textbook revision have been used to reconcile three almost incompatible versions of history that are presented in the history school books.

The International Community (IC) concentrated in the first phase of intervention and monitoring in the educational sector on physical reconstruction: rebuilding and refurnishing destroyed schools, classroom equipment, and so on. Only in a second step, since the year 2000, were the contents and methods of education taken into consideration. A commission with equal representation of the three constituent peoples, and supervised by international experts, examined the textbooks for history (and other so-called national subjects such as geography, religion, and languages) to eradicate "inappropriate," "offensive," and "inflammable" material that could be regarded as discriminatory from the point of view of one of the three constituent peoples or of international conventions on human rights issues. Authors and publishing houses were obliged to change the texts accordingly. The IC sent UNESCO officials, who in some cases were even accompanied by soldiers, to schools to make sure the incriminated passages in books already in use had been blackened. Needless to say, this kind of interference in school life aroused a wave of public protest and made the students all the more eager to read what was forbidden.

As a third step, the IC and ministries of education established more sustainable cooperation by setting up expert commissions that were to carry out yearly reviews of manuscripts before publication. Although the work of these commissions "neutralized" language and excluded extreme interpretations, and brought textbook experts from the three constituent peoples together for the first time to discuss contentious issues and to seek formulations that could be agreed upon by all sides, it neither changed the different angles of approach nor established common denominators; BaH still did not represent a common point of reference as each side defended its own narrative.

The procedure adopted by the textbook commissions reflected the structure of the divided society of BaH. Although the commissions dealt with conflicts within one state, they acted as if they were a trilateral body confronting three different nationalized versions of history and geographical issues (like contested boundaries). The members regarded themselves as representatives of their respective constituent people rather than as scholarly experts. It is unlikely that they would have met without the support of the IC, which played a major role in setting up the commissions.

The next step was intended to bring a major shift in approach: from negative screening of texts to supporting in a constructive way the writing of new textbooks. In 2003, a further expert commission was given the task of developing principles for future textbook authors that would foster a balanced, comparative, multiperspective representation of different narratives. The most important achievement of this commission may not even be the visible result: the "Guidelines for Authors of History and Geography Textbooks" was unanimously adopted and submitted to the ministries of education, which needed a further three years of political bargaining before signing them and making them a mandatory part of the textbook approval process. It was the process itself that counted and caused a change in attitude. In the course of the meetings, the members of the commission increasingly conceived themselves as experts who acted independently from a political agenda prescribed by local ministries or the IC, and who represented best pedagogical practice and subject knowledge, not "their" nation or people.

As positive as such an outcome may be, the reform process is still at risk. Although the experts acted in line with their respective ministries of education and the IC, it appeared that politicians are not yet prepared to defend the reform when it comes under criticism from influential pressure groups. When the first books written according to the new Guidelines were published and approved in 2007, the textbook approval agency of one canton revised its former decision and withdrew a textbook series from use in schools after the war veterans' organization publicly accused the authors of failing to mention the massacres the Serbs had committed against the Bosniak population in the First and Second World Wars. Of course, the authors did not deny Serb war crimes, but they did not want the students to be taken in by a stereotyped view of the Serbs, who, in other books, always had to take the blame and were depicted as the "eternal" culprit.

At present, the government of the Republika Srpska is still hesitant to openly and fully recognize that Serb units committed war crimes and genocide and is not helping to bring the culprits to court. Bosniak officials—who can rely on the support of a majority of the people in this regard—strongly defend the image of the "just and victimized" Bosniak whose historical mission was to bring together the different peoples of the region. Textbook authors who challenge this image have to face accusations of betraying their own people. The condition for rapprochement adheres to an unwritten sequence: without recognition of crimes, there can be no reconciliation.

Reconciliation as a Multidimensional Process

Considering the ban on history teaching in Rwanda and the low profile history teaching was granted in South Africa for almost ten years, one may wonder what role truth commissions played in both countries. Did the detailed knowledge about the conflict they brought to the public not have a positive effect on the status of history teaching? Surprisingly, both truth commissions as well as trials impinged only to a small extent on teaching materials. So far, we know of only some cases in South America where accounts from trials and commissions found their way into textbooks. In particular, victims' stories delivered to the Guatemalan Historical Clarification Commission have been published in booklets to be used as supplementary teaching material. In general, however, it seems as if the work of truth commissions played such a prominent role in public dealings with the past that they obviated the need for dealing with the issue historically in schools and thereby hindered the historical awareness of the people. Another hypothesis may well be that pedagogues are not used to interacting with the juridical sphere, where the deeds of individuals are questioned with the more general intention of delivering a comprehensive story encompassing a whole people over several decades or centuries.

Without recognition of crimes, there can be no reconciliation.

Trials and truth commissions address the issues of guilt, punishment, atonement, and forgiveness. When placed in the general historical context described by schoolbooks, accounts produced by trials and truth commissions may raise the fear that individual guilt or failure will be generalized and attached to the whole group for which the perpetrator stands. The South African truth commission was built on the value of individual voluntary confessions, which were accepted as atonement for the crime and guaranteed amnesty. After the confession, the individual case was closed and was not meant to be disseminated in society as a moral lesson serving pedagogical aims. The individual stories told in court or in a commission reveal exactly the topic that is often excluded from the curriculum. The history lesson and the trials or commissions address different dimensions of the crimes. Truth commissions in particular may contribute more to civic education than to history teaching, although they also refer to or revive traditional elements of justice. The "Gagaca" trials in Rwanda resemble a public hearing; they revitalize a traditional form of community-based consensus finding. They may sharpen the awareness of positive, cohesive elements in juridical procedures of the past in Rwanda and form part of the politics of history of the Rwandan governments, even though they do not influence considerably the way history is taught at school. It again proves that history *education* or the creation of *historical consciousness* is not to be equated with *history teaching*. Having acknowledged the different dimensions of juridical processes and history teaching, it is nevertheless astonishing that forms of controversial dispute and the establishment of truth through a communal communicative process prevalent in truth commissions have almost nowhere changed the restricted notion of the one and only objective truth that shapes the way history is presented in school textbooks. To explain the gap or to find the (missing) link between truth commissions, trials, and teaching deserves more in-depth research.

It is more understandable that textbook authors and curriculum experts object to using material from tribunals imposed on the country by foreign powers and located outside their own country, as these tribunals are widely seen as one-sided justice managed by the victorious foreign powers (Corkalo et al. 2004, 147). Their share in the reconciliation process is limited. This applies to Rwanda as well as to former Yugoslav countries. Biro et al. (2004, 200) concluded, "The overall survey results suggest that the role of the ICTY [International Criminal Tribunal for the former Yugoslavia] in promoting reconciliation in Croatia and BiH [BaH] is problematic." Although international courts are not held in high esteem by the perpetrators, a juridical verdict stating that crimes have been committed is nevertheless a condition for the victims to engage in a reconciliation process and dilute one-sided and adversary narratives of victimization and oppression.

The Future of Textbook Projects: A Concerted Transnational Approach

This article has concentrated on new forms of textbook revision in countries undergoing a postconflict situation; this section will again examine the more traditional patterns of binational or multinational consultations. Do they still provide a helpful framework for reconciliation between states? Are they still an effective instrument for building sustainable trust between peoples? The controversy over the presentation of the Second World War in Japanese textbooks that has been continuing in East Asia for decades should provide the battlefield. Official textbook talks between Japan, Korea, and China have not yet been held. On several occasions since the 1990s, UNESCO has tried to bring the three parties together, but Japanese government officials were never willing to join in. As there was no hope of reaching an agreement on an official level, NGOs, academic institutions, and individual researchers organized conferences to at least document how the issue is presented in Japanese textbooks, to compare this with results of recent research, and thereby to provide textbook authors with information that is as objective as possible. The failure of dialogue on an official level strengthened the voice of NGOs and established a link between traditional forms of interstate textbook consultations and the work of NGOs based on a civil society approach.

Nevertheless, well into the first decade of this century, the bipartite or tripartite debate within NGOs or scholarly groups also revealed remarkable shortcomings in contrast to textbook revision groups working outside East Asia. Recommendations or conclusions only criticized the Japanese side, which was implicitly perceived to be the only possible culprit; the role of the occupied people during the war—for example, instances of Korean collaboration or the civil war that took place in China, causing serious casualties and weakening Chinese resistance against the Japanese forces—were not mentioned. The participants did not even see the need to question their own history. Communication was asymmetrical. Only one partner was expected to make concessions and to change the textbook representation of the others' role, whereas the other two partners seemed to be sacrosanct. The activities of scholars and NGOs were firmly embedded in the political discourse, which deployed the same communication pattern: to convince Japanese politicians and to exert pressure to make them apologize. They legitimized through scholarly expertise the political claims of their own governments and of public opinion, which was in line with that of the politicians. It did not become apparent that their statements were grounded in an academic discourse that follows its own rules and is not driven by short-term political objectives or claims for justice, legitimate as they may be. It was therefore not surprising that scholarly seminars were rather seen as an appendage to the political debate rather than a driving force that could lend a new direction to the public discourse.

Continuous political pressure, intensified contacts between East Asian historians, and a thorough examination of textbook revision performed in Europe gradually changed the agenda and added a pedagogical dimension to it. In Europe, private publishing houses, international organizations such as the Council of Europe, and NGOs like EUROCLIO—the European Association of History Teachers—had embarked on an innovative way of pursuing international pedagogy: the writing of transnational history textbooks. Following this model, five bilateral or multilateral history textbooks have been written in East Asia in recent years, the most ambitious being a book written by a team of Japanese, Chinese, and Korean authors. These books cannot replace the obligatory history books; however, it would be a big step forward if students and teachers could use books that offer a wider view and do not only reflect a well-known and canonized national narrative. In addition to these activities, binational history commissions have been established between China and Japan as well as between Japan and Korea, such that official patterns can already be found alongside the work of NGOs. It goes without saying that, with these new premises, the communication process became truly bipartite or tripartite, for the Koreans and Chinese (albeit slowly) made their concept of history teaching and their history textbooks amenable to examination and critique from the other sides (Toshiki 2003).

The effect of innovations in transnational or transcultural activities on the agents who produce them may frequently be more significant than the impact of products on their users. The experience that it is possible to develop a joint history textbook is of value in itself, even if the book is not widely used. It has established a new paradigm that refutes the former opinion that the narratives are so different and so consistent with the respective national pride and historical canon of each nation that they cannot be changed by means of international comparative research and debate. Innovations do not exert direct and immediate influence on pedagogical practice; they spread out to many agents in the political arena, the academy, NGOs, and societal interest groups who may help to pave their way into the classroom. In this respect, the question of whether a Japanese-Korean-Chinese textbook commission should be set up can, at best, become obsolete if concerted efforts on the level of NGOs, universities, international governmental organizations, and pedagogical institutes can produce sustainable results.

Notes

1. The Web site of the Georg Eckert Institute for International Textbook Research offers biweekly press summaries on textbook issues (www.furl.net/members/GEI1, reviewed by Dr. Arunas Vyšniauskas).

2. Within the framework of the UNESCO Textbook Quality Improvement Programme, 8.75 million textbooks have been produced during the current conflict in Iraq (Textbook Quality Improvement Programme 2005).

3. The author of this article has gained personal experience in the field in the three latter regions.

References

Arlow, M. 2004. Citizenship education in a divided society: The case of Northern Ireland. In *Education, conflict and social cohesion*, ed. S. Tawil and A. Harley, 225-313. Geneva, Switzerland: UNESCO International Bureau of Education.

Becher, U., W. Borodziej, and R. Maier, eds. 2001. *Deutschland und Polen im zwanzigsten Jahrhundert. Analysen—Quellen—didaktische Hinweise*. Hannover, Germany: Hahnsche Buchhandlung.

Biro, M., D. Ajdukovic, D. Corkalo, D. Djipa, P. Milin, and H. M. Weinstein. 2004. Attitudes towards justice and social reconstruction in Bosnia and Herzegovina and Croatia. In *My neighbor, my enemy. Justice and community in the aftermath of mass atrocity*, ed. E. Stover and H. Weinstein, 183-205. Cambridge: Cambridge University Press.

Corkalo, D., D. Ajdukovic, H. M. Weinstein, E. Stover, D. Djipa, and M. Biro. 2004. Neighbors again? Intercommunity relations after ethnic cleansing. In *My neighbor, my enemy. Justice and community in the aftermath of mass atrocity*, ed. E. Stover and H. Weinstein, 143-61. Cambridge: Cambridge University Press.

Freedman, S. W., D. Kambana, B. L. Samuelson, I. Mugisha, I. Mukashema, E. Mukama, J. Mutabaruka, H. M. Weinstein, and T. Longman. 2004. Confronting the past in Rwandan schools. In *My neighbor, my enemy. Justice and community in the aftermath of mass atrocity*, ed. E. Stover and H. Weinstein, 248-65. Cambridge: Cambridge University Press.

Gasanabo, J.-D. 2002. L'histoire à l'école au Rwanda—Post-génocide, défis et perspectives. *Internationale Schulbuchforschung/International Textbook Research* 24:67-88.

Gemeinsame Deutsch-Polnische Schulbuchkommission: Empfehlungen für die Schulbücher der Geschichte und Geographie in der Bundesrepublik Deutschland und in der Volksrepublik Polen. 1977/1995. Rev. ed. Frankfurt, Germany: Diesterweg.

Giroux, H. A. 1997. *Pedagogy and the politics of hope. Theory, culture and schooling*. Oxford, UK: Westview.

Johannesson, B. 2002. The writing of history textbooks in South Africa. *Internationale Schulbuchforschung/International Textbook Research* 24:89-95.

Learning each other's historical narrative: Palestinians and Israelis (Part One). 2003. Beith Jallah, Israel: Peace Research Institute in the Middle East.

Longman, T., and T. Rutagengwa. 2004. Memory, identity, and community in Rwanda. In *My neighbor, my enemy. Justice and community in the aftermath of mass atrocity*, ed. E. Stover and H. Weinstein, 162-82. Cambridge: Cambridge University Press.

Pingel, F. 1999. *UNESCO guidebook on textbook research and textbook revision*. Hannover, Germany: Hahnsche Buchhandlung.

———. 2004. "Sicher ist, dass...der Völkermord nicht mit Hitler begann und leider auch nicht mit ihm endet." Das Thema "Völkermord" als Gegenstand von Unterricht und Schule. In *Genozide und staatliche Gewaltverbrechen im 20. Jahrhundert*, ed. V. Radkau, E. Fuchs, and T. Lutz, 98-112. Wien, Austria: Studienverlag.

———. 2006. Einigung auf ein Minimum an Gemeinsamkeit. Schulbuchrevision in Bosnien und Herzegowina. *Geschichte in Wissenschaft und Unterricht* 57:519-33.

Reid, J., and R. Siebörger. 1995. Conference report "Textbooks and the school history curriculum." *South African Historical Journal* 33:169-77.

Rutayisire, J., J. Kabano, and J. Rubagiza. 2004. Redefining Rwanda's future: The role of curriculum in social reconstruction. In *Education, conflict and social cohesion*, ed. S. Tawil and A. Harley, 315-73. Geneva, Switzerland: UNESCO International Bureau of Education.

Smith, A., and T. Vaux. 2002. Education, conflict and international development. Report commissioned by the UK Department for International Development, London.

Tawil, S., and A. Harley. 2004. Education and identity-based conflict: Assessing curriculum policy for social and civic reconstruction. In *Education, conflict and social cohesion*, ed. S. Tawil and A. Harley, 1-35. Geneva, Switzerland: UNESCO International Bureau of Education.

Textbook Quality Improvement Programme: Final report. 2005. Paris: UNESCO.

Toshiki, S., 2003. International exchange on textbooks in Japan: An interim report. In *Sharing the burden of the past. Legacies of war in Europe, America, and Asia*, ed. A. Horvat and G. Hielscher, 100-106. Tokyo: Asia Foundation—Friedrich Ebert—Stiftung.

Challenged Histories and Collective Self-Concepts: Politics in History, Memory, and Time

By
MARTIN O. HEISLER

Societies, like individuals, strive to have positive self-concepts. They endow stories of their origin and associate their course through history with ethical principles that attest to who they are and how they want to be seen. Such principles define the society for its members and for the world at large. But all societies must at some time confront evidence of actions undertaken in their name that violate their fundamental principles and conflict with their desired self-image. Following a glance at the basic elements of the politics of history and identity, the author suggests two sources of the tensions between "bad acts" and positive self-concepts. Both relate to shifts in developmental time. First, actions not considered wrong when they were undertaken in the past are inconsistent with current expectation. Second, transsocietal differences in normative frameworks lead to cross-boundary criticisms of behavior in which the critics' societies likely engaged at an earlier time. Accusations or criticisms generally meet with defensive, often hostile responses. Hypocrisy tends to rule in most cases, with little or no normative learning.

Keywords: violated self-concepts; normative shifts in time; criticisms of past acts

It is evident that disputes about the past can make for dramatic, often highly contentious politics, both within and between societies. But such disputes do not always have society-wide or even broader impact. There are important differences between conflicting accounts of recent events, for instance, and challenges to established narratives of a collectivity's history— deeply embedded, often institutionalized, memories bordering on the sacred.[1] In this article,

Martin O. Heisler, professor emeritus of government and politics at the University of Maryland, has worked in the fields of comparative politics and international relations, focusing on ethnicity and ethnic relations, transnational migration, security, and policy studies. He was special editor and contributing author of three previous volumes of The Annals. *His most recent publication, "Academic Freedom and the Freedom of Academics," appeared in the November 2007 issue of* International Studies Perspectives.

DOI: 10.1177/0002716207313436

I focus on politics associated with the latter—whether they are empirically grounded, mythical, or imaginary, or some mixture of these.

What triggers such contention? What is challenged or threatened by newly uncovered or publicized events in the past, and why are responses to such challenges so often pugnacious and quarrelsome? Disagreements about who said what to whom the other day may call into question personal integrity, while disagreements about the accuracy—"the truth"—of a people's history tend to be perceived (and are often intended) as critiques of the normative foundations on which a people's common identity has been built. We must ask how, if at all, past actions associated with or undertaken in the name of a collectivity threaten its self-concept or identity. What sorts of actions pose such threats, why are some not perceived as threatening, and what is a collective self-concept or identity? It is important to consider whether it encompasses all members of a population and, if not, what makes for exceptions.

These and related questions need to be addressed if we are to understand how and why history can become a significant source of political contention. But such questions are broad and complex; it would be arrogant to pretend even to try to answer them in a short article. I have a much more modest, two-part goal: to gain a better understanding of the implications of challenges to collective self-concepts through emendations of history; and to examine some of the practical, political qualities of collective self-concepts.

From Mythistory to the Essence of Peoplehood[2]

It is now commonplace to observe that history, memory, and identity are implicated in each other (see, e.g., Megill 1998; Kratochwil 2006). For some, memory has become a way, perhaps *the* way, of thinking about history; and identity is sometimes said to be produced by mixtures of real and imagined histories (see, e.g., Zerubavel 2003). But while these three concepts—often representing instrumental or purposive constructions—are intimately related, they are certainly not synonymous.[3] Nor can we say with confidence how they are related. All three are contingent on context and circumstance and on the instrumental purposes to which they can be put (Novick 2007; Kratochwil 2006), and all three provide hermeneutic possibilities to a wide variety of collectivities; to institutions such as the state, the church, and the ideological faction; and to the individual.

Furthermore—and this is my most radical claim—power to interpret and apply (use in instrumental ways) history, memory, and identity can be exerted at each of those levels, from the state and society at one end of the scale to individuals at the other (cf. Kansteiner 2002, 188-89).[4] The plausibility of this claim, like the statements about history, memory, and identity in the preceding paragraph, also depends on context: autonomy for individuals, associations, and institutions (below the level of the state) to exercise and act on choices covaries with the openness of the state, the degree of social modernity (Heisler 1990), and the space allowed by social control (see Janowitz 1978, chap. 2). The possibility that choice and power can be exercised at any or all of these levels makes the relationships of history, memory, and identity to each other even more indeterminate. With contingencies stacked on contingencies, Wulf Kansteiner's (2002, 184) comment that "memory's relation to history remains one of the interesting theoretical challenges in the field" is apt; and the same holds true for identity's relationships to both memory and history (Kratochwil 2006).

But grappling with the questions I posed at the outset does not require resolving these difficulties. *The current politics of the past* deals with history, engages memory, and may invoke aspects of identity, but, in fact, it *is a practical matter that unfolds in the present*. As Friedrich Kratochwil (2006, 6) has argued, "The understanding of 'politics' requires a historical awareness that is *sui generis*. Politics is inherently *practical* since it deals with doing the right thing at the right time in view of the particular historical circumstances." Viewed in this light, the task is less the determination of the bases in history of the attacks on particular positions, or which constructions of the memories of particular actions or events should prevail, than of the practical uses to which elements of the past can be put for current political ends.

History, collectivities, and their politics

Determining what those practical elements may be brings us back to context and contextualization. One way to pursue the task is to focus—in the language of the social sciences—on the independent and intermediate variables, or influences and mediating factors associated with particular outcomes or consequences, which are termed "dependent variables." Social scientists and many historians have come to view history, memory, and identity as dependent variables shaped by such political acts as elite-constructed stories of the past and collective memories or as socially or politically shaped objects, such as memorials and symbols. Here politics is the main independent variable or creative force that molds history, memory, and identity.

An earlier generation of scholars—many of them historians of European origin or education—held the alternative, now rather unfashionable, view that politics is largely a function of history, based on the harnessing of memory and appeals to identity. Writing in the mid-twentieth century, they focused on the subjective aspect of nationhood or national identity, a "we-feeling" that reflected a sense of a shared past presumptively grounded in history (e.g., Hertz 1944; Kohn 1955; Shafer 1955; but cf. Deutsch 1953, esp. 5-6). More recently, the anthropologist Benedict Anderson (1983) suggested that politics can be shaped by the sense of a shared past that is partly or mostly imaginary. In this view, politics is a dependent variable, and history and/or memory and identity are important independent variables.

Both views are correct, depending on circumstances. Politics is often a significant force in the construction of the past and the shaping of collective memory.

It can also exert influence on the contours and content of personal, political, and broadly collective identities, such as the cultural and eventually identitive integration of England in the mid-eighteenth century (Corrigan and Sayer 1985) or the making of "peasants into Frenchmen" (Weber 1976).[5]

An earlier generation of scholars—many of them historians of European origin or education—held the alternative, now rather unfashionable, view that politics is largely a function of history, based on the harnessing of memory and appeals to identity.

Time

The displacement of norms in time and dramatically shrinking normative and communicative space among societies are two important contextual factors. The former is evident in all those actions that were considered appropriate, even desirable, at an earlier time but that are now viewed as inappropriate or wrong in the same societies. Thus, the actions of the Australian government vis-à-vis the country's Aboriginal population, and especially its children, in the period between the world wars may have been considered appropriate to many (though surely not all) "reasonable people" at the time. They clearly are not now; and that gives rise to some of the most vigorous "history debates." Turkey's efforts to prohibit public use of the Kurdish language and culture seem "wrong" to many Turks (as well as to people outside Turkey), but they are essentially similar to the policies of the English government in the mid-eighteenth century, to which I alluded above.

What was acceptable or even preferable then is not acceptable now; but how, by whom, using what criteria can the dislocations in normative time be reconciled (Heisler 2001)? Such shifts in normative time are at the root of some of the most contentious politicized debates about the past.

Shrinking normative and communicative space across cultures (and societies) provokes disputes about the past that are at once similar and different. Whether we attribute the closing of distances between societies to vastly faster, more comprehensive, and cheaper communication and travel (including migration) or to sweeping structural shifts (read "globalization"), the boundaries of value systems and judgments about the behavior of those in other societies/cultures are easy to cross and are crossed often (Heisler 2001). Thus, members of collectivities whose perspectives have been widened through communication or time spent abroad, as well as people and governments in other countries, may demand that their society address elements in its past according to imported standards of accountability.

But the most important context for challenges to histories and collective self-concepts is internal, both to the collectivity and to its self-concept. It follows from what, again, in the title phrase of Rogers Smith's (2003) book, are the "stories of peoplehood" that undergird "the politics and morals of . . . membership." Since the language in which the central arguments are presented is connected to the content, I present portions in some detail.

Collectivities built on ethical foundations

To recall: the gist of the question that triggered my concern with the politics of the past is, "Who are we, as a people?"[6] The formulation of this question closest to my *problématique* can be found in Rogers Smith's (2003) *Stories of Peoplehood*. He frames the question in a way that, in my judgment, approaches the desiderata of *Gemeinschaft*—community—and does so in a fashion that relates it as closely to modern political, social, and cultural conditions as any work with which I am familiar. Smith's concept of "ethical stories of peoplehood" (elucidated below) partakes of some of the ideal-typic qualities of the classic *Gemeinschaft* construct but points to some important steps away from the utopian level toward the more mundane arenas of political life in modern societies—collectivities that more closely approximate *Gesellschaften*.

The stories a collectivity tells itself about itself at once indicate and form its self-image—its collective identity or sense of collective self. These stories narrate origins; and, more important, they mark the path the collectivity has traveled in history to become what it is now, or what it seems to stand for to many or most of its members. Smith is concerned with the formulation and reformulation over time of stories that constitute and maintain a collectivity's identity—the self-image shared in some manner and degree by most of its members.

The work is very rich in theoretical and analytic insights, but it is written at a relatively general level—necessarily so, considering its sweep and its goal of introducing a different way of thinking about the foundations of political membership. (Although illustrated from the experiences of various societies, in places it reads rather like an ideal or constructed type abstracted from the developmental history of the United States—a point to which I shall return.) At the same time, it is replete with openings to systematic research and to extending both its general theme and its more mundane connections to political life. Rather than attempt a synopsis of the entire argument, I highlight only the elements central to my concerns here.

Smith strives to identify the symbolic and substantive essences of public, usually authoritative, narratives that convey the sense of purpose and direction for large collectivities—that is, what they are about. As I noted earlier, he uses the terms "people" and "peoplehood" in part to avoid the diffuse conceptual and theoretical connotations of nation and society and in part because his conception of peoplehood can transcend the temporal, spatial, and associational boundaries of nation and society. A people can predate the nation, and it may include more or fewer persons than those who populate a nation or a society. Peoplehood denotes membership in a collectivity by those who identify with essential elements of its story and with the principles that story demonstrates. The story simultaneously represents and rallies the collectivity. Smith is concerned with *political* peoplehood; and while he recognizes the applicability to many levels and types of associations of the generative and sustaining qualities in such narratives, his focus remains at the macro or essentially societal level (Smith 2003, 151 ff.).

Peoplehood is a *political* state of being, and it has far-reaching political implications. It entails conscious association, based on reflection, not simply propinquity or economic interdependence (e.g., a Durkheimian division of labor); and by implication, it provides some degree of volition or choice (Smith 2003, 48; cf. Heisler 1990, 1994; Hollinger 1995; Schnapper 2003).[7] While most members of a society enter it through birth, peoplehood entails learning and socialization to a shared story and what it represents. It "is a type of activity that is carried on not by members of all human associations, groups, and communities, but by participants in what is still a rather larger and unruly subset of those groups" (Smith 2003, 19 ff.). Stories of peoplehood are instrumental in constituting collectivities; but more important for Smith and for my purposes, *they propagate the values and norms around which collectivities form, and with and through which their members identify*.[8]

Smith discusses three types of stories, sorted by the rationale they offer for the formation, cohesion, and collective purposes of peoples: political, economic, and ethical. Both in his explicit statements and by devoting most of the book to them, he makes clear that he is primarily interested in *ethically constitutive stories of peoplehood*. As he acknowledges (Smith 2003, 64), the meaning of this notion is not readily grasped. It is, therefore, best to quote his most direct statement. Such stories

> [refer] to a wide variety of accounts that present membership in a particular people as somehow intrinsic to who its members really are, because of traits that are imbued with *ethical significance* [italics added]. Such stories proclaim that members' culture, religion, language, race, ethnicity, ancestry, history, or other such factors are constitutive of their very identities as persons, in ways that both affirm their worth and delineate their obligations. These stories are almost always intergenerational, implying that *the ethically constitutive identity espoused not only defines who a person is, but who her ancestors have been and who her children can be* [italics added]. (Smith 2003, 64-65)

The effectiveness of such stories is not diminished by the seemingly circular way in which they delineate collectivities. Like Smith, I believe such stories are best grounded in history (Smith 2003, 186-98; also see Barton and Levstik 2004, 48 ff., 54 ff., and passim). But in many, perhaps most cases, origins are at least in part shrouded in a deep past; they may be mythical in part and replete with apocrypha. This renders the collective identities or self-concepts engendered by stories of peoplehood at once more malleable and more inflexible or dogmatic (Hughes 2003). Flexibility can give rise to the fuzziness or diffuse nature of origins, and rigid or dogmatic adherence to such elements of a story can reflect insecurities about their "objective truth" or their intersubjective validity.

Ethically constitutive stories are more likely to integrate collectivities and to provide rationale for coming and staying together than are political or economic arguments, and they make for stronger identitive links. They go beyond instrumental grounds for the existence of a collectivity and for associating with those in it, and they provide bases and foci for people's claims on the collectivity (see, e.g., Simon and Klandermans 2001; Brewer and Gardner 1996; Sedikides and Brewer 2001) and justify people's responsibilities to each other as well as to their common institutions. In sum, ethically based narratives offer more than instrumental or self-serving reasons for political loyalties.

Stories evolve over time, reflecting changing social, economic, political, and other conditions or the political exigencies faced by elites. The "updating" or revisions of the narratives are most commonly elite-driven. That is, formal or unofficial political leaders play active parts in constructing and reconstructing the stories; in fact, they are *political* leaders in part because of their roles in articulating such responses (Smith 2003, 42-43; Ong 1999, 70-72).[9]

Negative Actions Meet Positive Stories

I believe even more strongly than Smith seems to that stories of peoplehood must be positive stories (Smith 2003, 160).[10] As Michael Walzer (1994, 42) has argued, "Individuals need to maintain a high opinion of themselves, a sense of their probity and righteousness; and similarly the members of any society (especially the leading members) need to believe that their . . . policies are just." Even where stories of peoplehood are constructed around or reinforced by victimhood, the negative aspects of the theme are redeemed by testimony of survival and "overcoming," imparting a positive spin to past injustices or misfortunes. They convey strength of collective character derived from shared travails ("out of Egypt," "up from slavery").[11]

But how then are unpleasant—even morally repugnant—chapters in a people's past to be reconciled with stories that must have a positive thrust? Smith believes that

> most people will be more strongly motivated, rather than alienated, if they see their political identities as partly constituted by histories displaying both good and bad elements. Such histories will indicate, quite authentically, that it is now largely up to them to determine in their shared political lives whether and how the best parts of their heritage will be continued and extended, and the worst parts overcome. (Smith 2003, 160)

Smith does not discuss specifically, in detail, how such discriminating judgments will be made, either by publics or their leaders. The hope that such moral learning will take place is not uncommon and may well be justified; but it needs to be explored, if for no other reason than that, to date, it has not been systematically examined. The legal scholar Alan Dershowitz (2004) has asserted that societies and polities learn and embrace what is right from experience with wrongs—that in effect, rights can come from (previous) wrongs (also see Barkan and Karn 2006). But do they, and how would we know? Horrific acts in the past, done in the name of a people or particular ideas and ideals, seem not to have inoculated societies or their individual members; the massacre at My Lai did not protect against the acts at Abu Ghraib, much less those in other societies. The incidence of genocide has actually increased since the Holocaust and Stalin's mass murders; awareness that the unimaginable is possible seems to have made it more, rather than less likely (Bauman 1989/2000; Glover 2000; Katznelson 2003; Todorov 2003). Nor have such "lessons of the past" led to effective institutional impediments to such acts (Powers 2002).

Hypocrisy is rampant, and the cynical view that lying is a—or the—predominant way of dealing with unpleasant facts is difficult to avoid. Positive self-concepts, it seems, can be maintained in the face of betrayals of the principles on which they are based. Elites lie, as Michael Walzer (1994, 42) suggested, in their attempts to sustain the belief that they are virtuous in the minds of those they lead, lying "not only to others but also to themselves, their everyday evasions, and the veil they draw over the more ugly features of the world they have made."

Skeptical Conclusions

What if any lessons, then, do collectivities learn from actions that violate their avowed sense of who they are as a people, especially actions undertaken in their name or by their agents? At its most general, this is a timeless preoccupation with moral progress by societies. We must consider, should such progress exist, what its dynamics are.[12] My concerns here are much narrower and more down to earth, however: whether awareness of appalling acts in a collectivity's past, committed in its name, affects its self-image—and if so, how.[13]

Even this more modest question is daunting. Its complexity becomes evident when we consider its cognitive, epistemological, analytic, and moral elements. It is difficult to determine what past atrocities will be found to be traumatic by those members of a community who become aware of them. It is unclear whether we are justified in applying today's criteria for moral behavior to actions that occurred decades, even generations, ago. Should our assessments be relativistic or universalistic in time and place and across circumstances? Do the implications of our judgments of past behavior hold for social institutions at all levels—small groups, subcultures, entire societies, "civilizations"?[14] And what sorts of collectivities do we have in mind, anyway? We do not know who today associates herself or himself with the actions of those—perhaps just a few—who violated norms that are supposed to define an entire people and how they relate to such actions in the past. We may or may not be able to make a plausible case that moral progress occurs at an uneven pace or degree across, and perhaps within, societies or civilizations and how, if at all, such variation should influence our expectations and judgments. How do we ascertain *awareness and recognition* of the incompatibility between such atrocities as the wanton mass killing of innocent civilians or torture, on one hand, and the prevalent positive collective self-concepts all peoples have, on the other? In short, what must we know, when must we know it, and whose awareness or knowledge counts? And how should we react to such actions? Finally, what is a collective self-concept, and how, if at all, can we know it?

It is unclear whether we are justified in applying today's criteria for moral behavior to actions that occurred decades, even generations, ago.

A plausible case can be made that the behavior of some does not implicate all. It can also be argued that past bad behavior by some of its members does not encumber the collectivity today with formal (legal, political) or moral responsibility. Collective guilt is a morally tenuous proposition, in any case, and difficult to sustain culturally (Wohl and Branscombe 2005)—although collective shame may lead to long-term changes (Alweiss 2003). But at the very least, even the *implication* of collective guilt engenders ambivalence and ethical confusion; and it leads, not infrequently, to formal claims for material remedies (see, e.g., Barkan 2000; Deák, Gross, and Judt 2000).[15] In any case, the ways a collectivity deals with the guilt associated with some of its current or past members is an important political, social, and cultural issue (cf. Forst 1994/2002, 133 ff.).

A collectivity's response—through its public authorities, social or political elites, and educational system—to "news" of gross violations by its members can profoundly affect its domestic politics and international relations. In recent years, a large and still growing literature, general as well as academic, has focused on the political consequences of how the past has been addressed.[16] The "politics of history," "the politics of memory," and debates surrounding how and what history is taught[17] have become prominent themes in a number of disciplines in the humanities and social sciences, including psychology and international relations. They have also entered broader public discourse and even the judicial arena.

If such narratives are to retain their power to shape collective self-concepts—if they are to serve as the bases for responses to the question, "Who are we?"—they must be interpreted and frequently reinterpreted, edited, revised, or updated. Addressing these tasks is likely to lead to contestation among those with different interpretations of the thrust of the narrative and some of its elements.

Rogers Smith emphasizes throughout his book that such contestation is the stuff of politics (Smith 2003, passim but esp. 160), and therefore, it is to be welcomed as a normal part of the processes of collective life. He also avers that, through open discussion of negative elements in the collectivity's past, such politics may strengthen the normative core. In Walzer's (1994) more cynical, or perhaps more realistic, view, elites cope with challenges to the positive substance of the narrative by lying. In the absence of systematic empirical inquiry, these two views are likely to remain no more and no less than contrasting beliefs. But broadly comparative research and analyses seem to suggest that Smith's optimistic, though not unreasonable, surmise is more apt for cases such as the United States (which has been his principal scholarly focus) and western societies in general than for much or most of the rest of the world.

Notes

1. I use the term "collectivity" to avoid the accumulated connotations of such more thoroughly developed concepts as "nation" or "society," although these have several important elements in common with the notion of collectivity. In his seminal book, *Stories of Peoplehood: The Politics and Morals of Political Membership*, Rogers Smith (2003) uses the terms "people" and "peoplehood" for similar reasons. For heuristic purposes, my usage parallels the familiar, though increasingly controverted, notion of "collective memory," since it is implicated in the associated ideas of "collective self-concept" and "collective self-image."

2. "Mythistory" is the title essay in a collection of the great historian William H. McNeill's (1986) papers, denoting the blurring of distinctions between history based on scholarly research and imagined or distorted myths. The meaning of "peoplehood," from Rogers Smith's (2003) work, is indicated in the preceding note; the book is discussed at length below.

3. For different views, see Winter (2000, 2006, 2008 [this volume]); Kansteiner (2002); and a work that in some respects anticipated the tide of memory studies, LeGoff (1981). For a profound extended treatment of relationships between history and memory, see Ricoeur (2004).

4. Although the transnational level of "civilizations" is apposite to our time, I am reluctant to include it in this analysis. It is not clear that Islam (or, for that matter, Shiite or Sunni Muslims), "the West," "Christendom," or any other currently used referent for civilization is sufficiently and consistently coherent to resemble a collectivity as I use that term: as, for instance, an ethnic group, a society, a nation, or even the population of a relatively well-integrated state.

5. For a theoretical and more general view, see Hoover (1997, esp. part I).

6. This is essentially the same question with which the late Robert Wiebe (2002, xv) opened his Preface to his posthumously published *Who We Are: A History of Popular Nationalism*. For Wiebe, "who" had to do with identity and "we" with "connectedness."

7. Both Hollinger and I make a normative argument, based on bedrock liberal positions: that is, that in postethnic societies, affiliation *should* be determined by choice (see Hollinger 1995, passim, but esp. 116-17; and Heisler 1990, 1994).

8. Citizenship theory today seems concerned with citizen–state relationships, to the virtual ignoring of citizen-to-citizen ties. "Peoplehood," in Smith's (2003) usage, and especially as regards what he terms ethical stories of peoplehood, reiterates the importance of such person-to-person or citizen-to-citizen relationships in political theory.

9. Aihwa Ong (1999, 71-72) suggested that some Asian elites strive to imbue their populations with moral commitments to relationships and values that transcend the individual, thereby reinforcing identification with and loyalty to collectivities—beginning with the family and moving toward larger social institutions.

10. Smith (2003, 59) emphasizes "'ethically constitutive' stories" because "they have special capacities to inspire senses of normative worth."

11. If accompanied by benefits or claims for amends, they may enhance collective purpose (see Hollinger 1995, 46 ff.).

12. Michelle M. Moody-Adams (1999) succeeded admirably in moving forward the philosophical discourse on moral progress. Any discussion of moral progress in the context of the contemporary United States needs to draw a clear distinction between general philosophical and metaphysical concerns and their practical aspects, on one hand, and the recently amplified partisan political discourse on "moral values," on the other, which reflects the politicized value perspectives of much of the evangelical Christian right.

13. For useful discussions of the idea of collective self-image, see Brewer and Gardner (1996), Simon and Klandermans (2001), and Tutiaux-Guillon and Nourrisson (2003).

14. The widely publicized acts at Abu Ghraib prison in 2003 and 2004 can be used as illustrations of this "levels of affect" question: do—should—the inhumane treatment of prisoners in Iraq reflect on the few generally low-ranking soldiers who have been formally charged with having committed those acts, or the subculture of the civilian and uniformed military establishment; or the United States; or hypocritical Western societies; or . . . ?

15. Thus, states have provided, or have been the foci of claims for, restitution to entire groups (e.g., survivors or heirs of victims of German atrocities during World War II, Japanese Americans interned by the United States, and more recently the claims by some African Americans for reparations from the federal government for the slavery of their ancestors). Affirmative action programs, now in place or under consideration in more than ten countries, are also justified as collective reparations for collective wrongs. Consider also the recent and, in some instances, still ongoing "truth and reconciliation" efforts in many countries, as well as functionally related war crimes tribunals, from the Nürenburg War Crimes trials following World War II in Germany to the current tribunals dealing with war crimes in the former Yugoslavia, Rwanda, and elsewhere. For a penetrating analysis of the logic and morality of the notions of collective responsibility, collective guilt, and punishment that moves in a different direction from this discussion see Alweiss (2003).

16. There are many festering grievances and disputes around the world stemming from events six, seven, even nine decades ago. Consider, for example, recent tense exchanges between Germany and the Czech Republic regarding the Beneš decrees expelling ethnic Germans after World War II; protests by former Hungarian prime minister Orban regarding the treatment of their Hungarian minorities by the Czech and the Slovak republics, and his suggestion that their refusal to acknowledge those actions should hold up their admission to the European Union; and Turkish refusal to acknowledge, or even to discuss, the genocide of Armenians in the closing days of the First World War.

17. See especially Barton and Levstik (2004), as well as Hein and Selden (2000); Lerner, Nagai, and Rothman (1995); Ravitch (2003); Schissler and Soysal (2005); Stearns, Seixas, and Wineburg (2000); Zinn and Barsamian (1999); many research reports by the National Center for History in the Schools at UCLA; and above all, several works by Falk Pingel and the Georg Eckert Institute for International Textbook Research and, in general, its quarterly journal, *Internationale Schulbuchforschung/International Textbook Research*.

References

Alweiss, Lilian. 2003. Collective guilt and responsibility: Some reflections. *European Journal of Political Theory* 2 (3): 307-18.

Anderson, Benedict. 1983. *Imagined communities*. London: Verso.

Barkan, Elazar. 2000. *The guilt of nations: Restitution and negotiating historical injustices*. New York: Norton.

Barkan, Elazar, and Alexander Karn, eds. 2006. *Taking wrongs seriously: Apologies and reconciliation*. Stanford, CA: Stanford University Press.

Barton, Keith C., and Linda S. Levstik. 2004. *Teaching history for the common good*. Mahwah, NJ: Lawrence Erlbaum.

Bauman, Zygmunt. 1989/2000. *Modernity and the Holocaust*. Ithaca, NY: Cornell University Press.

Brewer, Marilynn B., and Wendi Gardner. 1996. Who is this "we"? Levels of collective identity and self representations. *Journal of Personality and Social Psychology* 71 (1): 83-93.

Corrigan, Philip, and Derek Sayer. 1985. *The great arch: English state formation as cultural revolution*. Oxford, UK: Basil Blackwell.

Deák, István, Jan T. Gross, and Tony Judt, eds. 2000. *The politics of retribution in Europe: World War II and its aftermath*. Princeton, NJ: Princeton University Press.

Dershowitz, Alan. 2004. *Rights from wrongs: A secular theory of the origins of rights*. New York: Basic Books.

Deutsch, Karl W. 1953. *Nationalism and social communication: An inquiry into the foundations of nationality*. Cambridge, MA: MIT Press.

Forst, Rainer. 1994/2002. *Contexts of justice: Political philosophy beyond liberalism and communitarianism*. Translated by John M. M. Farrell. Berkeley: University of California Press.

Glover, Jonathan. 2000. *Humanity: A moral history of the twentieth century*. New Haven, CT: Yale University Press.

Hein, Laura, and Mark Selden, eds. 2000. *Censoring history: Citizenship and memory in Japan, Germany, and the United States*. Armonk, NY: East Gate Books.

Heisler, Martin O. 1990. Ethnicity and ethnic relations in the modern West. In *Conflict and peacemaking in multiethnic societies*, ed. Joseph V. Montville. Lexington, MA: Lexington Books.

———. 1994. Some normative caveats in the pursuit of the rights of ethnic minorities. *Journal of Ethno-Development* 4 (1): 79-82.

———. 2001. Now and then, here and there: Migration and the transformation of identities, borders, and orders. In *Identities, borders, orders: Rethinking international relations theory*, ed. Mathias Albert, David Jacobson, and Yosef Lapid. Minneapolis: University of Minnesota Press.

Hertz, Frederick. 1944. *Nationality in history and politics: A study of the psychology and sociology of national sentiment and character*. London: Kegan Paul, Trench, Trubner & Co., Ltd.

Hollinger, David A. 1995. *Postethnic America: Beyond multiculturalism*. New York: Basic Books.

Hoover, Kenneth. 1997. *The power of identity: Politics in a new key*. Chatham, NJ: Chatham House.

Hughes, Richard T. 2003. *Myths America lives by*. Urbana: University of Illinois Press.

Janowitz, Morris. 1978. *The last half-century: Societal change and politics in America*. Chicago: University of Chicago Press.

Kansteiner, Wulf. 2002. Finding meaning in memory: A methodological critique of collective memory studies. *History and Theory* 41 (2): 179-97.

Katznelson, Ira. 2003. *Desolation and enlightenment: Political knowledge after total war, totalitarianism, and the Holocaust*. New York: Columbia University Press.

Kohn, Hans. 1955. *Nationalism, its meaning and history*. Princeton, NJ: D. Van Nostrand.

Kratochwil, Friedrich. 2006. History, action and identity: Revisiting the "second" great debate and assessing its importance for social theory. *European Journal of International Relations* 12 (1): 5-29.

LeGoff, Jacques. 1981. *Storia e memoria*. Turin, Italy: Einaudi.

Lerner, Robert, Althea K. Nagai, and Stanley Rothman. 1995. *Molding the good citizen: The politics of high school history texts*. Westport, CT: Praeger.

McNeill, William H. 1986. *Mythistory and other essays*. Chicago: University of Chicago Press.

Megill, Allan. 1998. History, memory, identity. *History of the Human Sciences* 11 (3): 37-62.

Moody-Adams, Michelle M. 1999. The idea of moral progress. *Metaphilosophy* 30 (3): 168-85.

Novick, Peter. 2007. Comments on Aleida Assmann's lecture. *Bulletin of the German Historical Institute* 40:27-31.

Ong, Aihwa. 1999. *Flexible citizenship: The cultural logics of transnationality*. Durham, NC: Duke University Press.

Powers, Samantha. 2002. *A problem from hell: America and the age of genocide*. New York: Basic Books.

Ravitch, Diane. 2003. *The language police: How pressure groups restrict what students learn*. New York: Knopf.

Ricoeur, Paul. 2004. *Memory, history, forgetting*. Translated by Kathleen Blamey and David Pellauer. Chicago: University of Chicago Press.

Schissler, Hanna, and Yasemin Nuhoglu Soysal, eds. 2005. *The Nation, Europe, and the world: Textbooks and curricula in transition*. New York: Berghahn Books.

Schnapper, Dominique. 2003. *La communauté des citoyens*. Paris: Éditions Gallimard.

Sedikides, Constantine, and Marilynn B. Brewer, eds. 2001. *Individual self, relational self, collective self*. Philadelphia: Psychology Press.

Shafer, Boyd. 1955. *Nationalism: Myth and reality*. New York: Harcourt, Brace and World.

Simon, Bart, and Brend K. Klandermans. 2001. Politicized collective identity: A social psychological analysis. *American Psychologist* 56 (4): 319-31.

Smith, Rogers M. 2003. *Stories of peoplehood: The politics and morals of political membership*. Cambridge: Cambridge University Press.

Stearns, Peter N., Peter Seixas, and Sam Wineburg, eds. 2000. *Knowing, teaching, and learning history*. New York: New York University Press/American Historical Association.

Todorov, Tzvetan. 2003. *Hope and memory: Lessons from the twentieth century*. Translated by David Bellos. Princeton, NJ: Princeton University Press.

Tutiaux-Guillon, Nicole, and Didier Nourrisson, eds. 2003. *Identités, mémoires, conscience historique*. Lyon-Saint-Étienne, France: Publications de l'Université de Saint-Étienne.

Walzer, Michael. 1994. Thick and thin: *Moral argument at home and abroad*. Notre Dame, IN, and London: Notre Dame University Press.

Weber, Eugen. 1976. *Peasants into Frenchmen: The modernization of rural France, 1870-1914*. Stanford, CA: Stanford University Press.

Wiebe, Robert H. 2002. *Who we are: A history of popular nationalism*. Princeton, NJ: Princeton University Press.

Winter, Jay. 2000. The generation of memory: Reflections on the "memory boom" in contemporary historical studies. *Bulletin of the German Historical Institute* 27 (Fall): 69-92.

———. 2006. *Remembering war: The great war between memory and history in the 20th century*. New Haven, CT: Yale University Press.

———. 2008. Historical remembrance in the twenty-first century. *The Annals of the American Academy of Political and Social Science* 617:6-13.

Wohl, Michael J. A., and Nyla R. Branscombe. 2005. Forgiveness and collective guilt assignment to historical perpetrator groups depend on level of social category inclusiveness. *Journal of Personality and Social Psychology* 88 (2): 288-303.

Zerubavel, Eviatar. 2003. *Time maps: Collective memory and the social shape of the past*. Chicago: University of Chicago Press.

Zinn, Howard, and David Barsamian. 1999. *The future of history*. Monroe, ME: Common Courage Press.

QUICK READ SYNOPSIS

The Politics of History in Comparative Perspective

Special Editor: MARTIN O. HEISLER
University of Maryland

Volume 617, May 2008

Prepared by Herb Fayer, Jerry Lee Foundation

DOI: 10.1177/0002716208316979

Q R S

The Future of Memory

Richard Ned Lebow, Dartmouth College

Background   This article is premised on three related assumptions:

- The first, an empirical one, is that elite and public opinion in at least some countries has become increasingly aware of memory as something that is problematic and often a source of contestation.
- The second assumption, theoretical in nature, is that elite and public opinion in at least some countries has become more receptive to the implications of this information.
- The third, also empirical, is that growing awareness by the elite and the ordinary public of both the malleability and politicization of memory will have consequences for future efforts to influence and control memory at institutional, collective, and individual levels.

First Assumption   The assumption has two components:

- awareness of memory as something that is not necessarily accurate, unchanging, and recallable; and
- recognition that groups with competing agendas often struggle to shape and control memory on at least the institutional level.

NOTE: In Western Europe, especially in Germany and Italy, the media covers controversial political issues, and in Europe these have not infrequently concerned questions of historical memory and memorialization. Issues like the Waldheim affair in Austria and the U.S. pressures on Swiss banks raised past events, often crimes in which the state was complicit and that official versions of institutional memory sought to hide.

Second
Assumption
The second assumption says that elite and public opinion in some countries has become more receptive to evidence indicating the malleability of memory.

- Many people recognize memory as a resource that groups in their society attempt to exploit, and they believe that this is feasibile.
- As memory is considered by most people to make them who they are, they are most likely to safeguard and defend their memories—individual, collective, and official—when they are confident about and content with their identities.
- When identity becomes problematic, people are likely to be less committed to memories and commemorations on which existing identities are based or from which they derive justification.

NOTE: The paradigmatic case in postwar Europe was the Federal Republic of Germany. National identity, previously strong, became uncomfortable for many Germans by reason of the country's Nazi past and the postwar division.

Third
Assumption
The third assumption is that growing awareness of memory as malleable and as a source of political contestation will have serious longer-term implications.

- It will affect the importance of memory for identity, the ease by which memory is reshaped or renegotiated, the means by which this is accomplished, and the shape and membership of communities.

Observations
The author observes a series of conditions, some of them in the form of hypotheses that are intended to serve as guides for future research:

- To the extent that people become conscious of any socialization process, they have greater potential to free themselves from it.
- Increased receptivity to self-congratulatory national narratives.
- The shaping and contestation of institutional memory by the state exercised through its control of the educational system and other vehicles for shaping mass opinion.
- International influences on institutional memory such as efforts of states and groups of states to shape the construction of official and collective memory in other states.
- Institutional memory as a form of reassurance.
- Shared remembrance—joint celebrations allow former enemies to recast the meaning of their relationship in a way that reduces dissonance and sustains the partially common identities former adversaries have come to develop.
- The proliferation of collective memory communities in states that include multiple nationalities or ethnic groups and multiple communities, institutional and some collective memories are more likely to clash to the extent that institutional memory excludes or deprecates these other nationalities or ethnic groups.
- The penetration of local collective memory by corporations and nonprofit organizations.
- Collective versus institutional memory is likely to become more apparent in authoritarian regimes as they find it increasingly difficult to maintain a monopoly over the flow of information.

**Q
R
S**

Conclusion

Scholarship on memory has focused almost entirely on reconstruction of the past for two reasons:
- It largely mirrors the conduct of the actual politics of memory.
- It is a field dominated by historians.

NOTE: There is no particular reason to think that future memory politics may be more future-oriented than in the past, but it is a possibility worth exploring. Either way, future memory is an important and neglected component, especially of individual and collective memory, and one worthy of serious investigation.

The American Past Politicized: Uses and Misuses of History

Michael Kammen, Cornell University

Background

Scholars are intrigued by the ways history has so often been written and revised for partisan policy purposes, a phenomenon hardly unique to the United States.
- The role of court historians required to record events in a manner pleasing to their masters is by now a long-familiar pattern.
- Presidents too often engage in "revisionism."
- Ever since Franklin Delano Roosevelt's presidency the focus of inquiry has tended to concentrate on presidential invocations of the past and their skeptics.

NOTE: One can take note of the Revolutionary founders' anxieties about the ways in which their deeds might be misunderstood or distorted, and how several of the most pivotal events in the national narrative came to be misremembered for politically self-serving reasons. Also note how the Supreme Court has often relied upon "law-office" history in support of outcomes the justices wished to achieve, and how prominent politicians have misread or misused history in making major policy decisions and in writing their memoirs.

Governmental Agencies

During the twentieth century several new governmental agencies increasingly provided official versions of key episodes and aspects of American history.
- In notable instances they gradually rewrote or reinterpreted the public's perception of the national past.
  - For example, the National Park system oversees a replica of George Washington's birthplace and a re-creation of the cabin where Abraham Lincoln was supposedly born, both of which are highly suspected of inauthenticity.

Presidential Revisionists

Presidents and their critics too often engage in "revisionism," sometimes unwittingly but most often deliberately to persuade others to support their policy preferences and retrospective judgments.
- Historian Ernest May has presented a strong critique of Truman and his advisors for facing the cold war using inappropriate analogies based upon events from the 1930s and World War II.

- Kennedy and Johnson both misused historical arguments to justify the deepening American engagement in Southeast Asia.
- Nixon's published memoirs show the whole Watergate episode as an unfortunate but minor blip in an administration filled with achievements, above all in foreign policy.
- In his memoir, Clinton glossed over some issues that really mattered, like the failure of his health care initiative and his pushing Sudan to expel bin Laden.

Supreme Court   The kind of historical treatise that Stephen A. Douglas wrote provides a fine example of what we commonly refer to as "law-office" history that omits anything germane that might be prejudicial to the case being argued.

- A notorious example of justices looking selectively to the founding of the nation for a rationale in decision making occurred in the case of *Dred Scott v. Sandford* regarding slavery issues and the interpretation of the Constitution as an exclusively white man's document.

Brown v.   John Davis of Lincoln University invited the help of two distinguished
Board of   historians in the case of *Brown v. Board of Education*—C. Vann Woodward
Education   and John Hope Franklin—to provide contextual material.

- In one instance Davis responded to Woodward, "Your conclusions are your own. If they do not help our side of the case, in all probability the lawyers will not use them. If they do help our argument, the present plan is to include them in the overall summary argument and to file the whole work as a brief in an appendix."
- Woodward and Franklin argued that the original equalitarian intentions of post–Civil War amendments had been eroded by political and economic pressures and extralegal tactics in the South.
- In this and many cases to follow, the Court made decisions based on "law-office history," intervening in what were essentially political issues involving state constitutions and accepted usage over time.

History   Our final example of American history being contested and politicized is
Standards   seen in the production of new National History Standards designed to improve the quality of history education in primary and secondary schools.

- The authors creating these standards were committed to a view of the American past that placed greater emphasis on women and minorities.
- There was criticism of the infrequency with which George Washington's name appeared compared to the frequency with which Harriet Tubman was mentioned.
- In 1995 the U.S. Senate was manipulated into voting 99–1 to condemn voluntary criteria. Later that year, when Senator Bob Dole attacked them, the Clinton administration, most notably the Secretary of Education, who had been supportive, rejected the standards—a candid acknowledgment that politics took precedence over history.
- A bipartisan commission review noted that most of the criticisms had not been directed against the standards themselves but against some of the teaching examples and activities.
  - It urged that the latter be deleted from the final edition, that certain subjects receive expanded treatment, that some concepts be clarified, and that ethnic and gender issues be more effectively connected to their historical contexts.

Conclusion   What took place between 1994 and 1996 was far more than a tempest in a teapot—it caused an entire nation to consider and reconsider how its history should be taught and understood in order to be meaningful and valued.

Blank Spots in Collective Memory: A Case Study of Russia

James V. Wertsch, Washington University in St. Louis

Background   "History" instruction in Soviet and post-Soviet schools, as well as in virtually every other country in the world, involves a complex mixture of what would be considered a sound interpretation of past events based on the objective review of evidence, on one hand, and an effort, on the other, to promulgate collective memory, or a usable past, as part of a national identity project.

- In this context, notions of history and collective memory overlap.
- Both of the above ways of representing the past deal with events occurring before the lifetime of the people doing the representing, and both assume that the accounts being presented are true.
- It is often difficult to separate history from collective memory, and textbooks almost always involve a mixture of the two.
- Formal history and collective memory must be kept distinct for several reasons:
  - Collective memory tends to reflect a single, subjective, committed perspective of a group in the present, whereas formal history strives to be objective and to distance itself from the present and any perspective that is currently in favor.
  - In addition, collective memory leaves little room for doubt or ambiguity about events and the motivations of actors, whereas formal history strives to take into account multiple, complex factors and motives that shape events.

Molotov-   With perestroika, and especially Gorbachev's admission in 1989 that secret
Ribbentrop Pact   protocols had been part of the Molotov-Ribbentrop Pact, the old Soviet version of the events of 1939 to 1940 could no longer be the official account.

- The most striking feature that distinguishes this from previous Soviet accounts is that the absorption of Latvia, Lithuania, and Estonia into the USSR was no longer formulated in Marxist-Leninist terms.
- Instead of focusing on the glories of the Soviet Union through the vision of the party, this account allows that mistakes were made.
- A striking feature of this account in the first stage of textbook revision is its awkwardness and ambiguity—new information appeared in a way that was inconsistent with the general flow of the text.
- During the second stage of textbook revision, a kind of "narrative repair" emerged to reestablish coherence based on a new narrative.
  - This new version moved beyond official Soviet accounts in that it made no attempt to deny the existence of the secret protocols of the Molotov-Ribbentrop Pact.

- In contrast to the narrative rift characteristic of the first stage, there is relatively little awkwardness or prevarication in this case, although some, to be sure, remains.

Schematic
Narrative

The schematic narrative template at work in the case of the Molotov-Ribbentrop Pact is one that occupies a central place in Russians' understanding of crucial historical episodes and includes

- an initial situation in which Russia is peaceful and not interfering with others;
- the initiation of trouble in which a foreign enemy treacherously and viciously attacks Russia without provocation;
- Russia almost loses everything in total defeat as it suffers from the enemy's attempts to destroy it as a civilization;
- through heroism, and against all odds, Russia triumphs and succeeds in expelling the foreign enemy, thus justifying its claims of exceptionalism and its status as a great nation.

NOTE: This template reflects traumatic events from Russia's past. At the same time, however, it is important to recognize that this is a cultural and cognitive construction, a particular way of pursuing what Bartlett called the "effort after meaning," and hence not the only possible way to interpret events such as signing the secret protocols of the Molotov-Ribbentrop Pact.

Conclusion

Deep collective memory is very conservative and resistant to change, something that runs counter to observations about the radically new public versions of the past that emerged with the breakup of the USSR.

- It is important to note that post-Soviet Russian history textbooks include assertions that would have earlier put their authors in prison.
- However, focusing on this alone fails to take into account the important difference between a surface level of narrative organization, where radical changes in specific narratives may be found, and the schematic narrative templates that mediate deep collective memory.
- While the specific narratives about the Molotov-Ribbentrop Pact may have changed in some surprising and seemingly radical ways, the underlying schematic narrative has been a very conservative force.
- When trying to resolve differences over the interpretation of past events, one useful means may be to introduce a heavier dose of objectivity and complexity into historical textbooks.
  - This suggests a different role for historians than is often assumed in academic discourse, and some historians resist precisely because they fear that it could lead to the elision of the distinction between collective memory and formal history that they have been so persistent in maintaining.

NOTE: The events surrounding the Molotov-Ribbentrop Pact show that people are not likely to arrive at a common understanding of the past simply because they are exposed to a common body of objective information. So the best hope we may have is to recognize the existence and power of the narrative templates as a first step and then proceed to harness formal history in an effort to adjudicate differences over "what really happened" in the past.

Q
R
S

Using the Past in the Nazi Successor States from 1945 to the Present

Jenny Wüstenberg, University of Maryland;
and David Art, Tufts University

Q
R
S

Background

This article focuses on how political elites used stylized histories of the Nazi past in the service of broader political goals, both domestic and international.

- The authors discuss debates about history, particularly in Germany, as a model for coming to terms with a traumatic past.
- They note that there are few studies linking ideas about history to broader political outcomes—this represents an area for future research.
- The article concludes by considering whether German memory politics will serve as a model for European memory.

Postwar Germanys

In both Germanys, the Nazi past played a crucial role in the struggle to regain legitimacy in the aftermath of humiliating defeat.

- Each state claimed to embody the correct lessons learned from the recent disaster, as well as a positive national tradition derived from previous democratic movements.
- The instrumentalization of the past prevented honest remembering:
  - The German Democratic Republic (GDR, or East Germany) fashioned itself as an antifascist state and repositioned itself on the victorious side of history.
  - The Federal Republic of Germany (FRG, or West Germany) used anticommunism and the need for reintegration into the West to justify neglecting justice and historical truth.

Reckoning with the Past

With the foundations laid by the Allies and isolated individuals, the reckoning with the Nazi past in West Germany was gradually transformed in the 1960s and 1970s—several developments explain this change.

- A number of legislative and societal discourses, most importantly those on extending the statute of limitations on the crime of murder (and therefore on many acts committed under the Nazi regime), as well as new trials against war criminals, carried the moral, judicial, and political issues concerning the Nazi past into the public sphere.
- Since the 1980s, propelled by prominent public debates and grassroots activism, the discussion of the Nazi past has moved into the mainstream of German society and culture.
- A generational shift has moved into prominent societal and political positions those who were not involved in the Nazi regime but who were influenced by their parents' and grandparents' selective remembering of the past.
- However, the reckoning with the past has been complicated by the merging of the Eastern and Western cultures of memory, by the growing need to confront other pasts, and by the realization that the experiential generation is fading. Since unification, leaders have stressed that their good

record of memory proves their reliability as an international partner and their legitimate presence in the halls of power.

Austria

As in both the FRG and the GDR, historical narratives of the Nazi past served concrete political goals in Austria.
- Deceptively classifying Austrians as the victims of the Germans helped Austria's founders to disentangle their nation's identity from that of their northern neighbors.
- The defense that Austrians were, like Jews, victims of Nazism was used to parry claims from Jewish groups for restitution.
- Unlike in West Germany, there was virtually no public debate in Austria about their Nazi past for forty years.

NOTE: After forty years, a small number of Green politicians, artists, and intellectuals demanded that Austria critically examine its Nazi past and accept some responsibility for Nazi crimes. Austrian academics produced a number of scholarly works that examined, and challenged, the victim narrative.

Collective
Memory Studies

The lack of empirical evidence connecting views of the Nazi past to support for democracy in the cases that have been most extensively studied points to a large issue in the field of collective memory studies: the lack of theorizing about, and testing of, memory's causal effects on politics.
- Despite a realization among political scientists that "memory matters," there are few studies that treat ideas about history as an independent variable and link it to distinct political outcomes.
- If the study of memory is still in its infancy within comparative politics, students of international relations have had relatively more to say:
  - Constructivists have been more engaged with the politics of history than other paradigms of international relations.
  - Since memory can be an important component of how domestic norms are framed and foreign policy is legitimized, it cannot be disregarded as a factor in international relations.

NOTE: In an example of how important memory has become in the negotiation of (inter)state power, Polish leaders stress that their memory work with respect to the massacres in Jedwabne signified Poland's status as a modern European state. Turkey's failure to confront the genocide of Armenians has repeatedly been cited as a reason to deny EU membership.

Conclusion

In Germany, the fact that the confrontation with the Nazi past has become not only a societal imperative but also a justification of state power makes an honest reckoning with history less subject to the political vagaries of the day.
- Does the German experience represent a form of "best practice" in the process of coming to terms with a traumatic past, one that deserves to be emulated by EU nations and others?
- Using Germany as a model would mean establishing an open and empathetic European dialogue in which "national histories are seen from a transnational perspective" and "external national borders [are] transformed into internal European ones."

Through a Glass Darkly: Consequences of a Politicized Past in Contemporary Turkey

Fatma Müge Göçek, University of Michigan

Background

It is known that nation-states develop their own official narratives of history in an attempt to sustain their present rule through the control of the past.

- In Turkey the state has created an imperfect and faulty perception of historical reality and in so doing has impeded its chances of becoming a truly participatory democracy.
- This creates problems in the resolution of the three major political problems faced by the contemporary Turkish nation-state, namely, the massacres of the Armenians in the past, the treatment of the Kurds at present, and the contested partition of the island of Cyprus.
- The author believes that challenging the temporal boundaries of this Turkish official narrative by delving into the period preceding 1919 or 1923 reveals a possible peaceful solution that may advance a more democratic Turkey.

The Sèvres Syndrome

The theme that connects the above three problems in the current Turkish official narrative is that they were initially produced by the West to fragment the Turkish nation-state—this is known as the Sèvres syndrome.

- The fear of loss of territory and the fear of abandonment not only became prominent themes in the Ottoman Empire, but also persisted into the Turkish nation-state and still influence its official narrative.
- As the syndrome further envelops these problems in the paralyzing emotion of fear, it renders their possible resolution even more difficult.

The Kurdish Problem

Among the three issues, the Kurdish problem dominates the other two in duration and significance: unlike the Armenians and the Greeks the Kurds still live in Turkey and make up 20 percent of its population.

- Turkey's Kurdish problem is currently defined outside of Turkey as the oppression and denial of rights by a majority group (the Turks) of an ethnic minority (the Kurds), resulting in a civil war.
- In official Turkish discourse, however, there is no mention of the Kurdish problem nor the civil war, but rather reference to a socioeconomic issue in the southeastern region of the country.
- The suppression was accompanied by the disappearance of the word "Kurd" from the lexicon, the ban of the Kurdish language, the replacement of the Kurdish names of towns with Turkish ones, and the denial of the right of parents to give Kurdish names to their children.

NOTE: Today, even though the growth of the public sphere and civil associations in Turkey are indicators of democratization and economic development, the engagement of the Turkish state and especially the military in northern Iraq very conveniently curb these positive transformations.

The Cyprus Problem

The most significant historical event in creating the Cyprus problem in Republican history was the 1974 invasion of the northern tip of the island of Cyprus by the Turkish military after the Turkish-Cypriot community withdrew from the government to set up its own political structure.

- The Turkish government justified the invasion by stating that it was acting in its capacity as one of the guarantor powers of the 1960 arrangement.
- The attitude of the Turkish nation-state toward the Cyprus problem mimics its stand toward Greece, which has severely hindered the possibility of conflict resolution.

Q
R
S

The Armenian
Problem

Two secret Armenian organizations decided to draw attention to the 1915 ethnic cleansing of the Armenians the Ottoman state had committed without subsequent accountability through a series of assassinations of Turkish diplomats and the bombings of Turkish sites.

- The attacks caused both the state and military to intervene by fostering, organizing, and institutionalizing the propensity to symbolic violence against the Armenians through a national historiography and a series of organizations with the overt purpose of studying and researching the Armenian issue.
- The Turks, rather than confronting their past and the violence contained therein against minorities in general and the Armenians in particular, chose instead to deny it by constructing an official counternarrative.

NOTE: The author argues that peaceful solutions to these problems could become possible only and primarily upon challenging the temporal boundaries of the official Turkish narrative.

Conclusion

Even though the Turkish state, including the military, constantly condemns the expansionist tendencies of European powers, the West does nevertheless continue to occupy a privileged place in the mind's eye of Turkish state and society, thereby contributing to the democratization process.

- Significant developments have been Turkey's transition to a multiparty regime in 1946; its alignment with NATO in 1952; and its opening up in the 1980s to the world economy and making significant efforts to alter its state-controlled, protectionist economic and political structure.
- Still, the military continues to consider itself the guardian of the state, established and maintained according to Republican and secularist principles to be protected not only against external threats but also against its internal enemies.
- The first step the Turkish nation-state ought to take toward the resolution of its Kurdish, Cyprus, and Armenian issues is to confront its history in its entirety rather than through fragments.

The Japanese History Textbook Controversy
in East Asian Perspective

Claudia Schneider, University of Leipzig, Germany

Background

Japan is criticized in most of the history debates taking place in East Asia for failing to come to terms appropriately with its past.

- The cold war alliance made it possible to leave many war-related questions unresolved, providing a lingering source of debate between Japan and its neighbors, who see themselves as its victims.

Q
R
S

- It was not until the 1980s, and particularly the 1990s, that many of these issues became contested.
- This article provides an overview of one of the most prolonged and notorious issues: the so-called "textbook controversy," the debates surrounding the treatment—essentially the noncoverage—of Japanese wartime behavior in the country's history textbooks.
- The textbook controversies attest to altered distribution of power in the region; changed state-society relations and prevailing national self-images; as well as the heightened significance of the past for the present—the global "memory boom."

History Texts   The transformation of history textbooks into objects of international debate dates from the summer of 1982.

- The debate was triggered by reports that the Japanese Ministry of Education (MOE) had ordered history textbook authors to make various revisions—changing the term "aggression/invasion" into "advancement" to describe Japanese military action in China.
  - The story was false, but a general problem of this sort did exist.
- Japan's neighbors had reasons to complain: not only was textbook coverage of Japanese military action rather evasive, the dominant consciousness in Japan was not primarily that of having been an aggressor toward Asian countries, but rather of having been a victim.
- Until then, however, Japan's neighbors had not complained. Thus, we have to look for reasons for the outbreak (and subsequent reiteration) not only in the Japanese, but also in the Chinese and Korean contexts.

The issue became both a source of and a potential challenge to government legitimacy.

- The hapless way the government handled it left such major domestic actors as the Ministry of Foreign Affairs (MOFA) and the MOE dissatisfied and contributed indirectly to Prime Minister Suzuki Zenko's resignation.
- For China and Korea, playing the "history card" was a tool for shaming, pressuring, and gaining leverage on the Japanese government.
- This further indicates that (1) the international controversy has always been closely tied to domestic issues and (2) mass media has played a significant role.

Neighboring   An immediate result of the above was the Japanese MOE's addition to the
Countries   criteria for textbook authorization of what came to be called the "Neighboring
Clause   Countries Clause."

- It stipulated that consideration should be given to neighboring countries' perspectives.
- The clause has been a source of discontent for conservative/right-wing forces who believe it is a sign that the Japanese are succumbing to diplomatic pressure on genuinely internal affairs. Conservative counterreactions include the writing of "revisionist" textbooks.

The 1990s

The 1990s saw a number of significant changes.
- In 1993, Prime Minister Hosokawa acknowledged that Japan had conducted a war of aggression.
- In 1995, a resolution in the Diet and a statement on August 15 by Hosokawa's successor, Prime Minister Murayama, contained formal expressions of apology and regret.

NOTE: Various revisionist groups were organized to counter this trend. They both contributed to and profited from a turn toward a defensive and defiant nationalism among parts of the Japanese population.

Korea and China React

South Korean and Chinese governments were put on the defensive by the textbook controversy.
- South Korean president Roh Moo-hyun launched diplomatic protests after pressure from the political arena and the public.
- The official Chinese reactions included the usual apolitical rhetoric and some cancelled visits, but no measures were taken with potentially negative long-term effects on their relationship with Japan.
- Popular nationalisms in both countries include strong anti-Japanese sentiments (caused by the wartime and colonial past).

Politics of Textbooks

The perceptions (and subsequent actions) of the involved actors, and of the general public, contribute largely to the tendency of textbooks to become objects of contention.
- First, because they are authorized or approved by the state, Japanese textbooks are imbued with a quasi-official character.
- Second, in many parts of the world, history textbooks are often seen as powerful symbols of a country's sincerity in dealing with a negative past.
- Third, their target audience, young children, causes them to be considered very influential in a double sense—both for the individual child's historical consciousness and for the nation's future.

NOTE: The promotion of patriotism remains a central goal of history education not only in the eyes of Japanese conservatives and revisionists but also in Korean and Chinese curricula.

Effects of the Textbook Controversies

In Japan, in dealing with the "fragmentation" of particularly contested and scrutinized issues, textbooks have displayed pendular movement, rather than a unidirectional trend.
- Textbooks *could* become somewhat more open in the treatment of other, related topics.
- Any insertions made in textbooks so far appear as signs of concessions in the political push and pull, not as reflections of revisions in the general agenda of the politics of Japanese history education.

In general, the two-sided controversy first raised awareness, but now tends to deteriorate mutual public perceptions.
- In Korea and China the controversy has fostered both counterreactions and introspection and established history textbooks as items worthy of reporting on, examining, and debating.

QRS

Conclusion

- Cross-nationally, the textbook controversies have prompted a number of initiatives by scholars and educators aiming at cross-national dialogue and mutual understanding.

Overall, Japan's strategy toward its neighbors is motivated by pragmatic concerns rather than by a moral conviction of the need to "settle the past."
- The country will thus continue to make indispensable concessions to accommodate criticism from other Asian countries, but no more.
- The ugly past does not go well with currently very vocal conservative calls for a more "patriotic education."
- Few Japanese see the country's relationship with its Asian neighbors as a high priority at this time, but a majority do acknowledge the need to reflect on Japan's past attacks and colonial rule over Asian nations.

NOTE: In sum, the author has sought to show that textbooks and textbook controversies are above all reflections of broader sociopolitical constellations and changes—more than just historically influential factors in their own right.

Disputes in Japan over the Japanese Military "Comfort Women" System and Its Perception in History

Hirofumi Hayashi, Kanto Gakuin University, Tokyo

Background

In 2007, then–Japanese Prime Minister Abe stirred up controversy by denying that "comfort women" were coerced by the Japanese military.
- He asserted that private agents, not the military, coerced the women.
- In contrast, Abe has been a fierce critic of the abduction of Japanese citizens by North Korea.
- Abe stated that he believes that Japan's war and the behavior of the Japanese military were righteous.
- Some of the main arguments in Japan are that the Nanjing Massacre was fabricated, that comfort women were regular prostitutes rather than victims of war crimes, and that Japan did not act aggressively.

The JWRC

The Center for Research and Documentation on Japan's War Responsibility (JWRC) advocates certain facts as documented in various materials:
- The former Japanese Army and Navy created the comfort women system to serve their own needs.
- The military decided when, where, and how "comfort stations" were to be established.
- The military was well aware of the various methods used to bring women to comfort stations.

NOTE: The JWRC expressed the strong hope that the world should acknowledge these facts and that a fundamental and final resolution to the comfort women issue would soon be reached. Yet the Japanese media ignored efforts of researchers and groups like the JWRC.

1991 Disclosure   The situation changed dramatically in 1991 when a former comfort woman from South Korea, Kim Hak Sun, broke nearly half a century of silence and made her story public.

- Her and others' bravery in stepping forward encouraged Japanese activists, especially female activists, to organize support groups.
- The Japanese government refused not only to apologize to or provide reparations for the women but also to carry out any investigation.
- However, in January 1992, unearthed documents in the National Institute of Defense Studies proved conclusively that the military had played a role in the establishment and control of comfort stations.
- As a result, Prime Minister Kiichi Miyazawa publicly admitted that the Japanese military was involved, and he apologized for the comfort women system for the first time.

NOTE: The suffering of the women involved did not end with liberation. Many comfort women were unable to return home. Some still remain where they were abandoned. Former comfort women have suffered the aftereffects of disease, injury, psychological trauma, and post-traumatic stress disorder, as well as social discrimination for their pasts.

The Mid-1990s   Ultrarightists began a systematic counterattack in the mid-1990s.

- They attacked textbooks that dealt with Japan's various atrocities, including the comfort women system, demanding that such material be deleted to recover a sense of national pride.
- Publishers of textbooks began to restrain the descriptions used.
- Later, the minister of education stated in 2004 that it was desirable for references to Japanese atrocities to be dropped.

NOTE: Against a background of economic depression and a climate of prejudice against other Asians, particularly the Chinese and Koreans, many Japanese have been influenced by these xenophobic campaigns.

U.S. Resolution   The U.S. House of Representatives passed a resolution in 2007 to the effect that the government of Japan "should formally acknowledge, apologize, and accept historical responsibility in a clear and unequivocal manner" for the military sexual slavery, known to the world as comfort women.

- The Japanese government refused to accept this resolution in any way.
- In response, civic groups in Japan issued a statement on July 31, 2007: "What would make a Japanese Government apology to comfort women unequivocal?"
- Most of the mass media in Japan responded unfavorably to the statement.
- Others claim that the Japanese government has already apologized.
- Now, the number of politicians of the younger generation in the Liberal Democratic Party (LDP) and the Democratic Party refuse to admit that the Japanese military was involved in atrocities or that Japan has responsibility for the war.

Q
R
S

Q R S

*Foreign
Neighbors'
Reactions*

There is a tendency for younger politicians to be more antiforeign, and it appears that the government of South Korea is at a loss as to how to respond, while the Chinese government remains silent in order to give priority to improving China-Japan relations.

- Although reconciliation is essential, attempts are being made at reconciliation without a formal state apology or individual compensation to victims.
- However, reconciliation needs to be achieved among the ordinary people of the Asia-Pacific region, including the victims, not among those in power.

The Politics of History and Memory in Democratic Spain

Carolyn P. Boyd, University of California, Irvine

Background

This article examines the political uses of history and memory in Spain since the death of General Francisco Franco in 1975.

- Once democracy was consolidated, professional historians clarified military responsibility for the civil war and documented the extent of the repression; the Right responded by reviving the Franquist myth of the civil war as a crusade against communism.
- "Memory" replaced history in public discourse with the breakdown of the transition consensus and the maturation of a generation with no recall of the war or the dictatorship.
- Demands for official condemnation of the dictatorship and public recognition of its victims culminated in the passage of the so-called Law of Historical Memory in October 2007.

Memory

Historical memory is a form of social memory in which a group constructs a selective representation of its own imagined past.

- Historical memory may legitimate or challenge the status quo, teach a lesson, validate a claim, consolidate an identity, or inspire action.
- There are as many stories about the past as there are social or political groups vying for power.

Spanish Model

The Spanish transition to democracy is viewed as a "model" transition because of its consensual, nonviolent character and positive outcome.

- The transition to democracy in Spain rested on a de facto "pact of silence" that avoided confrontation with those responsible for the dictatorship and denied public recognition of its victims.
- To avoid arousing the ire of the right, the first governments of the transition avoided purging Franco loyalists.
- Fear of military reaction and their own complicity in sustaining the dictatorship justified to many Spaniards the pact of silence.

The 1990s	By the 1990s, historians felt able to dispense with the myth of collective responsibility that had facilitated the Transition, and the historians began to investigate the policies and politics of the Franco regime.

- Persistent scholars began to document and quantify the human costs of the Franquist repression.
- The new statistics, which demonstrated conclusively that the victims of Nationalist repression vastly outnumbered those killed by the revolutionary Left, dealt another blow to the myth of equal responsibility.
- With the loosening of centralized state control, history textbooks had a greater variety of ideological perspectives on the past—most registered the hegemonic memory of the civil war as a fratricidal tragedy and showed the historical memory of the 1930s as a period when the political center was overwhelmed by extremists on the Left and Right.
- The socialists educational reform law (LOGSE) said history should enable students to "analyze and critically evaluate the realities of the contemporary world and the antecedents and factors that influence it."
  - The LOGSE sought to instill the habits of mind and behavior appropriate to a democratic society.
  - Most history textbooks written after passage of the LOGSE prioritized historical knowledge over mythmaking and historical distance over passionate moralizing.

1990s History Wars	After each of several regime changes in the 1990s, winners sought to reshape the historical memory of the civil war and the dictatorship.
The Memory Boom	After the turn of the century, "memory" began to occupy a larger share of public discourse on the past.

- The shift in preference for memory over history tracked the continuing shift in the balance of political power toward the Right.
- Equally important was the international debate over how democratic or democratizing societies should confront histories of violence, repression, and genocide.
- The revision of official memory to include the individual memories of those previously silenced was understood to be a necessary first step toward reconciliation and democratic consolidation.
- Public intellectuals willing to concede the functionality of "forgetting" during the Transition insisted that Spain's European identity depended upon official acknowledgement of the dictatorship's crimes.

The Present	The "fever for remembering," climaxed in 2006 when the Congress of Deputies endorsed a bill proclaiming the "Year of Historical Memory."
Conclusion	History cannot administer justice; its moral authority comes from its regard for truth-seeking and its social utility from its power to explain and interpret.

- The recent turn to cultural history suggests a politically attractive avenue of research.
- Historians may make the "past that does not pass" less the source of continuing friction than the reason for a renewed commitment to democratic coexistence.

Australia's History under Howard, 1996–2007

Andrew Bonnell and Martin Crotty, University of Queensland,
Brisbane, Australia

Q
R
S

Background

The conservative Coalition government led by Prime Minister John Howard was in power in Australia from March 1996 to November 2007.

- For a decade, Australian history was a battleground between the Howard government and its supporters and academic historians and other members of the so-called "left-wing intellectual elite."
- Australia's relations with its Indigenous people was the most emotive and controversial topic, but other aspects of Australian social and political history were also subjects of contention.
- Howard's advancement of a particular understanding of Australian history was guided by personal conviction and background—his upbringing was conservative and insular, and his understanding of Australian history reflected this.
- Howard sought to implement conservative social and cultural policies, while continuing to pursue neoliberal economic reform.
- The Howard government's efforts on the terrain of the so-called "history wars" served two combined purposes:
  - to contest the supposed hegemony in public debate of an unpatriotic and negative liberal-left intelligentsia in universities and the media; and
  - to assert a positive, nationalistic view of Australian history that would enable Australians to feel "comfortable and relaxed" during more potentially unsettling economic reform.

Influencing Public Debate

The Howard government used its control over funding for the higher education system and public broadcasting to influence public debate.

- Academics and public broadcasters were frequently weakened by funding cuts.
- The federal education ministry became more aggressively interventionist in universities, forcing changes in governance and workplace relations onto them.

Indigenous People

There are two main issues regarding indigenous people on which the Howard government took a markedly different position from its predecessor:

- native title to lands, and
- restitution for past wrongs.

NOTE: John Howard resisted the calls for a Commonwealth government apology on the basis that this generation could not be held responsible for well-intentioned errors of previous generations, and his government devoted considerable legal resources to opposing claims for compensation from members of what became known as the "stolen generations" (Aboriginal children moved to non-Aboriginal homes for a "better" upbringing).

Native Title

Another unwanted legacy in Indigenous affairs (as far as the incoming Howard administration was concerned) was in the area of native title.

- In 1992, the High Court of Australia handed down the *Mabo* judgment, which essentially found that under common law, a residual form of native title to traditional lands still existed.

- However, the incoming Howard government promised to roll back native title and provide certainty of tenure for rural landholders, the core constituency of the agrarian-based National Party.

Australian History

While issues concerning Australian Aboriginal history were among the most politically and emotionally charged subjects of the Howard years' "history wars," debate was not confined to these topics.

- The government also expressed concern with the way in which Australian history was represented to the public in, for example, the new National Museum of Australia, and taught to students in schools. Both areas became targets of government intervention.
- Activist Keith Windschuttle claimed that the zigzag ground plan of the museum's building echoed the new Jewish Museum in Berlin, conveying a subliminal message that Australia had a genocidal past.
- In terms of the teaching of Australian history, Howard has long expressed concerns that Australian children were being denied their rightful heritage of pride in their country's achievements and were too often finishing their secondary school years without a clear sense of the overall national historical narrative.

The End Results

Undoubtedly, the politicization of Australian history has been detrimental to academic and public debate.

- The reputation of academic historians has been tarnished by the constant vituperative attacks from conservation opinion writers, a development that has assisted, or at the very least hindered, resistance to the downgrading of the humanities in the tertiary education sector.
- While the history wars have provided background noise for the depletion of humanities faculties in Australian universities, and have accompanied the frustration of Indigenous hopes for more emancipatory government policies and for a genuine reconciliation process, their influence has hardly been decisive.
- It may offer some comfort to Australian historians that their commitment to liberal democratic humanism, to scholarship, and to their students has transcended the politics of their calling for the past decade—which is, ultimately, as it should be.

Democracy and Memory: Romania Confronts Its Communist Past

Vladimir Tismaneanu, University of Maryland

Background

How does Romania compare to other East European countries in terms of mastering its dictatorial past?

- The belated nature of Romania's decision to confront its communist totalitarian past was predominantly the consequence of obstinate opposition to such an undertaking from parties and personalities directly or indirectly linked to the previous communist regime.

- Both the National Liberal and the Democratic parties understood the importance of coming to terms with the past—the condemnation of the communist dictatorship has become one of the most hotly debated political, ideological, and moral issues in contemporary Romania.

The PCACDR

The Presidential Commission for the Analysis of the Communist Dictatorship in Romania (PCACDR) was continuously attacked from the extreme Left, the nationalist Right, and Orthodox clericalist and fundamentalist circles.

- The opponent's attitude was a sign that the Commission's chosen path was the right one, from an academic and moral point of view—a functional and healthy democratic society cannot endlessly indulge in politics of oblivion and denial.
- The work of the Commission was meant to pass moral judgment on the defunct dictatorship and invite a reckoning with the past via a painful, albeit inevitable, acknowledgement of its crimes against humanity and other forms of repression.
- The PCACDR comes close to the commissions for truth and reconciliation created in countries such as South Africa, Chile, Argentina, and Rwanda. In contrast to these commissions, the PCACDR had no decision-making power and no subpoena prerogative.

NOTE: For the first time in post-1989 Romania, the PCACDR rejected outright the practices of institutionalized forgetfulness and generated a national conversation about long-denied and occulted moments of the past.

The "Final Report"

The PCACDR Final Report identifies the nature of abuses and its victims, though not leaving aside the ideological context of the times.

- For the PCACDR, the communist regime represented the opposite of rule of law.
- Dealing with both the communist and fascist past must become a factor of communal cohesion as it imposes the rejection of any comfortably apologetic historicization.

NOTE: The main instrument for the process of mastering the past, employed by the PCACDR, was the deconstruction of the ideological certainty established by the communist regime upon which the latter founded its legitimacy.

Communist Condemnation

In Romania, the condemnation of the communist regime has taken place with a view to reconciliation, consensus, reform, and working through the past.

- It did not serve as a weapon of either President Băsescu against his enemies or as a means of rehabilitating any xenophobic and/or antidemocratic precommunist movements.
- An obstacle on the road to reconciliation is the fact that the perpetrators of Romania's communist regime have not been confronted, legally and institutionally, with their crimes.
  - Individuals identified as guilty of crimes against humanity or former members of Ceausescu's last Politburo have long been pardoned and continue to defend the old regime.

- The PCACDR, relying on President Băsescu's political commitment, created a document where responsibility for the past was claimed and individualized, but neither the Commission nor the president could impose reconciliation in the absence of repentance.

NOTE: The Commission's work and the intense debates surrounding it highlight one of the most vexing yet vitally important tensions of the postcommunist world: the understanding of the traumatic totalitarian past and the political, moral, and intellectual difficulties, frustrations, hopes, and anxieties involved in trying to come to grips with it.

Q
R
S

Can Truth Be Negotiated? History Textbook Revision as a Means to Reconciliation

Falk Pingel, Georg Eckert Institut für internationale
Schulbuchforschung, Germany

Background

The transfer of knowledge from one generation to the next through textbooks is controlled not only by scholarly, quality criteria and by pedagogical standards but also by political interests.
- To overcome narrow national and nationalistic approaches to historical interpretations and geopolitical visions of the world, international textbook revision became a politically acknowledged and scholarly activity after the shock of the First World War.
- The well-known traditional model of interstate textbook projects created in the 1920s is characterized by bilateral or multilateral cooperation on equal terms such as the German-Polish or the Italian-Slovenian Textbook Commission, to mention two contemporary examples.

Textbooks Today

After the dissolution of the communist system and the opening of borders, the topics and methods of textbook revision underwent remarkable changes.
- Oversight of textbook revision went from bilateral, quasi-official commissions set up by educational authorities to groups of experts linked to the work of nongovernmental organizations (NGOs) and agencies of civil society.
- Challenges to textbook revision shifted from controversies over the past to debate about current, open, and often still violent conflicts.
- Controversial topics extended from conflicts between states to conflicts between groups within a state or society (or from war to civil war).

South Africa

In South Africa after apartheid, two factions put forward their vision of a revised South African historiography.
- African teachers expected a new and uncontested "black" history that would tell the one and only true story in contrast to the distorted one they had been exposed to for so many years.
- A pluralistic model was favored by a group of historians who worked at universities long since known for their antiapartheid position, and they

advocated the use of new source materials about African history, innovative methodological approaches such as multiperspective interpretations, group discussion, oral history, and testimonies.

Bosnia and Herzegovina and Rwanda

The Parliamentary Assembly of the Council of Europe passed a resolution on "Education in Bosnia and Herzegovina" in the year 2000 that proposed a moratorium on the teaching of the war of 1992 to 1995.

- Contrary to the expectations of its creators, it has not stimulated enquiries into the war and its causes, but only created a vacuum that offers very little scope for intellectual curiosity and the development of new approaches to teaching issues of contemporary history.
- In Bosnia and Herzegovina almost all the different stages and methods of textbook revision have been used in their school books in order to reconcile three almost incompatible versions of history.
  - It was the process itself that counted and caused a change in attitude. The experts acted independently from a political agenda prescribed by local ministries or the International Community, and used the best pedagogical practice and subject knowledge.
- The same logic underpinned the Rwandan government's decision to abandon history teaching altogether until a new consensual concept had been developed—categorized as an approach-avoidance conflict.

Communication Process

Projects conducted by NGOs often aim expressly to break down communication barriers that politicians could not or did not want to overcome.

- The work of NGOs, which are composed of devoted intellectuals and teachers and parents, helps to create a nucleus for a civil society that can counterbalance backward-oriented political agencies.
- As a rule, the teaching units produced by NGOs are meant to provide additional material that does not replace regular textbooks.

Reconciliation

Considering the ban on history teaching in Rwanda and the low profile history teaching was granted in South Africa for almost ten years, one may wonder what role truth commissions played in both countries.

- The establishment of truth through a communal communicative process prevalent in truth commissions have almost nowhere changed the restricted notion of the one and only objective truth that shapes the way history is presented in school textbooks.

Japan, Korea, and China

Five bilateral or multilateral history textbooks have been written in East Asia in recent years, the most ambitious being a book written by a team of Japanese, Chinese, and Korean authors.

- These books cannot replace the obligatory history books—it is a big step forward to use books that offer a wider view and do more than reflect one's own well-known and canonized national narrative.
- The question of whether a Japanese-Korean-Chinese textbook commission should be set up can become obsolete if efforts on the level of NGOs, universities, international governmental organizations, and pedagogical institutes can produce sustainable results.

NOTE: That it is possible to develop a joint history textbook is a value in itself, even if it is not widely used. It refutes the former opinion that the narratives are so different and so consistent with the respective national pride and historical canon of each nation that they cannot be changed by means of international comparative research and debate.

QRS

Challenged Histories and Collective Self-Concepts: Politics in History, Memory, and Time

Martin O. Heisler, University of Maryland

Background

All societies at some time confront evidence of past actions undertaken in their name that violate their fundamental principles and conflict with their current self-image.

- The author suggests two sources of tensions between "bad acts" and positive self-concepts:
  - First, past actions not considered wrong when they were undertaken are deemed to have been inconsistent with current expectation.
  - Second, transsocietal differences in normative frameworks lead to criticisms of others' behavior, behavior in which the critics' societies likely engaged at an earlier time.
- Accusations or criticisms of actions in the past now considered deplorable generally meet with defensive, often hostile responses.

NOTE: History, memory, and identity are implicated in each other. For some, memory has become a way, perhaps *the* way, of thinking about history; and identity is sometimes said to be produced by mixtures of real and imagined histories. All three are contingent on context and circumstance and on the instrumental purposes to which they can be put.

Power and Choice

Power to interpret and apply (use in instrumental ways) history, memory, and identity can be exerted at all levels, from the state and society at one end of the scale to individuals at the other.

- The plausibility of this claim depends on context: autonomy for individuals, associations and institutions (below the level of the state) to exercise and act on choices covaries with the openness of the state, the degree of social modernity, and the space allowed by social control.
- The possibility that choice and power can be exercised at any or all of these levels makes the relationships between history, memory, and identity even more indeterminate.

NOTE: The task is less the determination of the bases in history of the attacks on particular positions, or which constructions of the memories of particular actions or events should prevail, than the practical uses to which elements of the past can be put toward current political ends.

Political Influences

Politics is often a significant force in the construction of the past and the shaping of collective memory.
- The displacement of norms in time and the dramatically shrinking normative and communicative space among societies are two important contextual factors.

Peoplehood

Peoplehood is a *political* state of being, and it has far-reaching political implications.
- It entails conscious association, based on reflection, not simply physical or psychological proximity or economic interdependence.
- Most members of a society enter it through birth, yet peoplehood entails learning and socialization to a shared story and what it represents.
- Stories of peoplehood are instrumental in constituting collectivities—they propagate the values and norms around which collectivities form, and with and through which their members identify.
  - The author believes that stories of peoplehood must be positive.
  - Individuals need to maintain a high opinion of themselves, a sense of their probity and righteousness.

Lessons Learned

What, if any, lessons, do collectivities learn from actions that violate their avowed sense of who they are as a people, especially actions undertaken in their name or by their agents?
- This is a timeless concern with moral progress by societies—the author's concerns here are much narrower and more down-to-earth, that is, whether awareness of appalling acts in a collectivity's past, committed in its name, affect its self-image, and if so, how.
- It is unclear whether we are justified in applying today's criteria for moral behavior to actions that occurred decades, even generations, ago.

Questions

How do we ascertain awareness and recognition of the incompatibility between such atrocities as the wanton mass killing of innocent civilians or torture, on one hand, and the prevalent positive collective self-concepts all peoples have, on the other?
- In short, what must we know, when must we know it, and whose awareness or knowledge counts?
- How should we react to such actions?
- What is a collective self-concept, and how, if at all, can we know it?

Effects on Domestic Politics

A collectivity's response—through its public authorities, social or political elites, and educational system—to "news" of gross violations by its members can profoundly affect its domestic politics and international relations.
- In recent years, a large and still growing literature has focused on the political consequences of how the past has been addressed.
- If such narratives are to retain their power to shape collective self-concepts—if they are to serve as the basis for responses to the question "who are we?"—they must be interpreted and frequently reinterpreted, edited, revised, or updated.

Worldwide Office Locations

United States of America

SAGE Publications, Inc.
2455 Teller Road
Thousand Oaks, California, 91320 USA
Phone: 805-499-9774
Fax: 805-499-0871
Email: journals@sagepub.com
Website: www.sagepub.com

Corwin Press, Inc.
2455 Teller Road
Thousand Oaks, California 31920 USA
Phone: 805-499-9774
Fax: 805-499-0871
Email: order@corwinpress.com
Website: www.corwinpress.com

United Kingdom

SAGE Publications, Ltd.
1 Oliver's Yard
55 City Road
London EC1Y 1SP, United Kingdom
Phone: +44 (0)20 7324 8500
Fax: +44 (0)20 7324 8600
Email: subscription@sagepub.co.uk
Website: www.sagepub.co.uk

India

SAGE Publications India, Pvt. Ltd.
B-42 Panchsheel Enclave
Post Box 4109
New Delhi 110-017
Phone and Fax: +91 11 2649 1290
Email: journalsubs@indiasage.com
Website: www.indiasage.com

SAGE Worldwide Website
www.sagepublications.com